Y0-BRM-437

Consensus and Global Environmental Governance

Consensus and Global Environmental Governance

Deliberative Democracy in Nature's Regime

Walter F. Baber and Robert V. Bartlett

The MIT Press
Cambridge, Massachusetts
London, England

© 2015 Massachusetts Institute of Technology

All rights reserved. No part of this book may be reproduced in any form by any electronic or mechanical means (including photocopying, recording, or information storage and retrieval) without permission in writing from the publisher.

MIT Press books may be purchased at special quantity discounts for business or sales promotional use. For information, please email special_sales@mitpress.mit.edu.

This book was set in Sabon by the MIT Press. Printed and bound in the United States of America.

Library of Congress Cataloging-in-Publication Data is available.

ISBN 978-0-262-02873-8 (hc); 978-0-262-52722-4 (pb)

10   9   8   7   6   5   4   3   2   1

To Carolyn and Sally,
who have done half the laughing for more than forty years

Contents

Series Foreword

Humans now influence all biological and physical systems of the planet. Almost no species, land area, or part of the oceans has remained unaffected by the expansion of the human species. Recent scientific findings suggest that the entire earth system now operates outside the normal state exhibited over at least the past five hundred thousand years. Yet at the same time, it is apparent that the institutions, organizations, and mechanisms by which humans govern their relationship with the natural environment and global biogeochemical systems are utterly insufficient—and poorly understood. More fundamental and applied research is needed.

Such research is no easy undertaking. It must span the entire globe because only integrated global solutions can ensure a sustainable coevolution of biophysical and socioeconomic systems. But it must also draw on local experiences and insights. Research on earth system governance must be about places in all their diversity, yet seek to integrate place-based research within a global understanding of the myriad human interactions with the earth system. Eventually, the task is to develop integrated systems of governance, from the local to the global level, that ensure the sustainable development of the coupled socioecological system that the earth has become.

The series Earth System Governance is designed to address this research challenge. Books in this series will pursue this challenge from a variety of disciplinary perspectives, at different levels of governance, and with a range of methods. Yet all will further one common aim: analyzing current systems of earth system governance with a view to increased understanding, and possible improvements and reform. Books in this series will be of interest to the academic community, but will also inform practitioners and at times contribute to policy debates.

This series is related to the long-term international research program Earth System Governance Project.

Frank Biermann, VU University Amsterdam and Lund University
Oran R. Young, Bren School, University of California, Santa Barbara
Earth System Governance Series editors

Preface

This book should be seen as part of two larger endeavors. First and foremost, it is appearing in The MIT Press Earth System Governance book series edited by Frank Biermann and Oran R. Young. This is only one of its connections to the Earth System Governance Project, which was launched in 2008 by the Scientific Committee of the International Human Dimensions Programme on Global Environmental Change as a core undertaking. The Earth System Governance Project encompasses a large number of research events, publications, affiliated projects, and research centers, and our own Norms of Global Governance Initiative (summarized in the appendixes of this book) is an affiliated project, aimed at identifying normative discourses that are fundamental to global environmental governance, mapping areas of consensus and disagreement, and contributing to the progressive development of global environmental norms. Since 2009 the Earth System Governance Project has sponsored an annual research conference. This gathering has greatly informed our thinking about global environmental governance and allowed us to present early drafts of several chapters of this book.

Second, this book is the most recent product of a research project we began in 1996. In *Deliberative Environmental Politics: Democracy and Ecological Politics* (MIT Press, 2005), we analyzed links between deliberative democratic theory and the practice of environmental politics. We assessed three major models of deliberative democracy—normative precommitment in public reason, public discourse-based communicative action, and full liberalism. And we looked at the potential and implications of each of these for institutions, citizens, experts, and social movements in what might emerge as a more ecologically rational environmental politics. For the most part we limited our critical analysis to local and national contexts, only briefly touching on the applicability of deliberative democracy to the international or global system.

In *Global Democracy and Sustainable Jurisprudence: Deliberative Environmental Law* (MIT Press, 2009), we focused entirely on the democratic deficit in international law and global politics. We explored the necessary characteristics of a meaningful global jurisprudence that could provide a firmer and more democratic foundation for international environmental law. We proposed a new approach for international law in the area of environmental protection: juristic democracy. We addressed several important foundational concerns. Juristic democracy emphasizes the role of the citizen as opposed to that of the nation-state as the source of legitimacy in international environmental law. For environmental regimes to be both politically sustainable and ecologically effective, three things are required. First, for environmental law to achieve the necessary global reach, global jurisprudence must be based on the collective will of citizens around the world rather than solely on what can be agreed on between nation-states. Second, the development and implementation of environmental rules must be rooted in local ecological knowledge if these rules are to be effective. Third, the political processes used to create international environmental law must be based on democratic deliberation and grounded in consensus. Fundamental to this approach is the surety that international law fails less often from a lack of coercive enforcement than from a lack of legitimacy.

We explained juristic democracy as a conceptual framework for the accelerated development of a global common law based on a foundation of norms and principles derived from the consideration by innumerable citizen juries of carefully cast hypothetical cases. Instead of merely seeking environmental law agreed to by nation-states, we argued that international environmental law creators and practitioners could and should aim to construct a global jurisprudence based on collective will formation. This reformulation would both improve the democratic legitimacy of environmental law and, in so doing, make international regimes more effective by making them more sustainable politically. We envisioned an approach that would allow for the progressive development of international environmental law through citizen engagement with one another across the globe in the process of resolving international environmental disputes. We ended this second book with an extended example of how existing international organizations, such as the International Law Commission, could oversee and manage the processes of drafting hypothetical cases, marshaling juries to deliberate them, and developing restatements of emerging decision principles.

Now this, our third book, continues the critical assessment of juristic democracy as a way of achieving some degree of democratic legitimacy for global environmental governance. Persons interested particularly in the relationship of the concept of juristic democracy to international relations theory and international law jurisprudence will find that addressed in *Global Democracy and Sustainable Jurisprudence*, and not repeated here. Likewise, we have not repeated that book's extended illustration of how existing international organizations could institutionalize the jurisprudence of juristic democracy in the existing framework of international law. This book builds on *Global Democracy and Sustainable Jurisprudence*, and goes beyond it by addressing the in-depth challenges that the practical requirement of consensus poses for any system of juristic democracy. We analyze the implications of deliberative consensus for the effectiveness of rule-bounded behavior, accomplishment of basic generic governance tasks, diversity and disadvantage in a politically divided and culturally plural world, and construction of whole systems of governance. Along the way, we also assess the state of social scientific knowledge about the potential and limitations of small-group citizen panels as contributors to the identification, and even development, of rationalized consensus. We conclude with an examination of the place of juristic democracy in what may emerge in future decades as a consensually federal system for earth system governance.

Specifically, this is how the book unfolds. In chapter 1, we explore how the characteristics of rule-bounded behavior determine what is required for global environmental governance rules to be effective—namely, they must be grounded in widely shared social understandings, authored by those they address, equal in their application to all addressees, capable of learning from (and adapting to) experience, rationally grounded, and internalized (or at least capable of being internalized) by those who participate in their adoption and implementation. These requirements create challenges for the identification and cultivation of consensus across at least three dimensions. In chapter 2, we map these challenges onto the kinds of dilemmas faced in three key governance tasks: the formation of regulatory norms, choice among models of change governance, and generation of plan-governed action.

In chapter 3, we discuss what international environmental law is now, what it might reasonably aspire to be, and what it is probably unreasonable to expect of it. We also relate the existing limitations directly to some of the basic characteristics of juristic democracy as they will be described in succeeding chapters. We describe a common law strategy for earth system governance. Here we explain the process of litigating concrete disputes, aggregating those decisions and "restating" them in the form of general rules, and developing models of governance from those rules. We then look at how this venerable approach to the progressive development of law can be applied to the challenges involved in environmental protection at the global level. In chapter 4, we address what is perhaps the most serious challenge to the deliberative democratic enterprise: the suggestion that deliberative techniques are hostile to diversity. In particular, we examine the claims that deliberation places historically neglected and disfavored interests as well as perspectives at a further disadvantage as a result of the constraints deliberation imposes on political discourse. Next, in chapter 5, we extend our discussion of earth system governance to the problem of promoting the objectives of environmental justice in the face of the political changes and economic transformations implicit in rapid globalization.

In chapter 6, we turn to the real-world implications of the use of juries as a deliberative forum. We are aided in this by the extensive research that has been conducted on juries as they are used in courts of law. Virtually all the concerns directed at the use of jury-size citizen groups as deliberative forums have long been familiar to lawyers and studied intensively by empirically minded legal scholars. In chapter 7, we explore how the legal process of restatement, augmented by the social scientific technique of content analysis, could be developed as a mechanism for aggregating the considered opinions of juries of deliberating citizens in ways that would allow progressive development of global legal structures for the rational governance of the human relationship to the environment. In chapter 8, we continue this analysis with a discussion of the role that citizen juries might play in the development and legitimation of an international administrative law for earth system governance. Our conclusion is that this approach to the formation of collective will has the potential to provide sorely needed democratic legitimation to the ongoing efforts of trans-national policy networks of environmental specialists. In chapter 9, we analyze the role that an administratively generated common law for earth system governance might play in the development of a form of consensual (or consociational) federalism in global governance.

We conclude in chapter 10 by again confronting the concept of consensus, which is (ironically perhaps) highly contested among democratic theorists, political professionals, and activists. There are those who think that consensus is beyond our reach, either because our divisions are too deep and numerous, or because our analytic capacities are insufficient. Others think that consensus, whether or not it is actually achievable, would be undesirable in any event. These theorists fear that consensus is either unavoidably repressive (because of the deliberative constraints necessary to produce it) or unavoidably prone to error (because small-group dynamics promote various forms of unreason). We close by looking at the degree to which the specific form of deliberation we propose protects itself from these problems. In three appendixes, we offer examples of the kind of posed conflicts in hypothetical scenarios that can serve as the substance of juristic democracy citizen deliberations, such as in our Norms of Global Governance Initiative affiliated with the Earth System Governance Project.

Juristic democracy is a conceptual framework for the accelerated development of a global common law based on a foundation of norms and principles derived from the consideration by innumerable citizen juries of carefully cast hypothetical cases. Juristic democracy offers the prospect of workable, democratic, environment-friendly, and rule-governed behavior within a system of global governance that is likely to remain (and perhaps should remain) anarchic in important respects. Because of its inherent democratic legitimacy, this method for creating, interpreting, and translating international environmental norms into law could in the initial stages bypass states, and unlike current international law, be universally recognized as both fact and norm (Habermas 1996). As such, it would constitute a rule-making system for earth system governance fully complementary with other governance approaches and strategies (Biermann et al. 2009; Dryzek 2009).

Acknowledgments

We thank the three anonymous reviewers for the MIT Press whose suggestions and recommendations led to improvements in this book. We offer special appreciation to MIT Press senior acquisitions editor Clay Morgan.

We are also grateful to a number of people who read parts of this book or listened to presentations thereof and offered valuable criticisms. We particularly thank John Dryzek, Simon Niemeyer, Robert Goodin, Priya Kurian, Debashish Munshi, Aarti Gupta, Frank Biermann, Ronald Mitchell, Ruben Zondervan, and Alex Zakaras.

Baber thanks the Commission for the International Exchange of Scholars and Italian Fulbright Commission for their support during his tenure as the Fulbright Distinguished Chair of Environmental Policy at the Politecnico di Torino, during which some of the early work for this project was accomplished; the Center for Deliberative Democracy and Global Governance at Australian National University for the visiting fellowship during which two chapters of this volume were drafted; and the Graduate Center for Public Policy and Administration at California State University at Long Beach for its generous support for research-related travel.

Bartlett thanks the University of Vermont College of Arts and Sciences for a research leave in 2012–2013 that greatly speeded this book's completion. The Gund Chair in the Liberal Arts provided crucial resources for the work, while the Department of Political Science offered a collegial and productive research environment. The cheerful assistance of both Candace Smith and Carol Tank-Day was invaluable to maintaining focus as well as sanity.

An earlier version of a portion of chapter 3 was previously published as Walter F. Baber, "Administrative Law and Discursive Democracy: Toward a Comparative Perspective," *International Journal of Public Administration* 34 (2011): 97–111.

An earlier version of a portion of chapter 8 was previously published as Walter F. Baber and Robert V. Bartlett, "International Law and Global Climate Change," in *The Oxford Handbook on Climate Change and Society*, edited by John S. Dryzek, Richard B. Norgaard, and David Schlosberg (New York: Oxford University Press, 2011), 653–665.

1
Nature Rules

The laws of nature are but the mathematical thoughts of God.
—Euclid

Forgive him, for he believes that the customs of his tribe are the laws of nature.
—George Bernard Shaw

As humanity fills every corner of the globe, and culture grows more universal in both form and content, no question looms larger than how we will accommodate ourselves to the impersonal and indifferent demands of nature. Rules will govern that relationship, no matter what form it takes. But it is left to us to decide what sort of rules they will be. Are we going to discipline ourselves to walk lightly and moderate our desires? Or will we continue to take as it suits us all that nature gives until the natural limits are met and our very survival is at risk? As we face this dilemma, an attitude of anthropocentrism is certainly forgivable—even healthy. This is true for at least two reasons. First, the biosphere is genuinely unconcerned about our fate. The earth will likely recover from much of whatever damage we have managed to do to it within only a few millennia of our disappearance. Second, the rules that must govern our relationship with nature are unavoidably social ones. The point is not to wait for the laws of nature to impose unavoidable costs on our actions but rather to constrain our own behavior in advance through freely adopted obligations.

What, then, are our alternatives in crafting a set of rules to govern our relationship with the environment? Should we aspire to the euclidean ideal, seeking to read the mind of God and establish environmental rules for ourselves that are both precise and sacred? Should we admit that all human efforts to order our affairs are a splendid conceit, crafted to hide even from ourselves the depth of our ignorance and impotence? Or is there a middle ground? Is it possible that human beings can puzzle out a set of rules that will guide them across the landscape, preventing the worst of their potential missteps and protecting the basic necessities that nature provides to them? The premise of this book is that the answer to this last question—concerning the possibility of successful global environmental governance—may be yes and that the working out of the details should be the guide to our future. So it may be useful to begin with a brief discussion of what social rules must look like if they are to protect the rest of nature from humans and humans from themselves.

The young man knows the rules, but the old man knows the exceptions.
—Oliver Wendell Holmes

Knowledge of the rules (or almost anything else) is most effective only when that knowledge is combined with experience. Making good decisions about how to behave under a specific set of circumstances requires us to know what issues those circumstances present, which rules are appropriate to those issues, and how to apply those rules to produce the appropriate conclusions. Repeatedly working our way through that analytic process is how we convert mere knowledge into reliable experience. It is how we come genuinely to understand the rules as well as the exceptions to them. This is certainly true of the individual, as she gradually trades the knowledge of youth for that of old age. If you add the capacity to record and transmit the insights of and discoveries made by individuals, you have a learned profession. Add again the doctrine of stare decisis, the notion that precedent should guide current decisions, and you have all the ingredients of common law systems. Stir this mixture vigorously for several centuries, and you have a collection of systems of social rules that governs much of the lives of the world's population.

Common law is common in more than one sense. In particular, the term has been used to refer to customs that prevailed in England prior to the Norman Conquest and imposition of formal law. It has also been used to distinguish between the law of the court and law as it applied to commoners (equals) in disputes where peers were not involved. It has been applied to legal doctrines that became applicable across the realm as circuit-riding judges started to spread evolving legal doctrines in a more uniform pattern—resulting in their becoming common to all. But perhaps most important, common law is common because it exists widely, in many human societies. Common law, as a loose and variable collection of legal as well as political practices rather than a determinate system of doctrine, recurs across both time and geography. It is an idea that works, and people everywhere and in every time have a survival incentive to be pragmatists.[1] Ancient understandings of common law have not been superseded by the contemporary view so much as they have been subsumed by it. The modern understanding tells us that common law is simply "a body of law that develops and derives through judicial decisions, as distinguished from legislative enactments" (Black 1990, 276). Common law is neither constitutional, nor ecclesiastical, nor statutory. It is a residual category of rules derived from precedent rather than positive enactment.

The fabric of common law has, in this contemporary view, grown somewhat monochromatic. But all the old threads can still be discerned in the tapestry. It is still understood that the decisions of the common law derive their authority "from usages and customs of immemorial antiquity, or from the judgments and decrees of courts recognizing, affirming, and enforcing such usages and customs" (ibid., 276). From the modern perspective, this formulation reveals that the common law satisfies the need for both primary and secondary rules of law—the first establishing some behavior as an obligatory standard, and the second explaining the grounds or procedures that justify that obligation (Hart 1994). Its basis in social understandings and the essential equality of its addressees (primary rules) as well as the universality of its ambit and respect for precedent as a guide for the development of new law (secondary rules) are all distinctive qualities of modern common law. Each of these qualities tells us something significant about the rules we need to govern our relationship with the environment.

Integrity has no need of rules.
—Albert Camus

That social understandings in the form of custom should be a basis for the legitimation of authority is not a new insight. Max Weber (1978, 226) described the authority of tradition as legitimate "by virtue of the sanctity of age-old rules and powers," the masters of which "are designated according to traditional rules and obeyed because of their traditional status." In explicating his view of traditional authority, Weber was able to provide examples of chiefs and kings from ancient Africa, Europe, and the Orient who understood themselves as well as their authority in much the same way that he did. This account of legitimate authority (domination, in Weber's terminology) offers both the primary and secondary rule forms required by H.L.A. Hart (1994) for a system of rules to be characterized as law. Tradition supplies both the obligatory norms of behavior and authoritative power of enforcement. Indeed, it would be difficult to offer an example of a traditional society of such cultural integrity that it could do without this Janus-faced assertion of obligation and justification.

Tradition and the modes of authority it grounds have distinct advantages. By assembling administrators, household officials, and favorites from the ranks of kin, the traditional authority figure is able to craft institutions of uncommon stability. When both the rules and rule giver issue from the same immemorial source, the very idea of challenging either seems unnatural. There are, however, certain drawbacks. Most obviously, a traditional system of authority is difficult to reconcile with the essential equality of addressees typical of a common law (or any modern) system of governance. That is far from the only problem. In a system of traditional authority, it is (officially) impossible for law or administrative rule to be deliberately created. Rules that in fact are innovations can be legitimized only by the taxing claim that they have been "valid of yore," but have only recently been recognized by means of the special "wisdom" of the traditional leader (Weber 1978, 227). Moreover, traditional authority structures are hostile to economic modernization. Under the influence of such institutions, "economic relationships tend to be strictly tradition-bound. The development of markets is obstructed, the use of money is primarily consumptive, and the development of capitalism is impossible" (ibid., 238). So in the long run, systems of social rules that rely entirely on the tradition of custom pay a high price for such stability as they enjoy.

In addressing these problems with traditional authority, one of the options discussed by Weber is equally as problematic. Recourse to charismatic authority offers a solution to the problem of introducing new rules, with personal inspiration as a reinforcing narrative in this system of authority. But charismatic authority is no friendlier to modern economic relationships than traditional authority, and it is even more hostile to equality before the law than is traditional authority. The remaining option, then, is to construct a system of obligation on rational grounds and situate it in a system of legal authority.

You have to learn the rules of the game.
And then you have to play better than anyone else.
—Albert Einstein

The core concept of rational/legal authority is that "every body of law consists essentially in a consistent system of abstract rules which have normally been intentionally established. Furthermore, administration of law is held to consist in the application of these rules to particular cases; the administrative process in the rational pursuit of interests which are specified in the order governing the organization within the limits laid down by legal precepts and following principles which are capable of generalized formulation and are approved in the order governing the group, or at least not disapproved in it." The typical person in authority "is himself subject to an impersonal order by orienting his actions to it in his own dispositions and commands" (ibid., 217). Thus, all the addressees of the rules constituting a rationally grounded body of law stand before that law as equals—including those tasked with the creation and enforcement of law.

In the hands of most of his students, Weber's identification of rational/legal authority leads inexorably to the subject that he himself in fact next took up: the creation of monocratic bureaucracy. One of Weber's observations is central here. The development of bureaucracy, he claimed, greatly favored "the leveling of status," which could be shown as its normal tendency. In the interest of equality, bureaucracy tends to eliminate "the office-holder who rules by virtue of status and privileges" as well as those who "hold office on an honorary basis or as an avocation by virtue of their wealth." In this way, "everywhere bureaucratization foreshadows mass democracy" and equality before the law—whatever the source of that law (ibid., 226). Here we find the grounds for the unique, if unexpected, capacity of the common law to reconcile custom and tradition with equality and democracy.

When those in authority are prevented from appropriating the sources of the power that they wield, ownership of custom and tradition remains popular. In principle, at least, free and equal citizens retain the right to identify the issue of obligation arising from the circumstances that confront them, determine which of their shared understandings govern the resolution of those issues, apply those understandings, and judge the consequences to see whether the rules that they live by are in need of amendment. As such, respect for custom and action to satisfy the need for change come together in the moment of democratic self-governance. This reconciliation, though, does nothing to guarantee the universality of rules. Indeed, Weber tended to think of the development of rational/legal authority as necessarily a phenomenon of the nation-state. Consistent with the continental tradition of law, Weber tended to agree with Hans Kelsen ([1949] 2006) that law (properly speaking) is a function of positive enactment rather than a result of the gradual accretion of precedents. To secure the necessary ambit for environmental law and ensure that it has a robust learning capacity, an additional element is required.

The chessboard is the world ...
the rules of the game are what we call the laws of nature ...
and the player on the other side is hidden from us.
—Thomas Henry Huxley

The final element necessary for successfully playing the game of rule-bounded global environmental governance is internalization. There is considerable debate in the social scientific literature about what rule-bounded behavior actually consists of and why people agree to it. One view, which can trace its lineage back to Thomas Hobbes and Immanuel Kant, is that people agree to be bound by rules for instrumental reasons. Their motivation is purely self-interest, but it is a more informed, long-term self-interest than that found in the popular imagination and primitive economics. On this account, rule followers know that if they do not curb their self-interested behavior, they will defeat their ultimate objectives over the long run. Decision theorists often use the tragedy of the commons and prisoners' dilemma to concretize this mode of thinking, and in those forms, the problems associated with narrowly conceived self-interest are quite familiar. Yet one crucial element of rule-governed behavior is difficult to explain under the instrumental view.

Suppose that your neighbor and you agree to take in each other's mail whenever one of you is out of town. Your agreement is casual, but explicit.

Through customary practice, you each make it clear that no more is required to avail yourselves of this benefit than a timely and courteous request. Moreover, this agreement has become part of an overall pattern of "neighborliness" that extends to many different matters, and has proven to be both beneficial and satisfying to you. Imagine further that over the course of several years, your life patterns have diverged to such a degree that you now travel more than your neighbor (although she was most recently out of town). At this point, you make a request for mail service from your neighbor that extends over a longer period than usual for either of you. What are reasonable responses for you if she declines?

Probably all could agree it is time for you to reassess the basis on which you interact with your neighbor. Assuming that you have no other convenient options for dealing with your mail, your neighbor has imposed a significant disutility on you precisely when you were expecting to enjoy a benefit from your previous agreement. At a bare minimum, your neighbor appears to have recalculated the relative costs and benefits involved in this form of neighborliness, and it seems reasonable that you should do the same. But most would agree that it would also be reasonable for you to have an emotional rather than exclusively rational reaction. You might be quite reasonable in regarding your neighbor's renunciation of your prior arrangement to be blameworthy. Granted, over the years she may have come to benefit less from the agreement than she initially had (in relative terms at least). It may be easy enough for you to see that your neighbor (being both intelligent and rational) has taken your possible reactions into account and amended her estimation of the value of neighborliness in itself. You may even be willing to concede that she is within her rights to make both those decisions. Yet you may still find her action to be blameworthy. Clearly, an instrumental account of rule-governed behavior has trouble explaining (much less justifying) that reaction.

Thomas Scanlon (1998, 2008) develops an account of moral obligation that does a better job of explaining the "blaming" aspect of rule-governed behavior. He contrasts a view of blame as a sanction (closely related to punishment) with one that sees blame as the calling out of relationship-damaging behavior. If blame is merely a sanction, then there is nothing objectionable about someone who prices that sanction into her behavior and decides to disappoint your legitimate expectations anyway. On the other hand, if blame is a more complicated matter of calling a person to account for violating the underlying assumptions that sustain a specific form of relationship (such as neighborliness), then a different and more emotionally consequential reaction is warranted. It is inconsistent with the internal character of neighborliness to subject that relationship itself to an ongoing instrumental reappraisal.

It might still be unclear to some, however, where the blameworthy element of subjecting neighborliness to instrumental reappraisal lies. What makes that relationship (and other similar ones) sacrosanct? The answer, perhaps, lies in the conditions under which such relationships come to exist. When you agree to a "take in the mail" arrangement with your neighbor, you are doing more than simply agreeing to purchase a good or service from one provider instead of another. You are establishing a condition of reciprocity that you expect your neighbor to not only follow but also internalize (Gaus 2011). Part of the value of such a relationship is that it can be relied on in a way that exchange relationships between businesses and consumers cannot be. Just because your local car dealer gives you a better price than another dealer across town, it does not follow that she should do so again the next time you shop for a car—and it would be unreasonable for you to blame her if she did not. But when a neighbor unexpectedly begins to treat your relationship as one limited to its exchange value, her action is blameworthy precisely because she is aware of the internalized nature of your relationship, has profited from it in the past, and has depended on and exploited your internalization of those relationships norms. If she wishes to renounce the obligations arising from that internalized relationship, she is obligated (by the essential character of the relationship) to do so under the same circumstances of reciprocity that existed when the relationship was established. If, on the other hand, your neighbor failed to internalize the relationship norms in the first instance, then she is probably a sociopath. In either event, her action is blameworthy because it has given you a false impression of the other player in your rule-governed game.

The golden rule is that there are no golden rules.
—George Bernard Shaw

Bringing what has been said about rule-bounded behavior to bear on global environmental governance (and in anticipation of the discussion of "good neighbor" principles in international law in chapter 5), an effective set of social rules (under conditions of modernity) must be grounded in widely shared social understandings, authored by the addressees, and equal in its application to all addressees. In other words, it must be democratic. Furthermore, an effective set of rules must be capable of learning from (and adapting to) experience, rationally grounded, and internalized (or at least capable of being internalized) by those who participate in its adoption and implementation. It must, in short, be deliberative. The importance of these qualities of environmental rules can best be demonstrated by an illustration of the problems that arise when they are absent. For this purpose, we briefly take up a topic that we will return to often in the following chapters: the problem of global climate change.

The proposition that the earth is undergoing a significant process of warming, due at least in part to human activity, is denied only by fringe political actors and those who live in the opinion enclaves created by them. Agreement regarding what should be done about this problem is, unfortunately, less universal. The latest reminder of how far we have yet to go in coming to grips with climate change is the widespread disappointment with recently negotiated agreements. This disappointment is "inextricably linked to failure to establish a universal legally binding agreement modeled on the Kyoto Protocol containing negotiated targets and timetables" for the reduction of greenhouse gas emissions (Bäckstrand 2011, 669). The soon-to-expire Kyoto Protocol was supposed to be replaced at the 2009 Copenhagen meeting with a new set of standards for a new compliance period. It was also meant to be the occasion when the international climate change policy community welcomed the United States back into its fold.

A central element of the developing climate regime was the conviction that in the absence of true global democracy, strengthening the values of democratic procedure could enhance transnational legitimacy (Buchanan and Keohane 2006). Democratic accountability could be promoted through the development of shared global publics (nongovernmental organization [NGO] contestation), professional norms and transnational epistemic communities, and market mechanisms, such as rating agencies and corporate standards (Keohane and Nye 2003). This set of ideas represents a response to legitimacy deficits arising from the weak accountability of political elites and international negotiators, who increasingly have to justify their decisions to both national and transnational publics (Zürn 2004). From this perspective, the US opposition to the Kyoto Protocol and resistance to a new binding treaty are viewed as manifestations of the broader phenomenon of the democratic deficit. But an alternate perspective is possible.

The climate regime, beginning with the United Nations Framework Convention on Climate Change (UNFCCC) and extending through the negotiation of the Kyoto Protocol, has been plagued by a lack of goal clarity along with the failure to develop principles of fairness that are satisfactory to all the major parties and grouping of parties. This weakness has revealed itself in the failures to develop adequate systems for monitoring, reporting, and verification, establish credible funding mechanisms, and meet the need for flexibility in the ongoing process of regime development (Young 2011). Perhaps the proponents of the Kyoto Protocol have erred, though, by failing to complete the necessary transition from an executive multilateralism that privileges elite discourses to a societally backed multilateralism that ensures full multimedia coverage of as well as broad public access tp the process of policy development (Zürn 2004).

That failure to democratize the regime process fully would account for the fact that a critical dimension of global climate policy to date has been an evident gap between what is fair and what is economically acceptable to key countries (Baer 2011). Viewed against this backdrop, the 2009 Copenhagen Accord and 2010 Cancun Agreements would not have to be regarded as complete failures. The accord's pledge and review process, for example, could be interpreted as a turn toward a bottom-up and decentralized climate policy architecture in which voluntary pledges from major emitters and groups of emitters replace multilaterally negotiated targets (Stavins and Stowe 2010). Any climate regime that hopes to be effective must be able to count on the member states themselves to take the lead in dealing with matters of implementation, enforcement, and adaptation (Young 2011). In other words, the rules embodied in that regime must be capable of being internalized by the addressees. The likelihood that the rules will be depends significantly on whether they are based on equality among their addressees, universal in scope, and grounded in widely shared social understandings. The rules of that regime must be rationally grounded obligations as opposed to calculated advantages that are capable of evolution over time as our evaluations of what is fair develop and we encounter new challenges to our shared objectives.

Works of art make rules, rules do not make works of art.
—Claude Debussy

We might be forgiven if we are troubled by the suggestion that there is no golden rule for the development of international environmental regimes—that all we can hope to do is muddle through the endless process of crafting and revising new rules to replace those that have become normatively problematic or outdated in purely practical terms. To the extent that negotiating international agreements is an art rather than a science (the rules involved being less the thoughts of God than the customs of our tribe), perhaps the very idea of rule-governed behavior is alien to global governance. Perhaps every experience in that area of human endeavor is a one-off, unique experience from which no lessons for the future may be learned. It is certainly beyond our capacity to evaluate that possibility. We do, however, have sufficient confidence in the power of human intellect that we are skeptical of arguments that put any achievement permanently beyond its reach. Even a sincere and well-founded sense of futility does not require complete resignation. Low probability outcomes justify considerable effort if the consequences of success are sufficiently valuable. So even if genuinely effective agreements to address international environmental challenges like global climate change would be rare and improbable works of art, maybe those few successes would provide the rules (of thumb at least) that we need to replicate that kind of achievement with increasing frequency. To continue our exploration of that possibility, it is necessary to look more closely at how rules of behavior become concretized in international law along with how that process might be democratized. This is the task that we take up next.

2

Mapping and Developing Consensus for Global Environmental Governance

The linkages among society and the environment generate normative challenges across at least three distinct dimensions. First, environmental change imposes costs (both individual and collective) that fall disproportionately on some social groups—often those that have historically suffered from disadvantage and disenfranchisement. Second, the necessity of creating institutional arrangements for managing environmental change, and integrating those decisions with collective choices in other areas, poses value-laden questions of policy design. Third, the human causes and consequences of environmental change and collective choices they involve pit citizens along with their understandings of the world against one another at the level of social action.

The task confronting environmental governance analysts in responding to these challenges is to describe accurately as well as progressively develop the normative, political, and social consensus necessary for managing society–environment linkages in ways that are both ecologically sustainable and democratically legitimate. The work of deliberative theory offers options for matching techniques to tasks mapped onto these human dimensions of environmental change. Deliberative democrats can, for instance, analyze the issues of distributional justice and social equity by using hypothetical case scenarios in juristic deliberation exercises to describe existing elements of normative consensus regarding general legal principles. They can employ techniques of deliberative polling to measure support for alternative policy paradigms that institutionalize policy goals and objectives related to the society–environment linkage. And deliberative democrats can promote stakeholder partnerships that allow contending local discourses regarding the implementation of environmental policies to be reconciled through the coproduction of regulatory programs and procedures.

Although there is undoubtedly much to be said for the achievements associated with incompletely theorized agreements (Sunstein 1999), a complete indifference to theorizing our successes ultimately leaves us less able to replicate them. It is in this respect that the efforts of governance and policy theorists can be especially useful. What is needed most is a basic road map allowing environmental actors to identify the techniques of deliberative democracy that best fit the challenges they face at each stage of the policy process—the formation of basic regulatory norms, choice among competing models of governance of environmental change, and production of concrete plans of action. A first cut at mapping and specifying such an approach to developing a normative consensus for governance is summarized in table 2.1.

Normative Principles, Policy Models, and Action Plans

Deliberative democratic practice has generally focused either on choices between competing policy models (such as direct command and control regulation versus market-based regulatory strategies) or the development of local implementation agreements within the context of an existing regulatory scheme. We suggest that a process of juristic deliberation could be used to identify widely supported normative principles and general propositions of law through the adjudication by citizen juries of hypothetical cases involving disputes over environmental issues (Baber and

Table 2.1
A normative consensus for governance

Governance challenges	Deliberative technique	Deliberative problem	Deliberative product	Regulative standard
Distributional justice	Juristic deliberation	Hypothetical cases	General legal principles	Normative consensus
Institutions and policy integration	Deliberative polling/policy juries	Alternative policy paradigms	Policy goals and objectives	Political consensus
Social causes/consequences of change	Stakeholder partnerships	Contending local discourses	Implementation plans/regulatory coproduction	Social consensus

Bartlett 2009a). It is relatively easy to construct such hypothetical disputes. One can, for example, devise hypothetical scenarios that pit the doctrines of *prior appropriation* (according to which rights to water are established by a "first in time, first in right" rule) against claims of *equitable utilization* and state necessity (based on a "public trust" doctrine under which resources like water are held in trust for general use). This can be done across a wide range of factual circumstances without directly engaging the perceived interests of the citizens who participate in such deliberations.

Norman Frohlich and Joe Oppenheimer (1992) offer a point of departure for this approach. Their empirical research in ethical theory involved a series of negotiations among small groups of individuals (normally five persons) who were asked to choose among four possible schemes of income distribution to be applied in a simulated economy. Their choice was then implemented in a series of simulations in which participants were asked to perform work for which they were paid, and then their incomes were adjusted according to the policy they had previously adopted.

Juristic deliberation research and practice differs from Frohlich and Oppenheimer's approach in several respects. Because participants are asked to choose among several regulatory norms rather than among redistributive policies, a more complex hypothetical situation is needed. As opposed to a simple distribution of income, it is necessary to present participants with a more richly detailed set of circumstances involving the loss of an environmental good caused by one actor and imposed on a different actor. What can be simulated is a hypothetical legal case—complete with parties to be heard, pleadings to be weighed, and philosophical problems to be resolved. This approach is suggested by the work of Kenneth Culp Davis (1969a, 1969b). The factual circumstances of the cases can be developed to require participants to choose between hypothetical outcomes that represent some of the underlying normative principles of environmental protection, and environmental change and governance.

Moreover, because it is more difficult to simulate regulatory actions than instances of income and taxation, it is necessary to create a survey instrument to capture the experiences of participants and relate them to deliberative outcomes. Instead of focusing on the reactions that participants have when they experience the consequences of their policy choices, juristic deliberation concentrates on the deliberative process that produces those choices and the participants' level of normative commitment to the principles eventually chosen. One might have a series of scenarios in which neighboring states lodge disputes against one another in a "court" over the use of a river that makes up their shared border (such as presented in appendixes B–C). One of the disputes might involve whether the existing pattern of resource utilization (which significantly favors one state) should be respected or whether that pattern should be altered to allow both states to exploit the river's resources more equally (based on factors like their size and population). The advantage for environmental governance is clear. When resource utilization issues implicate basic normative questions (as they generally do), a preliminary deliberative experience with consensual norm building offers a foundation of mutuality that has the potential to expedite agreement at later stages of the policy process. This process of juristic deliberation using hypothetical legal cases to identify basic normative principles is represented by the entries in the first row of table 2.1.

Deliberative democratic techniques are now more commonly used at another stage of the policy process: the choice among competing policy models. Within the deliberative democratic experience are "minipublics" (Goodin and Dryzek 2006)—innovations that seems generally well suited to selecting from among competing policy paradigms. These techniques include planning cells, consensus conferences (Smith 2009), deliberative polling (Fishkin 1995), and policy or citizen juries (Huitema, van De Kerkhof, and Pesch 2007). They involve convening deliberative assemblies of from ten to several hundred individuals who are presented with information regarding an existing public policy and the leading alternative approaches. Deliberative polling brings together a stratified random sample of citizens in the sponsoring jurisdiction to participate in both small-group discussions and larger plenary sessions, thereby allowing them to assimilate substantial and balanced information about a pending issue of public policy, exchange views on competing policy alternatives, and come to considered judgments (as opposed to unreflective opinions) about what the group considers to be the most reasonable course of action (Ackerman and Fishkin 2003). In effect, average citizens are permitted to play the role of legislator for a limited period with respect to a single policy problem involving a limited number of alternative solutions. Although the results of such exercises are not binding on actual legislators, eventual policies that deviate markedly from patterns of decision revealed by deliberative polls are immediately suspect, and may be avoided by elected and appointed officials for precisely that reason (Gastil and Levine 2005). Larger assemblies can be then divided into "juries" of twelve to fifteen persons, and each jury deliberates the choices it has been presented. In some cases, a jury is asked to come to the most inclusive consensus that it can. In other instances, no conclusion is asked of the jury. The participants are instead surveyed after their deliberations to determine their "considered opinion," as opposed to their initial preferences.

In the context of watershed governance, a policy jury might be presented the choice between a piecemeal approach to the constituent problems of soil conservation, species protection, and so forth, or a policy model that emphasizes the development of a comprehensive resource utilization plan encompassing within it the entire scope of the watershed. Or perhaps the choice might be between a series of command-and-control mechanisms of environmental protection and a collection of market-based strategies for resource conservation. As an example, biodiversity policy in the United States has long been dominated by the Endangered Species Act, which imposes strict (some would say draconian) restrictions on the taking of living beings once their species has been designated as endangered. Another paradigm is the biodiversity policy of Italy, which stresses a comprehensive planning approach in which both the direct and indirect effects of government decisions across a wide range of policy areas are evaluated for their impacts on plants and animals. As one might have guessed, the Endangered Species Act has often been criticized for its narrow and belated focus on species that have become "terminally ill," whereas the Italian approach has been faulted for not having sufficient enforcement capacity to actually protect anything. It should be equally unsurprising that a broader "biohabitat" perspective has developed in the United States, and that Italy has taken steps to put more teeth in its biodiversity policy. This convergence is due, at least in part, to the emergence of an underlying consensus among Americans and Italians on the general contours of what an effective biodiversity policy requires.

Observers of deliberative democratic practice see both promise and peril in our collective experience with deliberative polling. On the one hand, policy juries have been lauded for offering us our best glimpse into the preferences of a more informed and engaged electorate—preferences that usually differ markedly from those expressed in conventional polls, the voting booth, and legislation engineered by self-interested lobbying groups (Ackerman and Fishkin 2003). On the other hand, deliberating groups are prone to error as a consequence of group polarization (Sunstein 2006). Even critics, however, concede that their concerns apply largely to homogeneous deliberative groups that are weighing questions susceptible to empirically verifiable answers. There is little to suggest that politically diverse policy juries are less able than elite decision makers to achieve ecologically rational results (as that phrase is being used here), and the advantages of such broadly democratic approaches in terms of political rationality should be evident. When methods of selection are used that provide demographically and ideologically heterogeneous deliberative groups, there is no reason to doubt the authenticity of the political consensus that emerges. A deliberative democratic approach is preferable to other approaches because it contains within itself the means of revising both its procedures and products at the initiative of either the organizers or participants (Gutmann and Thompson 2004). The second row of table 2.1 represents this process of deliberative polling at the stage of choosing between contending policy paradigms in order to identify basic policy objectives.

Finally, deliberative democracy is already a familiar feature of governance at the action plans and policy implementation levels in the form of stakeholder partnerships (Sabatier et al. 2005). Subnational stakeholder groups of this sort have already engaged the interests of deliberative democratic theorists (Baber and Bartlett 2005). These structures of governance can best be understood as arrangements for organizing and reconciling competing local discourses about the implications of general legal requirements when applied to local questions. The objective is to develop implementation plans at the subnational level that will achieve national (or international) objectives through the coproduction of regulatory governance. One example of this approach has been described as "collaborative learning" (Cheng and Fiero 2005).

Collaborative learning, a recent innovation in public participation that departs from the traditional focus on issues and interests, is an approach designed specifically to address the complexity and rancorous conflict that frequently are a feature of the governance of public lands. It is characterized by a systems approach to understanding environmental change and governance issues, the promotion (instead of avoidance) of dialogue about differences among stakeholders, and an emphasis on feasible improvements in concrete circumstances rather than idea outcomes over the longer term. Unlike deliberative polling, which seeks stratified random samples of the population, collaborative learning employs landscape-based working groups that represent key stakeholder groups. An outstanding illustration of such groups is the watershed partnership (Clark 1997). These voluntary groups convene at the local or regional level to discuss issues of watershed governance. Possessing no formal authority, watershed partnerships are open to anyone wishing to participate. But they generally attract large landowners and corporations whose behavior substantially affects watershed outcomes, environmentalists who can take up or forgo their right to sue under a variety of statutory schemes, and government officials who want to find safe ground in between.

Perhaps the leading example of stakeholder partnerships, watershed partnerships are a well-understood and thoroughly documented technique for involving local participants in the management of a region's natural resources. Yet whether this is a widely deployable social technology is open to question. Stakeholder participation generally enjoys the advantage of small scale as well as relatively high levels of social and cultural homogeneity. Under these circumstances, a shared sense of community plays a significant role in the success of issue-specific planning processes (Young 2008). These circumstances, though, are seldom present when the environmental challenge at hand is international in character. The adequacy of funding and institutional capacity understood as critical to the success of stakeholder partnerships in the developed nations (Leach and Pelky 2001) can rarely be counted on to be available elsewhere in the world. Although transfers of technology and resources are possible, they implicate other groups of stakeholders, taking policymakers further from the relative simplicity of conventional watershed governance. There is a fear that low levels of literacy and political empowerment in the developing countries of the world will depress levels of stakeholder involvement, particularly among subgroups of the population that are already neglected or exploited (Gupta 2008; Lubell et al. 2002). Fully participatory democracy, it is sometimes suggested, is a luxury that few countries can afford and few citizens even value. How can each of these concerns be answered?

International problems of environmental governance unquestionably place more complex demands on processes of collective action than do strictly local issues. But at the same time, international issues are even less amenable to command-and-control solutions than are problems arising in individual communities. Watershed partnerships, like all cooperative decision processes, have distinct limitations. Positive outcomes are always dependent on existing stocks of human, social, and financial capital (Lubell et al. 2002). But watershed partnerships enjoy distinct advantages as a result of their ability to coalesce and operate in the absence of assertions of governmental authority. These organizations come in several varieties: government centered, citizen centered, and mixed membership. Furthermore, the secret to their success is not a traditional sense of community per se. It is that participants see themselves as members of a community of fate. The pressing demands of their shared environmental challenge give them the motivation necessary to seek out collaborative solutions, regardless of whether they share social and cultural commonalities, or are subject to the same legal mandates (Hardy and Koontz 2009). It is the nature of the challenge that determines the character of the partnership.

Resource adequacy is, in some ways, a more difficult challenge than the absence of social solidarity or state sovereignty. It is an unhappy coincidence (and perhaps not so coincidental) that the most troubled regions of the world from an environmental perspective also face the most daunting economic challenges and possess the most limited institutional capabilities. Sometimes regarded as the poster child for environmental lost causes, the Philippines is a case in point. After decades of neglect, Philippine biodiversity is on the verge of collapse. Ecosystems have been pushed beyond their limits, often with tragic consequences for human populations. Philippine spending on environmental protection has been miniscule. When capacity building has been attempted, the economy rather than the ecology has been its focus. In spite of this, research suggests that signs of hope are emerging. Locally based stakeholder partnerships, with the financial and technical support of international organizations, have made progress in water quality, forest conservation, and species protection. Noticeable gains have also occurred in the production of science-based environmental publications and the building of institutional capacity for environmental governance in civil society (Posa et al. 2008).

There is no reason to believe that either literacy or political efficacy is a prerequisite to participation in a stakeholder partnership for environmental governance. Environmentalists have enlisted construction workers in Panama in the effort to rescue animals threatened by expansion work in the Canal Zone. Not only have the construction workers been capable and reliable, they have begun to show an independent commitment to the effort (Correa, Carver, and Master 2008). The mangrove ecosystems of the north Brazilian coast have been converted from de facto open-access areas subject to excessive exploitation into user-regulated and user-managed common pool resources (Glaser and Oliveira 2004). Most promising of all, the management of Kenyan wildlife resources by stakeholder partnerships has been enabled by the creation of an innovative political framework, development of the capacity for self-organization within rural Kenyan communities, and incentives created by the existence of group ranches within various wildlife dispersal areas (Mburu and Birner 2007). None of these features of Kenyan society are dependent in any direct or significant way on the literacy or political influence of local residents.

Experience with the role of watershed partnerships in developing governance action plans is particularly illuminating. It suggests that effective partnerships must be full ones. Regardless of the provenance of the watershed group (citizen based, agency based, or mixed), the appropriate matching of partnership structure and operation to their roles is key (Moore and Koontz 2003). This can be accomplished only by involving the local community in the underlying research that defines the policy problem at hand, because the watershed partnership fills the gap between what public institutions can achieve on their own and what the community itself needs (Arnold and Fernandez-Gimenez 2007; Shandas and Messer 2008). But to achieve this level of autonomous input, community members of resource management partnerships need to be full partners. The regulatory environment within which they operate must be characterized by a low level of command-and-control enforcement by central authorities (Lubell et al. 2002), and they must enjoy the political clout and legal standing necessary to engage agency representatives as equals as well as insist on the development of consensual (or nearly consensual) resolutions of regulatory problems (Cronin and Ostergren 2007). It is this peculiarly *social* consensus that sustains the development, implementation, evaluation, and redesign of regulatory action plans during the numerous iterations through which they must pass. This process of using stakeholder partnerships to sort through contending discourse among local contributors to policy implementation is represented in the third row of table 2.1.

Observations on Deliberative Practice

There is nothing so distinctive about the issues of environmental change and governance that it puts them out of the reach of democratic deliberation. New techniques like juristic deliberation can easily be imagined as tools for exploring the contours and limitations of normative consensus about the exploitation and conservation of natural resources. Well-tested techniques such as deliberative polling can readily be used to elicit a more reflective public opinion on contending models of watershed governance. Of course, watershed partnerships are the preeminent example of stakeholder planning and the coproduction of regulatory implementation. Thus, at each successive step of the process of developing environmental governance and policy, deliberative techniques are readily deployable and offer significant advantages over less fully participatory approaches, especially in terms of the political durability of the solutions that they produce.

The desirability of greater public participation in the formation of international environmental regimes has long been recognized. The involvement of citizens in the development of environmental policy through domestic administrative rule making has been found to increase governmental accountability, improve the information base of public decision makers, and enhance the efficiency of the policymaking process by revealing public sentiment at an earlier point than would otherwise be the case. The need to realize all these advantages is just as great at the international level (Wirth 1996).

Citizen juries, in particular, offer some special advantages for environmental decision making. As a complement to more traditional approaches to data gathering on public preferences, citizen juries allow for both the description of *considered* opinions and an assessment of the adequacy of the knowledge base underlying those opinions. This is especially helpful in addressing the "citizen value" versus "consumer value" arguments that so often arise in this policy arena (Kenyon, Hanley, and Nevin 2001).

Discourse-based techniques like citizen juries allow us to escape the paradox between the public nature of ecosystem values and their measurement through the isolated expression of individual preferences. Because the allocation of environmental goods to one party affects the welfare of others, raising significant normative and ethical questions, discursive groups of this sort would seem to be an especially appropriate forum for airing the issues of social equity that environmental decision making inevitably involves (Wilson and Howarth 2002).

The story of citizen juries is not one of unlimited promise, however. Assembling appropriately composed groups is always a challenge. The role to be played by experts and government officials, and accountability mechanisms associated with their participation, must also be considered (Kenyon 2005). More important still, there is an ever-present danger that deliberative discourse will degenerate into mere pluralistic bargaining. Whereas some of our experiences with citizens' juries suggests that they provide significant gains in citizen learning and have a positive effect on participants' sense of political efficacy, there are also worrisome signs of recurring problems with groupthink. But an awareness of these tendencies on the part of those who construct these "minipublics will allow for more consistent and reliable jury design (Huitema, van De Kerkhof, and Pesch 2007).

The fact that democratic deliberation can be deployed at every stage of the process of environmental governance leads to another observation: deliberative democracy has the potential to greatly add to political legitimacy. This is significant because environmental governance is likely to involve issues of distributive justice. This characteristic of environmental governance makes it difficult but essential to broaden involvement to include representatives of historically underrepresented groups. In the United States, for example, the political and economic disadvantages of Native American tribes mean that they are not often involved in watershed partnerships. Yet their involvement (when it occurs) leads public officials to deploy financial and human resources in ways that better manage watersheds across a full range of social values, resulting in more equitable and defensible regulatory outcomes (Cronin and Ostergren 2007). Thus, the realization that every step in the processes of environmental governance can include substantial citizen participation means that a virtuous circle of public confidence and public involvement can be created to legitimize ecologically sound outcomes that might otherwise be rejected because they may disappoint some stakeholders.

Recognizing that democratic deliberation has a role to play at every stage of governance is just a short step from realizing that the linear assumption inherent in the very concept of the policy process needs to be overcome. In any broadly participatory political process, arriving at consensus is a recursive proposition. Yesterday's normative agreement can be unwound by today's political dissent or tomorrow's social discord. Skilled policy analysts and experienced public managers, perhaps to a greater degree than theorists, are aware that all conclusions are tentative and no victory is final. That is why the leaders of collaborative watershed partnerships frequently find themselves grappling with challenges of organizational development and maintenance rather than the environmental issues that originally brought them to the table (Bonnell and Koontz 2007). Collaborative governance is at least as much a matter of organization building as it is environmental protection. A long-recognized strength of deliberative democracy is its tendency to build social capital (Shandas and Messer 2008). It does so in at least two ways.

First, well-implemented democratic deliberation makes it possible to achieve an "economy of moral disagreement." Democratic deliberation requires citizens to justify their political positions to one another by seeking a fully public rationale—one that all deliberators could (at least in principle) accept. This requirement minimizes the outright rejection by deliberators of positions that they oppose by discouraging a reliance on comprehensive moral or religious doctrines in favor of more limited rationales allowing for the eventual convergence of their views with those of others (Gutmann and Thompson 2004). Second, democratic deliberation has the tendency to turn a collection of separate individuals into a self-identified group whose members see one another as cooperators in a shared project instead of opponents in a zero-sum contest. Among the norms that deliberation promotes is group cooperation, which is frequently strong enough to discourage members from clinging to their positions for transient or entirely personal reasons (Miller 2003). For the environmental practitioner, it means that deliberative exercises conducted iteratively in any given community are likely to increase that community's ability to resolve problems in a collaborative way. Together these two features of democratic deliberation (its tendency to reduce moral disputes and promote consensus) can reduce the costs of organizational maintenance in a stakeholder partnership by narrowing the grounds of disagreement among the participants, thereby reducing the range of possible policy outcomes with which any final decision procedure must deal. When this result is achieved, more of the resources of environmental professionals can be turned to solving environmental problems as less time is spent overcoming the forces of organizational entropy. Ultimately, a tipping point is reached where gains in democratic legitimacy are no longer paid for with losses in organizational effectiveness.

An as yet unrecognized advantage of deliberative approaches to governance and policy formulation is that when looked at collectively, they constitute a deliberative system that lends a greater degree of coherence to the often-messy business of integrating citizen participation into the policy process. When one examines table 2.1 closely, one can discern the outlines of a governance cycle. To begin with, normative choice based on the adjudication of hypotheticals requires that those hypotheticals be drafted. The social scientist or environmental governance professional is the obvious choice to do the drafting. But this need not be an exclusive step in the process. Beyond the legitimating role played by disinterested citizens (as final arbiters), representatives from both the development and conservation sides of the debate can be asked to provide such input as is required to ensure that the hypothetical represents the arguments of actual stakeholders at their best. In this context, consensus does not mean agreement about the ultimate results of adjudication. It is an agreement among interested parties instead—a normative consensus that the hypothetical case to be presented is valid as a test of the competing philosophical positions.

The next deliberative step, the choice by policy juries among competing paradigms of regulatory policy, necessitates a different sort of consensus. What is required is an agreement among the advocates that the political goals and objectives of their favored policy option are accurately represented. Explanatory material provided to juries in support of each policy design must, by general agreement, be grounded in reliable research and valid inference. Certainly, administrative law judges possess the capacity to weigh the adversarial filings of "friends of the court" and summarize those materials in ways that are adequate to the needs of citizen decision makers. Judicial institutions have developed extensive bodies of legal doctrine regarding the admissibility of evidence and appropriate instructions for jurors. This body of knowledge is readily available to any administrator who requires guidance on how to present competing policy paradigms in an evenhanded manner to citizen juries. Juries can support a *political consensus*, but one necessarily bounded by the structure of the decision choices presented.

The policy approach eventually adopted will require the development of implementation plans that are specific to each region and jurisdiction where the problem underlying the policy arises. For instance, watershed governance may be undertaken within the context of a state or national policy mandate, but its implementation is an outstanding example of the aphorism that policy is procedure. Watershed partnerships have shown a marked capacity for translating broad policy mandates into environmental governance plans that are durable and workable, because they are local and consensual. Deliberative democracy, at this level, does not pretend to impartiality nor require it of the participants. Involvement in the planning process is voluntary and open to all. The resulting action plan is intended to capture not an ideal outcome but rather a *social consensus* about what compromises and accommodations will be required for those involved to move forward in a sufficiently cooperative fashion such that the convening authority will not withdraw its support of the partnership.

An additional advantage to viewing deliberative democratic techniques as elements in a governance cycle is that it allows us to address problems of democratic legitimacy. This is particularly true in the area of international law and policy. Jürgen Habermas (1996) argues that democratic legitimacy results when behavioral rules have the qualities of *normativity* and *facticity*. A rule is legitimate, according to this view, when those it addresses can regard it as both morally justified and practically effective—in other words, as both a social norm and social fact. International rules therefore suffer from both their lack of any genuinely democratic provenance, and their frequent failure to be fully developed and executed. A deliberative governance cycle offers solutions at each of these levels.

Transnational deliberations that allow representative samples of the global public to resolve concrete (but hypothetical) disputes over important ecological values would provide an opportunity to discover areas of normative agreement about basic principles of environmental protection and the use of natural resources. Where normative consensus is lacking, such deliberations would allow for the more accurate "mapping" of citizens' considered opinions—resulting in an "economy of moral disagreement" (Gutmann and Thompson 2004) that would reduce international tensions and promote cooperation in areas where cooperation is actually possible.

At the level of the development of paradigms of regulatory policy, the deliberative polling of representative citizen groups at the national level would allow for the democratic legitimation of choices among the available alternative approaches to environmental protection and governance. If the alternatives presented are each plausible manifestations of a normative consensus identified earlier in the transnational governance cycle, the resulting choices might be expected to constitute a form *of* common but differentiated responsibility that would enjoy greater political viability because it possessed greater democratic legitimacy. James Fishkin's (2009) deliberative polling in the People's Republic of China shows that these techniques do not require high levels of education, economic development, or previous democratic experience.

Finally, at the level of policy execution, the use of stakeholder partnerships to develop implementation plans holds promise for transnational governance. These decentralized approaches to environmental protection and governance have been particularly useful in circumstances where national governments either lacked the capacity to impose national solutions or were reluctant to do so for political reasons. The implication for international law and policy are clear. Where enforcement options are of limited utility or entirely lacking, voluntary compliance can only be enhanced when those whose conduct is to be regulated are centrally involved in defining what compliance actually amounts to in practice.

So when viewed in a systematic perspective, the model of deliberative policy development presented here offers a coherent picture of a participatory planning cycle that provides a significant level of citizen involvement at each stage of the governance process. It legitimates and rationalizes the involvement of interest groups and other NGOs in the policy formulation. And it lends concreteness and plausibility to the idea of consensus as something more than a political ideal.

Is Deliberation Worth the Cost?

Each of the aforementioned deliberative practices imposes costs, both in terms of financial and personnel resources as well as the political risks attendant to broader public participation in environmental governance. Why should professional managers, already short on resources and long on controversy, spend either organizational or political capital on these efforts? Three major justifications suggest themselves.

First, environmental regimes must meet the standard of ecological rationality if they are to be effective in practice. Though not especially bold, this is an important assertion because it carries with it a certain amount of freight. One could describe many forms of rationality (Bartlett 1986). Some of these forms of rationality are at least partly incompatible. In some instances, they may even conflict in fundamental ways. Moreover, they are not all of the same order of importance. But two of them are critical to this argument: political and ecological rationality.

Paul Diesing (1962) contends that political rationality takes precedence over other forms because the solution of problems of governance makes possible an attack on other problems within which concerns over other forms of rationality arise. A serious deficiency in political rationality thus can undermine our ability to pursue, much less achieve, any other form of rationality. But John Dryzek (1987) views ecological rationality as fundamental. The failure to preserve and promote the integrity of the environmental and material underpinning of society would render ineffectual, and even irrelevant, our efforts to achieve other forms of rationality. Bearing in mind that Diesing did not explicitly consider the status of ecological rationality, it is a small step from Dryzek's assertion to the claim that ecological rationality is a Janus-faced concept. Ecological rationality subsumes the concepts of both environmental and political sustainability, viewing each as an essential element in the long-term protection of humanity's ecological resources and an essential prerequisite to the pursuit of other forms of rationality (Baber and Bartlett 2005).

A second justification for democratic deliberation is that its elitist- and interest-group-driven alternatives are inadequate. To satisfy ecological rationality's need for political sustainability, a more robust form of democracy than contemporary interest group liberalism is required. Although it may be true that reports of liberalism's death have been greatly exaggerated, it is not generally disputed that the patient is suffering from an illness. The diagnosis that liberalism is inherently incompatible with environmental protection because it takes human interests as the measure of all values (Matthews 1991) does not have to be entirely correct for us to recognize that some new form of democracy may be called for. We need only acknowledge that there are real tensions between preservation and conservation—between protection and wise use—and that the consequences of ignoring those tensions are potentially serious.

Both elite meritocracy and interest group oligopoly fail the test of ecological rationality. A meritocracy of science-based elites will ultimately fail to translate its understanding of environmental problems into effective environmental policy. Simply as a practical matter, the dynamics of the policy process requires experts to express themselves in ordinary language, adopt the lay perspective when engaged in collective decision making, and offer reasons for the positions they take in the public arena that are fully accessible to the other actors they encounter there and hope to influence (Baber and Bartlett 2005). To overcome this problem without surrendering these elites' claim to special authority, a meritocracy would have to sell itself to (or actually become) the alternative that William Ophuls (1997) has posed it against: an interest group oligopoly. But that form of governance will also fail to achieve ecological rationality because it is politically unsustainable in modern societies and cannot produce the broadly held ecological consensus that successful environmental governance requires. Problems of environmental governance generally are so thoroughly interpenetrated with questions of individual choice that new moral, conceptual, and affective frameworks must be developed (Valadez 2001). A mutualistic and cooperative view of nature is required, in which human social, economic, and political life can be reconciled. Only through the creation of institutions of governance that are more (not less) democratic than the existing practices of interest group liberalism can that result be achieved (Baber and Bartlett 2005).

Finally, democratic deliberation is justified by a number of developments, often discussed under the general heading of globalization, that impede the ability of national governments along with their subunits to address problems of environmental governance associated with resource and environmental regimes alike. A range of increasingly powerful agents, including NGOs, transnational advocacy networks, communities of scientific expertise, and social movements of global reach, are challenging the conventional sovereign state for control of the environmental agenda. The resulting tensions are clearly visible in the transnationalization of governance as it increasingly becomes the subject of international environmental regimes (Conca 2005). Problems of soil conservation, water management, and the preservation of species diversity that challenge national and subnational governmental institutions are merely localized manifestations of the loss of vital ecosystem services at a global scale (Galaz et al. 2004). These challenges manifest themselves at both the subnational and supranational levels of governance, calling into question basic principles of environmental protection, contending models of environmental regulation, and competing plans of environmental action.

Deliberative democratic processes have immense potential to inform and legitimate environmental governance at each of these levels in ways that respond to the challenges of ecological rationality, popular participation, and globalization (Baber and Bartlett 2005, 2009b). Techniques of democratic deliberation are at the disposal of those whose duty it is to regulate the human dimensions of global environmental change. If environmentalism is to find its "third way" (Minteer 2006), if it is to develop a common language in which to construct environmental governance regimes possessed of a genuinely democratic provenance, that breakthrough is most likely found at the level of practice—in the iterative innovations in problem solving developed by those on the front lines of environmental change, environmental protection, and governance. At the global level, the near impossibility or severe underdevelopment of other modes of problem solving means that any heavy lifting to address the ensemble of interrelated environmental problem will continue to be undertaken in much same way as has been the case for the last half century: by developing the norms, rules, and institutions that constitute international law, with all the limitations, baggage, and potentiality inherent therein.

3

Legislation by Consensus: The Potential of International Law in Global Environmental Governance

Like many political concepts, governance is an encompassing term lacking agreement about its core elements. Minimally, it refers to processes of societal collective action (governing) without implying, including, or excluding authoritative institutions (government). Although the concept is highly useful for understanding domestic politics and the contributions made to problem solving by civil society (governance beyond government), it is particularly valuable to the understanding and design of transnational collective action, which occurs in a political system whose singular characteristic is the absence of an overarching government apparatus. National sovereignty, even if somewhat attenuated by the forces of globalization, treaty commitments, and international institutions such as the United Nations and European Union, precludes anything resembling global government. Governance encompasses action and interaction by expert and activist networks, intergovernmental organizations (IGOs), NGOs, state governments, multinational corporations, and transnational regimes, creating and using the rights, rules, practices, procedures, mechanisms, and shared belief systems that at the global level, collectively constitute a political system (global governance without global government). A centrally important component of this evolving governance system is international law.

If law is understood to be nothing more than rules formally promulgated by a unified sovereign authority, then of course international law is an oxymoron. Indeed, it is easy to find scholars who argue that international law is not really law. But this is based on a misappreciation of what constitutes domestic (municipal) law within recognizable nation-states. Although constitutions and legislation are the most salient sources of municipal law, many other sources can be identified in most societies—such as, for example, administrative edicts, adjudicatory decisions, and long-standing traditions. There are no constitutions in international law; the rules most comparable to legislation are the regionally limited directives and regulations of the European Union. Nevertheless, international law has several other identifiable and acknowledged sources (Peel 2011; Di-Mento 2003), including: thousands of treaties, conventions, and protocols, traditionally between states, but in recent decades sometimes recognizing nonstate actors; customary norms and rules accepted as binding; the case law of international courts and tribunals; the binding acts of international organizations; general principles of law; and nonbinding principles, guidelines, and recommendations adopted by states and international institutions (soft law).

Thus international law is not distinctive in its sources; analogies can be identified in the municipal law of many societies. Particularly in the United Kingdom and many of its former colonies, the bulk of what constitutes municipal law is common law, consisting of binding customary norms and rules derived as well as codified from the decisions and practices of judicial tribunals over centuries—analogous to customary rules and case law above with respect to international law. Common law is not unique to Britain and countries once colonized by it. For instance, an earlier system of common law based on Germanic customs and then codified in Latin can be traced back as far as between the sixth and eleventh centuries (Lupoi 2007). The term common law is not ordinarily used in the international sphere, although it would not be misleading to do so. There are two especially crucial differences between existing domestic common law and the coevolution of customary law and international tribunal case law. First, international law, unsupported by formal democratic institutions and processes, has a fundamental legitimacy problem. Second, there are many domestic arbitration cases in any given system, but historically there have always been few international cases (totaling at most a few dozen per year). Consequently, international law can draw on only limited context or experience, and no compelling legitimizing justification, from identifying norms and elevating them to the status of law. Although municipal common law progresses slowly and conservatively, it nevertheless does so with a rapidity and breadth that has not been possible for case-law-based international legal development, which continues to be dependent on only about two hundred actors (independent nation-states) to generate cases. Needed are both the raw material of many more concrete cases and a jurisprudence that justifies the creation along with application of law based on democratically legitimated norm articulation.

The Contours of International Environmental Law

At the most general level, existing international law is a collection of agreements that represent the will and consent of nation-states with respect to the rules governing their relationships. It might best be understood as the law of a single global polity that consists of only about two hundred individuals, each corporate in character. One finds the law of this polity in a number of places.

Treaties, the nearest thing that the international community has to legislation, are the increasingly predominant form of international law (Weiss et al. 2007). Unlike domestic legislation, however, enacted treaties must pass through two distinct legislative procedures. The international negotiation that produces the text of the "legislation" is followed by a ratification process in which each of the signatories employs domestic legal institutions to commit itself formally to the agreement, which that signatory usually has already participated in negotiating and has signed. For example, the UNFCCC was negotiated prior to the 1992 United Nations Conference on Environment and Development, where 154 countries signed it. But the convention did not enter into force until after the fiftieth country (the minimum specified in the treaty itself) had ratified it in December 1993. It is as if law is actually adopted by way of a formal promise of obedience from each of the polity's members, acting in what Hans Kelsen ([1949] 2006) characterized as their international legal personalities. In this way, treaties share more in common with contracts than with domestic laws, which are the expression of will of a single legal personality. Treaties codify an agreement to behave in a certain way, yet admit no necessary obligation to do so. In fact, treaties are something even less than a formal contract. They are more nearly similar to a letter of intent, creating a record of the agreement in more careful language than everyday speech, clarifying the terms of cooperation, and providing a basis for mutually beneficial interaction, but anticipating no form of external enforcement (Goldsmith and Posner 2005). In the environmental arena, one can chart a progression in the use of treaties from simple bilateral accords, like those between the United States and Canada respecting their boundary waters, to multilateral agreements designed to confront genuinely global challenges, such as the protection of marine life or prevention of atmospheric ozone depletion.

International law also can be found in international custom. Customary law consists of that set of norms derived from the actual practices of states undertaken in the belief that those practices are required of them by law (Weiss et al. 2007). Customary international law therefore is located at the intersection of habitual behavior and mutual obligation. Customary law is recognized (at least in principle) as obligatory by nations and legal scholars alike, in spite of the fact that it may never have been memorialized in writing (Young 1994). Customary international law is more difficult to invoke than is treaty law, though. One must be able to both articulate the terms of the putative law and then show that the law is accepted by states as law (Hunter, Salzman, and Zaelke 2007).

A number of observations about this process are helpful to an understanding of its potential and limitations. First, the invocation of customary law is an empirical process rather than a normative one. It attempts to describe existing rules that govern the interaction of nations rather than to propose new rules. Second, invoking customary law requires showing that state compliance with the rule is both extensive and virtually uniform, and that it particularly includes the state(s) affected by the case at hand. It must be clear that state conduct inconsistent with the putative rule has generally been treated as a breach of international obligations. Third, the pattern of compliance must be attributable to a sense of legal obligation (*opinio juris sive necessitatus*). It is insufficient that states follow the putative rule either out of a sense of moral obligation or in pursuit of political expediency. Fourth, even if these requirements are satisfied, states may insulate themselves from the application of customary law if they can demonstrate that they have been persistent objectors. If a state can demonstrate a consistent record of conduct reflecting an unwillingness to be bound by the rule or recognize it as law, it can exclude itself from any obligations under the rule (Bodansky 1995).

Examples of customary law in the environmental area might include the principle that a state should not use its territory in a way that causes environmental harm outside that territory. The precautionary principle has been suggested as another candidate for customary law status, despite the fact that this putative rule is subject to significant contestation (Peel 2011). Both principles have been invoked with respect to climate change, for example, but there is no evidence that either has yet guided actual behavior. The difficulty in proffering illustrations of customary law thought to be at work in the environmental area reflects the limitations implicit in this form of law. It is difficult, say, to determine whether a reluctance to cause harm outside one's territory is grounded in a sense of legal obligation or merely a desire to maintain positive relations among neighboring states. The precautionary principle may eventually fail as customary law because its application to concrete circumstances raises concerns of overregulation that undermine its universality as a rule. Thus, customary international law is plagued by both an inability to characterize accurately the behavioral regularities that are its foundation and fundamental ambiguity about how to apply its rules to contested cases (Goldsmith and Posner 2005). The real influence of customary law principles may be "to frame the debate rather than to govern conduct" (Bodansky 2010a, 203).

International tribunals issue rulings that interpret and apply treaties and customary law, and as such, influence the evolution of international law. But the potential of prior decisions actually to guide the development of international law is largely unrealized, and will remain so until international jurisprudence makes them relevant by recognizing the doctrine of stare decisis—as noted earlier, that decisions are precedents binding on future decisions, and precedents should not be ignored or overturned unless there are strong reasons to do so (Bhala 1999, 2001)—and until the number of decided cases rises to the level that makes possible the drawing of generalizations about what they teach.

Additional sources of international law are worthy of mention, although they continue to be of lesser importance than treaties and customary law. General principles of law are behavioral rules widely recognized in nations with formally organized legal systems. By definition, these principles are characteristic of all (or nearly all) domestic legal systems, and for that reason, enjoy a presumptive validity at the international level. An example, perhaps, is the "polluter pays" principle, encountered widely in domestic law, and so well received among nations and international organizations that it has become virtually synonymous with environmental dispute resolution (Larson 2005).

International administrative law is what governs the authorization and operation of IGOs. Largely procedural in character, this form of law is relevant to environmental protection only indirectly and only to the extent that it structures the actions of organizations with environmental responsibilities (Weiss et al. 2007). For instance, much of the monitoring, reporting, and other technical work of the UNFCCC Secretariat is done pursuant to rules not contained in formal treaties. Under the provisions of the Vienna Convention for the Protection of the Atmosphere, the Montreal Protocol, and its amendments, some high global warming potential gases—notably hydrochlorofluorocarbons—are regulated in part through adjustments made to annex lists of chemicals and control levels rather than through formal amendment of the treaties themselves.

Finally, soft law occupies an ambiguous status. It can be manifested in aspirational or hortatory language contained in an otherwise-binding document, or in apparently obligatory language in a document that is not itself binding (ibid.). Significant examples of soft law are the 2009 Copenhagen Accord and 2010 Cancun Agreements, which were adopted by the UNFCCC Conference of the Parties in the face of an inability to agree on terms of a substantive protocol to succeed the Kyoto Protocol. It is worth remembering, however, that soft law can stand in one of several relationships to hard law. It can serve as a next-best alternative to hard law where no hard law has been developed and, occasionally, even encourage the development of hard law. It can also be a complement to hard law, facilitating dialogic as well as experimentalist transnational and domestic processes that are transformative of norms, understandings, and perceptions of state interests. But the presence of distributive conflicts among states, in particular among powerful states, coupled with the coexistence of hard- and soft-law regimes within a regime complex, can undermine the smooth and complementary interaction of hard and soft law to such a degree that the two become adversaries (Shaffer and Pollack 2010). Whether this oppositional relationship is positive or negative depends, of course, on one's estimation of the legitimacy and effectiveness of the hard law involved. The hard law can represent either a creative tension that gives the regime a necessary reflexive capability or source of internal contradiction that promotes gridlock. It will be some time before it becomes apparent, say, whether the impact of the Copenhagen Accord and Cancun

Agreements on the development of hard international climate change law will be significantly positive or negative, or both.

Discussing in broad outline what international law is raises the question of what international law is not. What elements of domestic legal systems are not to be found in the international legal system? Three observations occur immediately.

First, as a system of governance, international law lacks the capacity to grow. Its capability for extending its reach and developing new solutions to problems as they arise in the policy environment is severely limited. Any new competencies that the system ever enjoys are introduced from outside. This stands in marked contrast to domestic systems of common law, which can develop new legal doctrine as well as behavioral norms by working their way through a large number of concrete cases, breaking legal ground and experimenting with new rules as they go (Baber and Bartlett 2009a). International law is not prevented from doing this by the lack of institutional infrastructure. International tribunals like the International Court of Justice (ICJ) exist and deal with cases, often guided (as Article 38 of the ICJ Statute provides) by the writings of eminent legal scholars and decisions of judges in national courts, though none of those sources are international law in themselves. The United Nations International Law Commission (ILC) is fully capable of restating ICJ rulings in the same way that, for example, the American Law Institute (ALI) restates the common law in a wide variety of fields for the guidance of legal practitioners in the United States. It is true that the ICJ and ILC do not enjoy the same huge "database" of court decisions that exist in countries like the United States. But even that limitation (which like the inexperience of youth would correct itself over time) is not the heart of the problem. The critical element missing from international law that prevents it from learning and growing is the absence of the doctrine of stare decisis (Hunter, Salzman, and Zaelke 2007). The decisions of international tribunals, even those of the ICJ, are binding only on the parties to the dispute at hand. Although it is true that prior decisions are used by later courts as guides in finding the content of the law, the fact that international adjudications are not binding even on the courts that render them encourages exception mongering by parties to future disputes and discourages progressive development of the law through the careful analysis of precedent that characterizes common law legal systems. Some commentators view this as a largely mythical problem or self-inflicted wound, born of the fact that international jurists hue to "nonbinding" precedent while maintaining the fiction that their prior decisions are not actually binding (Bhala 1999). Be that as it may, the more pertinent observation from our current perspective is that a de jure doctrine of stare decisis in international adjudication would help assure a coherence in international environmental law that both states and international organizations should expect if they are serious about building a well-ordered multilateral system of environmental protection (Bhala 2001).

Second, as a form of political praxis, international law lacks democratic legitimacy. In the leading forms of democratic government, democratic legitimacy is grounded in an elected legislature. The key feature of both parliamentary and presidential systems is that citizens choose representatives to legislate on their behalf. Whether one affirms a democracy that is representative or directly participatory (Barber 2003), the essence of the matter is that citizens are empowered to live under laws of their own choosing. "To govern oneself, to obey laws that one has chosen for oneself, to be self-determining," is the objective of democratic practice (Dahl 1989, 89). Contrast this emphasis on democratic legislation with the observation that at the international level, the legislative function is the least well developed. International "legislators" lag behind their judicial and executive counterparts for a variety of reasons, "ranging from constituents' suspicion of 'junkets' to their own inability to stay in office long enough to develop enduring relationships with their foreign counterparts" (Slaughter 2004, 127). Notwithstanding the Campaign for a United Nations Parliamentary Assembly, it is unclear how one would go about restructuring international institutions to create elected legislators with more meaningful roles, even assuming that such institution building would be desirable and the difficulties arising from domestic political circumstances could be overcome. A more fundamental question is precisely what legislators should be doing within the confines of an international legal system, envisioned as part of a larger system of "global governance in a disaggregated world order" (ibid., 130)?

Third, as a form of environmental problem solving, international law lacks sufficient implementation mechanisms. Within the context of international law, the issue of implementation is sometimes reduced to nothing more than a question of coercive enforcement and promptly dismissed as impossible in an international polity that remains fundamentally anarchic. This is unfortunate for at least two reasons. One is that coercion and cooperation are not discrete categories, even at a conceptual level. In many respects, the two are functionally identical, consisting of "acts, threatened acts, or offers of action" directed at one state by another with the intent of inducing a change in the latter state's behavior (Goldsmith and Posner 2005). Conflating implementation and coercive enforcement is also to be avoided because it obscures the fact that the implementation of international agreements is a varied collection of specific actions that international actors (both states and IGOs) take to make international agreements operative in national legal systems (Faure and Lefevere 2011). Ignoring this obstructs our efforts to imagine and perfect implementation mechanisms that do not depend on conventional adjudication, which has not been and is not likely to become an effective means of inducing compliance with international environmental obligations (Knox 2001). Finally, the inadequacy of implementation mechanisms in international environmental law leads to the system's inability to adapt to changing circumstances. If every element required in implementing the mandates of international law must be negotiated in detail by the principals, that system will be inflexible and slow to react to new challenges. This will be a particularly serious flaw for environmental matters such as climate, which is subject to nonlinear and sometimes-abrupt changes (Young 2011).

In summary, international environmental law exists within a system of governance that features institutions answering to the general description of courts, legislatures, and executive agencies. But those institutions each lack at least one essential element of their domestic counterparts. International courts lack the ability to bind themselves (and potential future litigants) through their decisions and to accumulate binding decisions into a coherent superstructure of legal norms that can be studied and perhaps codified. They must wait to be supplied with legal rules by "legislation" to an extent that courts in common law countries need not. International "legislatures" lack the democratic legitimacy provided by the electoral processes that have come to be regarded as the sine qua non of democracy at the domestic level. The paths of public accountability between citizen and the government official who represents them in international negotiations are so attenuated that the results are immediately suspect from the democratic perspective. International executive agencies are hamstrung by the absence of authority to craft appropriate implementation mechanisms. Without this form of authority, which has made the modern regulatory state possible, it is hard to imagine how systems of global environmental regulation could ever be developed or maintained.

What International Law Probably Cannot Do

Few things in the world of human endeavors are genuinely impossible (given sufficient time for experimentation and observation). But it seems clear that the current processes of international law make certain desirable outcomes implausible. We focus here on three such implausible outcomes, things that international law would seem incapable of doing, and current limitations in the practice of international environmental law that are both significant obstacles to progress yet theoretically within our ability to address. These limitations correspond to the general shortcomings of international law described above.

First, international environmental law as a practice is generally unable to derive substantive norms from its own concrete experiences. The norm of common but differentiated responsibility, for instance, did not emerge organically from the practice of resolving environmental disputes. A comparison to common law practice may be useful to show the importance of this point. The doctrine of contributory negligence was used to deny damages to plaintiffs whose own lack of ordinary care had contributed to their loss. This doctrine, which originally developed to avoid rewarding people for their own carelessness, eventually produced such troubling results in so many cases that it was replaced by the doctrine of comparative negligence. The new approach did not deny recovery to a careless plaintiff, as had the doctrine of contributory negligence. Rather, it reduced any damages by the proportion representing the plaintiff's contribution to her own injury. It could be argued that the international law doctrine of common but differentiated responsibility operates as a mirror image of contributory negligence. As applied to climate change, for example, it excuses those parties whose contribution to climate change has been relatively slight so far from any responsibility for the problem. It allows what is different in the climate change problem to obscure what is common, to the detriment of responsibility as a whole. Because it was developed as an abstract principle rather than within the context of a continuing process of problem solving, it lacks any compelling provenance and is not susceptible to refinement through cumulative experience.

Second, despite an enormous turnout of civil society representatives, the Copenhagen Accord and Cancun Agreements were developed as well as adopted behind closed doors with little or no opportunity for those represented by the negotiators to be heard when it really counted (Bodansky 2010b). This is not a feature unique to the UNFCCC Conference of the Parties, however. The democratic deficit in international negotiations is systemic and pervasive. Indeed, given the evidence that the Kyoto Protocol enjoyed the support of most Americans at the time of its negotiation, a failure of democratic representation would seem to have created the background conditions that made the later Conference of the Parties negotiations so intractable in the first place. If a democratic deficit of this sort is allowed to continue, the results could be particularly serious because addressing climate change implicates the most basic processes of modern industrialized economies. Reliable public support for whatever preventive measures are developed will be vital, but ultimately unavailable, if the policy process has been nondemocratic.

Finally, the Copenhagen Accord and Cancun Agreements might be regarded as an important step forward because they recognize a limitation of international environmental law that the Kyoto Protocol ignored. They establish a bottom-up process of climate policy development in which signatories list their national actions internationally and subject them to some as yet underdefined process of global scrutiny (Bodansky 2010b). Although it is difficult to know precisely how this process will be developed in the coming years, it represents a realization that implementing any climate change regime will be unavoidably dependent on the member states to play the leading role in matters of implementation (Young 2011). Again, this dependence is neither unique to the area of climate change nor a fatal flaw. It is, rather, an implicit recognition that the implementation capacities required to make any environmental governance regime effective must exist (or must be developed) at the level of the state and below, or even beyond the state. Financial and technical assistance can be organized internationally. Effective action to prevent environmental degradation probably can never be.

State Sovereignty, Legitimacy, and Accountability

International law is constantly in search of legitimacy. As a general matter, law's legitimacy depends on the ability of its addressees to regard it as both a fact and norm (Habermas 1996). Law must be seen to establish behavioral requirements backed up by effective compliance mechanisms. Moreover, those requirements must reflect values produced by collective will formation that is fundamentally democratic, broadly participatory, and free of any form of coercion. This standard of legitimacy is well understood by students of contemporary democratic theory and forms the normative basis of deliberative democracy.

A deliberative theory of environmental politics is grounded on the fundamental assumption that no regime of environmental protection can achieve the goal of ecological sustainability if it does not also satisfy these basic requirements of democratic legitimacy (Baber and Bartlett 2005; Dryzek 2009). This assumption further suggests that a consensus criterion for decision making is essential as a regulative norm of democracy, not just as a practical means for overcoming the network of mutual vetoes that characterizes the relationship in which global environmental actors often find themselves.[1]

This general account of environmental democracy, originally developed at the nation-state level, poses several challenges for adapting the conceptual demands of deliberative democracy to environmental protection at the international level. But not all the news is bad. Deliberative democracy's commitment to consensual decision making fits well in a political framework containing the idea of sovereignty as a defining characteristic of the parties involved. The challenges nevertheless are significant, including problems of democratic deficiency, delegation of implementation, legal jurisdiction, and underdeveloped jurisprudence.

International environmental governance is plagued by a democratic deficit. Any democratic heritage of international decisions can usually be traced to the existence of democratic processes within the countries that participated in those decisions. Thus, international democracy is derivative instead of direct and participatory. If one has accepted the premise that democracy is a constitutive element of ecological sustainability, this shortcoming becomes especially troubling.

Furthermore, the implementation of international decisions cannot simply be delegated to a regulatory agency, as we frequently do at the domestic level. Because the parties to international environmental agreements are mainly states, but the actors ultimately targeted by those agreements are generally private organizations and individuals, enforcement is inherently problematic. International environmental law cannot merely impose its requirements, which might be just as well because that law is not the result of a democratic legislative process to begin with.

International courts lack both the jurisdiction and jurisprudence necessary to adjudicate the complex disputes that would arise under a system of international environmental law (Baber and Bartlett 2009a). This problem contributes to the inability of international environmental law to pose a social fact to those actors whose behavior it seeks to regulate. It also adds to the incapacity of international negotiations to develop the kind of normative commitments that would represent the values held by those who such agreements seek to protect.

The relative ineffectiveness of international environmental law has undermined the efforts of domestic political leadership to translate general enthusiasm for environmental protection into support for stringent multilateral environmental accords (VanDeveer 2003). Difficulty in creating political support for environmental accords can also be traced to the inherent elitism of the international political process. As an illustration, progress toward an agreement on ozone-depleting chemicals stalled until the chemical companies that were the source of the problem assumed a leading role (Falkner 2005). Economic and technological power gave those corporations an advantage over other actors in shaping the policy discourse that characterized early development of the ozone regime. As positive as the eventual outcome may have been, it is impossible to argue that the process was particularly democratic.

Adequate coverage in international environmental agreements can fall victim to state sovereignty and its status as the primary organizing principle in international politics. As natural and inevitable as it may seem today, the modern nation-state is a historically contingent development (Brooks 2005). Nation-states are not especially well adapted to the challenges of environmental protection in the age of globalization. Scientific advancement, economic integration, and population growth demand the universalizing of basic ecological responsibilities without respect for national boundaries (Caldwell 1999).

Taken together, these challenges can cause multilateral environmental agreements to fail to protect the environment adequately because the terms of the agreements often contain weak obligations at the outset (Crossen 2004). International regulatory structures must be more than mere compromises among environmental stakeholders. They must be transnational efforts to develop forms of governance tailored to specific markets or policy arenas (Andree 2005). To be fully effective in protecting the environment, governments, international organizations, and NGOs need to focus on particular ecological issues, but do so with a greater regard for their broader contexts and implications.

International law based entirely on interstate relations is unable to effectively address global and transborder issues. State interest, state sovereignty, state equality, and state responsibility are concepts largely irrelevant to resolving problems such as global warming. Addressing such issues requires that we attend to not only interstate and interpersonal justice but also intergenerational justice (Yokota 1999). Even when international norms can be identified, they are difficult to express in the form of effective law, for which the only legal principals are states. This helps explain a pattern of multilateral environmental agreements that achieve high levels of compliance because they require only low levels of cooperation (Crossen 2004). It also explains a situation in which norms of international behavior fail to develop into an effective system of prevention and remediation of international harms (Garrett 2005).

Different problems are presented by nations that would comply with international environmental norms if they could. Developing states often can argue persuasively that if they were held to high environmental standards, their economic development would be severely curtailed. Imposing such standards would work a serious injustice on those sectors of the world's population least able to assert themselves in international political debates (Najam 2011). Long-term, nonstate alternatives that might be appropriate to such circumstances require much stronger global governance institutions than those that currently exist (Park, Conca, and Finger 2008).

Ultimately, institutional change depends on political will, which can be sustained only with popular political support. The failure of international agreements among states undermines support for further agreements (Soroos 2011). State-based transnational environmental protection requires nations to agree to international inspection, performance audits and public reporting, and a common adjudicatory authority. Standards of conduct and methods to facilitate compliance, captured in legal principles recognized and observed as law, are necessary elements of global environmental governance (Peel 2011). Coercion would be less necessary if environmental values were more universal. This brings us back to the key failing of international environmental law: its failure to develop normative consensus through a genuinely democratic global politics.

What We Might Change

The development of fundamental environmental norms, democratic choice among competing policy prescriptions, and organization of implementation plans are probably beyond the reach of international environmental law as presently conceived. It is possible, though, to imagine means by which these limitations could be addressed, if not completely overcome.

Law is shaped by both tradition and change. It is inherently conservative. Its continuity and predictability contribute to the stability as well as survival of the polity. But today legal traditions are being challenged by social change of such magnitude that the conservative function of law requires that it adapt to meet new, evolving circumstances (Caldwell 1999). The challenge is more pressing still when we add the idea that law should reflect a normative consensus resulting from the agreement of those who it seeks to govern. Here we again confront the central political challenge to international law: the democratic deficit.

The democratic deficit is not unique to international law. All assessments of the state of democracy around the world find that a majority of countries are not free or only partly free. Transnational corporations typically have control structures that subvert any exercise of democratic control by employees, customers, the public, or even stockholders. Transnational environmental NGOs subject themselves to few democratic processes. The European Union—the most fully developed example of international cooperation consisting entirely of democratic states—faces a significant democratic deficit of its own. Many international regimes,

conferences, and treaties have experimented with ways of including actors from civil society. But without mechanisms to ensure the democratic
character of that participation and its impact on policy outcomes, the
potential of those efforts is limited. Only a small number of innovations
allowing direct citizen participation, such as the citizen submission process of the North American Agreement on Environmental Cooperation,
disturb this discouraging pattern (Dorn 2007; DiMento 2003).

The development of a global public sphere is in its infancy. Yet the
introduction of elements of direct democracy in specific environmental
policy arenas is a promising start (Feld 2005). Opportunities for direct
participation are important both as a source of democratic legitimacy
and matter of political acceptability (Giorgi and Pohoryles 2005). The
development of a global civil society based on contestation and communication within as well as across minipublic spheres is both good for
environmental democracy and more consistent with imaginable political
scenarios than comprehensive (and utopian) proposals (Hunold 2005;
Friedman, Hochstetler, and Clark 2005).

As we have previously observed, international law (unlike domestic
common law systems) is incapable of generating legal norms internally by
adjudicating a large number of cases under the doctrine of stare decisis.
Generally speaking, the influence of precedent in international law has
been limited by the myth that stare decisis does not apply in that system.
But even if the doctrine were officially adopted, development of international law would proceed at a glacial pace compared to that of municipal
common law simply because so few cases arise when there are only about
two hundred legal personalities in the jurisdiction (even if they are unusually litigious when compared to the more than seven billion natural
personalities they represent).

One partial solution, which could be complementary to other potential ideas, is for IGOs to initiate a process of adjudicating hypothetical
disputes, each of which would be crafted so as to present clear choices
between contending legal norms. Numerous citizen juries, on a worldwide basis, would be asked to resolve such disputes consistent with their
collective sense of justice. Legal scholars would than analyze and summarize the verdicts in the same way that lines of case law are subjected to
"restatement" (Baber and Bartlett 2009a). Such restatements could then
provide the precedential foundation for international tribunals to resolve

real-world disputes over environmental issues in ways leading to the progressive development of international environmental law. If international environmental law could teach itself to learn in this manner, the results might be quite valuable. In the United States and many other countries, a majority of environmental cases are filed under common law theories. Moreover, the common law provides the conceptual foundation for most legislated and decreed law. Legislators and bureaucrats alike rely on the common law to fill in gaps in public law, and guide both courts and agencies in their interpretation of statutes and rules (Plater et al. 2004). Restatements of this sort might also serve as the raw material for a process of codification (through conventional international negotiations) that could produce results with a stronger democratic pedigree than is currently typical.

Citizen juries represent an attempt to realize in practice some of the advantages claimed for deliberative democracy in theory. Groups of citizens are brought together in sessions that allow them to receive well-balanced information about a policy issue, exchange competing points of view, and come to considered judgments as a group. Citizen jurors work to arrive at consensus through a collective, interactive discourse. This process is easily distinguished from the kind of reasoning typical of traditional moral philosophy. It is an effort to find a workable definition of a problem that yields a solution that can command the unforced assent of the average citizens. These concrete problems are characterized by what Hilary Putnam (1995) calls the interpenetration of fact, value, and theory. Experience with citizen juries suggests that the approach enjoys a number of significant advantages over other deliberative processes.

Service on a citizen jury is not especially demanding, and yet allows for a high level of democratic participation and is far more educative than ordinary political campaigns (Gutmann and Thompson 2004). Citizen juries tend to produce consensus rather than polarization (Fishkin and Luskin 1999). This is because citizen juries begin their deliberations with discussion rather than votes. The risk of polarization is further reduced by the fact that the plenary groups within which citizen juries sometimes operate are large enough to contain representative samples of public opinion, and are led by moderators who ensure that all perspectives are heard, experts are available to clarify questions of fact, and participants receive extensive and balanced information on the subject in advance (Gutmann and

Thompson 2004). Unlike representative institutions that are closely identified with the particular experiences of national populations, the citizen jury is a broadly deployable approach that can resonate in a wide variety of cultures. Indeed, the use of citizen juries is one of the few techniques allowing us to imagine a form of world assembly in which citizens could deliberate as members of the whole order of humanity rather than as representatives of nation-states (Laslett 2003). The deliberative form of rationality that citizen juries promote is more than just talk. It is an intrinsically valuable achievement, forged by the direct efforts of citizens to take responsibility for concrete, practical problems and produce judgments that transcend the interest aggregation typical of liberal politics (Baber and Bartlett 2005). For these reasons, the deliberative process of citizen juries is an especially appropriate response to the global environmental problematique.

But using deliberative democratic procedures like the citizen jury to address problems of environmental protection at the international level is not without difficulty. It is hard to imagine a more challenging set of policy issues, more entangled with special interests, than those involved in earth system governance. When one compares this policy arena with most others, it is easy to become discouraged by its complexities. To date, international environmental negotiation has produced a body of generally unenforceable law, with which the parties comply only because it requires little of them beyond what they were already willing to do. International environmental law is more a collection of contracts than a body of law, yet even in a world governed largely by contracts, there must be a background of obligatory law. After all, the law "does not enforce every promise which a man may make" (Holmes [1881] 1991, 253). In a common law tradition, it is the collective genius of generations that allows us to decide, on the basis of many thousands of practical judgments, which promises should be enforced and which should not. Although most of those rulings were arrived at by judges not juries, the work of trial juries suggests that the effectiveness of judges can be approximated by the rest of us if we possess sufficient information and act within a properly structured decision environment (Vidmar and Hans 2007).

The common law of contracts is similar to all other areas of common law in that it is simply a series of limited responses to concrete problems encountered by the parties to actual legal disputes. The coherence and legitimacy of the common law does not result from tackling big issues with big ideas. The common law is a bottom-up enterprise, much as empirical science tends to be. It involves repeated "observations" of what our senses (especially our sense of justice) tell us about particular sets of circumstances (Baber and Bartlett 2009a). The practical impossibility of grappling comprehensively with problems of environmental policy in all their imponderable complexity points to just such a modest approach. Our challenge is to create transnational environmental law grounded in our shared understanding of reality, but demanding enough to actually protect the global environment.

A useful approach can be found in an idea intended to assist administrative law judges in their efforts to deal with the complexities of regulation through rule making. Kenneth Davis (1969a) suggested that administrative law judges could bring the practicality of the common law to the complexities of regulatory policy by using hypothetical cases in administrative rule making. These cases would pose important although limited problems of regulatory policy. They would allow administrative law judges to rule on narrow and carefully crafted questions. Most significant, these rulings would supply the precedents that regulators could rely on in exercising their rule-making discretion. This approach to rule making would neither leave regulated parties wondering what specific obligations they faced nor require decision makers to deal with questions they felt unprepared to address.

Rule making through hypothetical adjudication can be adapted to the use of citizen juries. Instead of asking citizen juries to choose between competing solutions to actual entangled policy problems (like global climate change), they can be presented with hypothetical disputes that would arise under a variety of regulatory approaches and then can be asked to apply the same common sense of justice that many already use when serving on legal juries. Citizens would enjoy both the educative and expressive advantages associated with direct political participation. With a sufficient number of properly selected juries ruling on the same case around the world, the global community would engage in a process of collective will formation unmediated by any elite. Once citizen juries have adjudicated concrete but hypothetical cases of international environmental disputes, that collection of decisions can be aggregated to form a system of legal doctrine in the same way that the results of actual cases are first restated and then later codified in systems of common law.

Developing a transnational form of common law would require, of course, improving on the haphazard pattern of development that characterizes historical systems of law if we are to produce useful results over a reasonable period of time. Policy specialists working in existing transnational networks could develop and administer such adjudicatory proceedings. In the area of environmental protection, the United Nations Environment Programme has the technical capacity to commission hypothetical cases touching on any aspect of major environmental issues, and the Commission on Sustainable Development could oversee deliberation in any of the hundred countries where it supports local organizations. Aggregating citizen jury decisions into a coherent body of legal doctrine would be a natural extension of the ILC's ongoing responsibility for the codification and progressive development of international law (Baber and Bartlett 2009a). In fact, this new avenue for restatement and codification might redeem the ILC from the accusation that it has become an outdated institution (Tomuschat 2006).

The question, then, is not whether juristic democracy is feasible for developing a global common law for earth system governance. It is whether states can be persuaded to allow their prerogatives to be usurped by their own citizens. Juristic democracy, as a form of deliberative democracy, assumes "mutuality" as a background condition of discourse (Gutmann and Thompson 2004). To the extent that this condition is absent (as it is where sovereign violence, institutionalized discrimination, or vast disparities of discursive resources plague given societies, or constrain participation across borders by members of those societies), deliberative process are either degraded or rendered impossible. In the context of global politics, however, the formal equality of nation-states themselves promotes mutuality between them. It also allows societies that are less than fully democratic to participate in international deliberative arrangements in productive ways—representing the normative commitments of citizens to the degree that their domestic limitations allow.

Juristic Environmental Democracy in a World of Sovereigns

Any critique of juristic democracy would likely begin with defenders of state sovereignty claiming that the "legalization" of international politics can never be effective. In this view, law without enforcement cannot really *be* law because it is never recognized *as* law. Critics of international law generally argue that "international law scholars exaggerate its power and significance." They claim, for example, to "know of no global democracy approach that spells out how or why states, especially powerful states like the United States (or, for that matter the EU), would submit to a broader form of genuine global governance" (Goldsmith and Posner 2005, 225, 223).

Thinking of law as no more than rules backed by coercive force is a long-standing habit, and one that some international relations theorists are no more or less guilty of than journalists, politicians, and the lay public. But why *must* the entity that pronounces legal judgments also be responsible for the enforcement of judgments? A number of societies that we would not call stateless, including those of ancient Greece and Rome along with Anglo-Saxon England, left the prosecution of criminal cases to private individuals, and in yet other societies all judicial decrees were enforced, if at all, privately (Posner 1995). In fact, all that any form of enforcement ever does is raise the costs of noncompliance. Coercive law simply overlays normative expectations with threats of sanctions in such a way that "addressees may restrict themselves to the prudential calculation of consequences" (Habermas 1996, 116). Likewise, the "enforcement" mechanisms of international law (such as those of the World Trade Commission) combine dispute settlement processes with the existence of provisions allowing aggrieved states to pursue private enforcement under the color of official adjudication. Coercive enforcement thus does not necessarily equate with compliance or effectiveness (Faure and Lefevere 2011). Similarly, in well-functioning states municipal law depends relatively little on coercive enforcement, relying first and mainly on social and psychological controls—providing information about social norms and natural consequences, and increasing the benefits of compliance. Recent developments in international treaty law therefore have emphasized noncompliance procedures intended to facilitate compliance instead of acting on the adversarial assumption that noncompliance is "the result of a willful desire to violate" (ibid., 185). So it might be fair to say that if advocates of sovereignty have erred in any respect, it is not in underestimating the robustness of international law but rather in exaggerating the essential differences between international and municipal law.

A second sovereignty-based argument is that sovereign states protect important individual rights in ways that international regimes cannot. As such, democrats should not actually want to develop such regimes. Democracy, in this view, is a function of constitutional government and any drift toward global governance is a threat to that one true foundation of democracy. Absent a sovereign to enforce the law, the citizen's obligation to obey evaporates, and the remaining choice is between anarchy and arbitrary coercion (Rabkin 2005). But this argument also exaggerates the difference between international and municipal systems of law by highlighting coercion instead of the more subtle effects of law as a cumulative system of behavioral incentives. A useful exploration of this contrast is the analysis of law in "primitive" societies advanced by Richard Posner (1981).

Posner's discussion of "primitive" legal systems is helpful for our purposes because these systems develop in the absence of a sovereign state or any of the formal institutions normally associated with them. His description of the legal traditions of the Yurok tribe of California is especially interesting. When a dispute arose among the Yurok, each of the principals would retain the services of two to four disinterested individuals, who would pass back and forth between the parties collecting accounts of the dispute. These private "jurors" would then render a judgment. A losing party who refused to abide by the judgment would be condemned to be the wage slave of the prevailing party. Continued resistance rendered the recalcitrant an outlaw (ibid.). Throughout history, informal institutions of this sort have allowed stateless societies to develop sophisticated systems of individual rights. Moreover, because early criminal law was no more effective (generally speaking) than primitive systems of private law in protecting individuals, protecting individual rights would appear not to be part of the original bargain between sovereign and subject. Posner's explanation for the development of criminal law is that sovereigns "owned" an interest in their subjects that was impaired by acts that reduced their productive capacity. This economic interest was not accounted for in the private system of compensation, so the sovereign established criminal sanctions that served as "a method of internalizing this externality" (ibid., 204). This view suggests that an abrogation of sovereignty is not a necessary corollary of global environmental governance. Efforts to regulate the transboundary relationships between individuals can be considered an evolving system of quasi-private law meant to acquit limited and specific rights through mechanisms of collective action intended to preempt environmental harms.

A final point regarding the impact of juristic democracy on sovereignty is that the primary advantages of introducing forms of participatory democracy into international lawmaking would likely accrue to states that operate at a political disadvantage under the current system of nationalist power politics. Weaker states wishing to impose a regime of environmental protection to their advantage would reap significant public relations benefits from deliberative democratic experiments that lend scope and substance to general public sentiments in favor of environmental protection. They might even be able to introduce new environmental norms into existing agreements that currently govern disputes in other areas such as trade and human rights. But why would powerful states, particularly environmental recalcitrants, subject themselves to such processes? The admittedly hopeful answer is that even nations with something to lose in a thoroughly democratized global politics still have more to gain. Those potential gains can be summarized in one word: reciprocity.

The concept of reciprocity knows no logical limit. It "extends to all individuals, not just to citizens of a single society" (Gutmann 1999, 309). It reaches across the full range of policy arenas. Yet it carries special weight in environmental governance. Environmental problems depend on far more "cross-national deliberation" for their resolution than can be accomplished within any single set of domestic political institutions (Gutmann and Thompson 2004, 61). This casts doubt on the ability of individual states to achieve even their own domestic environmental objectives. Environmental goods can be provided to a national population only if its government "negotiates and consistently maintains agreements with other governments for the purpose" (Laslett 2003, 217).

In an age of increasing global interdependence, deliberative democracy's emphasis on justifying collective decisions to the people who must live with the consequences of those choices argues for extending the requirements of democratic deliberation to the international arena. Conventional aggregation of interests across boundaries is hard to conceptualize, but "deliberation across boundaries is straightforward," and deliberative theory would seem to be more useful in the international system precisely because it lacks "alternative sources of order" provided by sovereign authority (Dryzek 2000, 116).

Abundant examples of deliberative democracy's various institutional elements can be identified on the international environmental stage (Meidinger 2008). Much of the recent progress in international environmental governance, children's rights, population control, and social development have been due to the involvement of global civil society in collective decision making (Friedman, Hochstetler, and Clark 2005). These activities have evolved from their earlier reactive forms to seize the policy initiative in a number of areas (Snidal and Thompson 2003).[2]

So experience does not show that deliberative participation in international civil society is futile. Rather, it suggests that to be fully effective, deliberative practices must penetrate international governance more deeply and be less mediated by elite-dominated NGOs (McCormick 2011). Dryzek (2009) proposes the development of a networked deliberative system, based on exactly the existing institutional models we have been discussing. A fully developed system of juristic democracy would constitute one such network that could contribute significantly to better earth system governance through the identification, clarification, and eventual formalization of transnational environmental norms.

Bounded, Realistic Optimism

How can any continuity in the outcomes of juristic democracy experiments across national and cultural boundaries be explained? Why might people in different parts of the world see environmental protection the same way? How can that continuity be useful in protecting the international environment?

Environmental problems, complex as they are, enjoy one distinct advantage over many other problems of collective will formation. To the extent that protecting the environment is a scientific question, some responses will be objectively better than others. Given the prevalence of environmental challenges and growth of global communications technology, there is every reason to expect that the successes and failures of various responses will become part of the wider public consciousness.

All societies share a common heritage of chthonic legal tradition. The chthonic tradition is an ancient system of law centered on the sacred character of the cosmos (Glenn 2010). It emerged from the most basic of human experiences, primarily with the development of human morality and memory. According to H. Patrick Glenn, it is the oldest of all traditions, and can be understood as the law of a culture or tribe. As contemporary examples, Glenn refers to the laws of indigenous peoples, who he believes live in closer harmony with the earth than other human populations. At a broader level, he uses the term when referring to law that is a part of the custom or tradition of a people, and in this regard is distinguishable from the traditional definitions of law as positively adopted and enforced rules. Regardless of their relative level of development or specifics of their current legal regimes, modern human societies can trace their origins to a form of life that was tribal and view of the universe that was mythical. People saw themselves as living lives integrated with those of their fellows and situated in a natural environment of which they were an integral part. The informal and oral rules of behavior that evolved from that worldview formed the backdrop against which modern legal traditions ultimately developed (Lupoi 2007). So it should not be particularly surprising to find commonalities among those legal traditions today. They may be nothing more (or less) than the "artifacts" of our common history.

To the degree that elements of our chthonic legal heritage survive in modern legal traditions, we should not be surprised, either, to find them expressed in the area of environmental protection. Chthonic law is conspicuously thin in areas like contract and tort. People living close to the land and each other had little use for such concepts. But environmental claims of a chthonic character have been advanced by tribal populations in modern judicial institutions. For example, the Supreme Court of Canada has incorporated the civil law concept of usufruct (a limited property right arising from intermittent use) into the common law tradition in upholding the traditional rights of indigenous peoples (Glenn 2010). Elements of chthonic law have thus earned their survival by proving their adaptive ability. Chthonic law is environment friendly in a way that later legal traditions often are not. "It is not just green; it is dark green" (ibid., 73).

Since at least the time of John Locke, Western legal thought has shown a pronounced aversion to custom. Replacing fealty to tradition with rational legislation has been its brief. Over the centuries, this process has nearly demolished the credibility of custom as a source of normativity in the law (Tully 1995). The emergence of legal positivism can be interpreted in this light. Perhaps international law is more "primitive," though—and healthier for it. International law explicitly recognizes custom as a source of valid law. Custom, in this context, is understood to be the customary behavior of states toward one another. But if certain basic normative principles are found to recur across national and cultural boundaries, there is nothing to prevent international tribunals and legal bureaucracies from taking note of those general principles, and then incorporating them into their analysis of what is customary within the whole order of humankind.

Even in the most democratic polities, humans make mistakes. It may turn out that the poet Piet Hein was correct when he said that we are all "global citizens with tribal souls" (Barnaby 1988, 192). Optimism may be wholly unjustified. Yet to the hopeful mind, the repeating themes and recurring chthonic legal traditions that typify the world's many tribal societies (Glenn 2010) are enough to suggest that we may be able to discover our obligations to one another and embrace what we have in common, if we distance ourselves sufficiently from all that differentiates us.

Of course, all that differentiates us is no small matter, and the tremendous diversity and differences of humankind have profound implications for democratizing global governance.

4

Reconciling Diversity and Consensus in Democratic Governance

A persistent complaint lodged against deliberative democracy has been that its preoccupation with achieving reasoned political consensus makes it inimical to diversity. A society characterized by deep moral divisions and cultural pluralism cannot, some argue, produce the kinds of agreement that deliberative democrats seek without unacceptable levels of minority disenfranchisement (Connolly 1991; Honig 1993; Mansbridge 1990; Mouffe 1996, 2000; Sanders 1997; Schapp 2006; Young 1996, 2000). To the degree that this criticism is true, the deliberative democrats' dream of extending the range of their theories to global earth system politics would seem doomed from the outset (Young 2007). If the level of cultural complexity and political division characteristic of the pluralist nation-state is beyond its capacity, then deliberative theory must certainly fail as an answer to the democratic deficit on a global stage, characterized by diversity orders greater than that of any single nation-state. At least one prominent voice in the deliberative chorus has expressed just such a worry (Habermas 2006), but more hopeful perspectives on this issue abound (Bohman 2007; Brunkhorst 2002; Dryzek 2000, 2006; Thompson 1999; Young 2007).

It is vital, then, for deliberative democrats to respond in direct and persuasive ways to the complaints of difference democrats, if the grandest hopes for deliberation are to be sustained. But to do so, the complaints of difference democrats must be understood as precisely as possible. How is it that the views of women, racial and ethnic minorities, and other historically underrepresented groups might find no translation in the language of deliberative discourse? Is it simply the trouble that any small voice has in making itself heard? Is it the challenge that a viewpoint alien to the dominant perspective has in making itself understood? Or is it the problem of a radically new vision finding a way to attract converts and advance itself through persuasion alone? It is important to understand the role that each of these dimensions plays in the complaints of difference democrats if global governance is ever to be legitimized by more deliberative forms of democracy.

While much of the theorizing in the environmental movement has been heading in a deliberative direction, environmental practice has presented a series of contrasting developments in the form of distinctly nondeliberative forms of expression (Humphrey 2007). At least three such categories of environmental expression can be distinguished.

First, it is possible to identify a range of speech acts (actions intended and reasonably understood to be expressions of opinion) that are not persuasive in either the classical sense of the word or the way that deliberative democrats use the concept. Environmental activists, for example, concerned that their voices are not being heard, have long engaged in various forms of street theater. Many of these actions are nondeliberative inasmuch as they are designed specifically to engage people's emotions, ranging from humor to horror. Activists dressed as threatened animals turning up in incongruous places is a tried-and-true method for securing a few minutes of coverage on the news, or attention on YouTube or social media. Who could deny that this obviously nondeliberative tactic can be a crucial means to attract people's attention to, for instance, a contested land use decision that more might oppose if only they knew about it? The activists' direct action does little, of course, to improve the level of public knowledge about the issue. But environmentalists have long understood that giving voice to an issue is a preliminary step in educating the public and motivating it to action (Torgerson 1997).

A second illustration of nondeliberative expression in environmental politics is the boycott. Borrowing a page from civil rights movements, environmental groups have boycotted virtually every product imaginable. The archetypal case is perhaps the boycott against canned tuna. This certainly can also be seen as giving voice to an issue (drift net fishing, in this case). Yet the boycott goes beyond merely drawing attention to a concern through dramatic action. It also seeks to impose a cost on the actor whose behavior the environmental activist wishes to contest. The point of such cost levying is not primarily to convince the fishing industry of the folly of its behavior but rather to simply raise the cost of that behavior until rational self-interest accomplishes what persuasion cannot. Even if no one's interests or preferences are changed, the shared understanding of the situation has been altered by the introduction of a new variable into the model that the parties use to think about their positions. Although it is not sufficient in itself, a shared understanding of the situation is fundamental to the process of collective will formation (Habermas 1987b).

A third category of nondeliberative speech acts consists of those intended actually to persuade other parties to the deliberation. One example is the linkage of practices involved in the raising of livestock for meat to the Holocaust (Humphrey 2007). A book like *Eternal Treblinka* (Patterson 2002) is offered as a form of expression not designed to add anything to the deliberative process but instead to so overwhelm the emotions of readers that their moral worldview is changed. No democrat—deliberative or otherwise—condemns the fact that books, motion pictures, television programs, speeches, marches, videos, and other public expressions do actually change the views of individuals. Rather, deliberative democrats care about how those newly acquired individual perspectives are then promoted to others in the process of collective will formation (Gutmann and Thompson 2004). If those involved in a discussion about whether farm price programs should continue to support the production of meat are unmoved by the reasons offered by animal rights activists (as many surely would be), the question would remain as to whether that disagreement should be resolved through deliberation, aggregation of interests, or some undemocratic method. At that point, animal rights activists who found themselves still in the minority might well conclude that deliberation (as undramatic and unsatisfying as it is) and the discursive limitations that deliberation might impose would nevertheless be preferable to simple voting or autocracy.

Having identified these three levels of possible disadvantage that the strictures of deliberative democracy might impose (voice, understanding, and persuasion), it is necessary to determine which of these (alone or in combination) lies at the heart of the complaints of difference democrats. To do so, it is helpful to relate the specifics of the critiques of deliberation in a systematic way to the dimensions of difference. With respect to the challenge of providing a voice to difference, one of the most contested elements of the deliberative regime is its focus on achieving consensus. This objective, in itself, has been indicted for its tendency to push difference aside. The emphasis within the deliberative tradition on the offering of public reasons for one's policy preferences has been thought to further disadvantage already-disadvantaged interests by depriving them of the full range of the personal commitments and perspectives they might use to make themselves understood. Democracy itself has been indicted (in both its deliberative and aggregative forms) as a system that institutionalizes contestable policy regimes by insulating them from challenge by opinion groups that might be regarded as permanent minorities within any given polity and so already face disproportionate burdens of persuasion. We examine each of these critiques in greater detail.

Voice and Consensus: Street Theater and Its Critics

Being heard is a central concern of virtually everyone who attempts to be active politically, regardless of interest or orientation. This is particularly true of those who perceive themselves to be representatives of a minority viewpoint. It is easy for any political message to become lost in the cascade of issues and groups clambering for attention, yet more so for those who have to shout from the periphery of the public stage. Ensuring that every perspective's voice gets heard is the first concern of virtually every democrat, so that does not really distinguish difference democrats from democrats of either the deliberative or aggregative sort. Difference democrats really begin to set themselves apart when they take on the mantle of agonistic democracy (Mouffe 1999).

Advocates of agonistic democracy contrast themselves with democrats of other sorts, particularly deliberative democrats, by emphasizing their commitment to making room in the political arena for protests, emotional appeals, civil disobedience, and other expressive actions designed to shock dominant groups as well as open their eyes to previously ignored concerns (Young 1999). The pursuit of reasoned consensus and civilizing norms of deliberative democracy, difference democrats argue, submerge the genuine injustices suffered by "other voices" who can express themselves only through rhetorical acts that enlarge rather than diminish a polity's region of moral disagreement (Parkinson 2006). Whereas it would be difficult to find a deliberative democrat who would outlaw nondeliberative communications of this type, it is true enough that most would likely agree with Robert Goodin (2000) that a point is inevitably reached when additional theatrics begin to crowd out reasoned discourse, regardless of anyone's good intentions. Agonistic democrats would disagree, or even regard that crowding out as a positive good.

Difference democrats often advance a slightly different argument: that the search for consensus is oppressive in a more general way. Although it is especially harmful to the challenging perspectives of marginalized groups (Sanders 1997), a broader mischief results from a search for agreement that suppresses conflict and encourages the creation of a false unanimity (Mansbridge 1983). When added to the inevitable conflicts of a society characterized by vast inequalities of resources, status, and privilege, this can only lead to an oppressive and ultimately unstable form of consensus that does not genuinely deserve the name (Mouffe 1996). There is at least some evidence that the pursuit of unanimity in deliberative exercises can tend to push aside conflict rather than resolve it, leading to both self-censorship and the suppression of disagreement with the attendant loss of voices and reduction of discursive scope (Button and Mattson 1999).

There at least four important responses to this criticism. First and most simply, a false consensus is not the objective nor is it in the interests of deliberative democrats. Theorists in this tradition have been every bit as quick to caution against the exclusion of minority perspectives as have been their agonistic colleagues (Bohman 1996; Gutmann and Thompson 1996, 2004).

Second, deliberative democrats have gone beyond their agonistic colleagues to develop methods of avoiding the tyrannical pursuit of consensus without giving up on the objective of reasoned agreement. For instance, Dryzek (2001) has suggested that the search for consensus can be rendered less likely to repress difference if the number of deliberative occasions is appropriately restricted (to constitutional questions or those of basic social structure), the number of people involved is restricted and their representativeness is carefully ensured, or internal (that is to say, private) deliberation is substituted for some interactive deliberation. Cass Sunstein (2003) has observed that deliberation produces quite different results in the cases of heterogeneous and homogeneous groups. In the latter, deliberation tends to reinforce previously existing views instead of testing contending perspectives against one another. Where a homogeneous group represents a dominant political discourse, the result is nearly always unfortunate. But this sort of "enclave" deliberation can be helpful to historically disadvantaged groups in developing and refining the themes they need to engage the broader political community. Indeed, much of the experience of civil rights movements can be interpreted in this way, and it reinforces the deliberative democratic theme that the organizations that compose civil society should pay as much attention to the democratic quality of their internal debates as they do to that of the broader dialogues in which they participate. Of greater relevance for our present purposes, it suggests that some combination of enclave deliberation with traditional representative deliberation would be useful in drawing out as well as refining the discourses of marginalized groups, such as women in traditional cultures or minorities in societies burdened by a history of racism.

Third, the tyranny of consensus may be an overstated problem in the first place. Our experience with consensus conferences and policy juries is still relatively limited. Deliberative democracy's role in the processes of forming the public will is a recent, incompletely developed phenomenon. Deliberation with consensus as its goal, however, is a far older and more studied human tradition in the area of legal juries. Research in this area allows us to draw several relevant conclusions about the rule of unanimity in a deliberative environment (which we explore in greater depth in chapter 6). The requirement of unanimity in the criminal jury is a source of considerable frustration for jurors. But their capacity to develop civic skills and take a positive attitude away from the jury experience depends little on their ability to achieve unanimity. Those cardinal outcomes rely far more on whether individual jurors believe that their own views were attended to respectfully by fellow jurists—something that is encouraged by the consensus requirement. Positive results in this respect are generally correlated with an atmosphere of mutual respect in which facts and reasoned judgment were paramount (Gastil et al. 2010). In the legal justice context, an inability to reach a unanimous verdict is treated as a completely valid deliberative outcome in spite of the fact that all involved are aware that consensus is the goal. This particularly important element of jury practice is readily adaptable to deliberative democratic processes more generally, and many of the emerging practices of deliberative democrats parallel features of the jury system that have long been relied on to improve the quality of collective decision making (Sunstein 2002, 2005). Empirical research available on the work of juries does not generally bear out concerns that historically disadvantaged or underrepresented interests are neglected in the jury room (Vidmar and Hans 2007), because centuries of experience have produced deliberative processes that resist that tendency. If similar caution is taken in structuring deliberative democratic practices, similarly positive results should reasonably be expected.

Fourth, for all their criticisms of deliberative democratic practice, difference democrats have failed utterly to explain how majority rule aggregative democracy would produce equally good, let alone better, results from the minority perspective. A form of democracy that stresses the pursuit of consensus would seem far preferable to minority groups (which might as a practical matter then enjoy some form of qualified veto) than a system in which preferences are regarded as immutable and aggregative. This is, of course, precisely the logic that led Arend Lijphart (2008) to conclude that societies characterized by deep and persistent cultural divisions are far better served to adopt a consociational form of democracy than either the Westminster or Washington models. Consociational democracy protects minority perspectives (of whatever sort) by both reducing the number of wasted votes in mass elections and encouraging the development of broad coalition governments that magnify the influence of small parties (Lijphart 1977, 1999). Why these effects of an emphasis on consensus are ultimately bad for minority viewpoints is far from obvious and made no clearer by the work of difference democrats.

Understanding and Public Reason: From Action to Communication

If the consensus orientation actually advances the interests of minorities, perhaps the dangers of deliberative democracy lie elsewhere. Another candidate for the role of villain in the difference democrat story is the requirement of "public reason." Generally speaking, deliberative democrats call on speakers to offer reasons for their positions that anyone in the polity might accept if they found them to be persuasive. In particular, reasons that require the addressee to adopt the comprehensive view of the good held by the speaker (whether religious, ideological, or cultural in nature) are to be avoided (Rawls 1971). Needless to say, this would also preclude the proffering of reasons grounded in a speaker's narrow personal or financial advantage (if there were a temptation to offer reasons of that sort).

Because of the burden that public reason is supposed to impose, many deliberative democrats (in the tradition of John Rawls) limit the requirement to fundamental political questions, and only when people take on certain kinds of political roles (Dryzek 2001). The purpose of the public reason requirement in this context is to allow political representatives to discover institutional arrangements that could comprise an overlapping consensus among the reasonable comprehensive visions within a given society. The intent is not to move people away from their comprehensive moral commitments but rather show them areas of real (or potential) agreement by requiring them to support their positions with reasons true to their own stances, although not obnoxious to the comprehensive perspectives of others.

Other deliberative democrats are less reserved in their application of the public reason requirement, extending it (in theory at least) to almost any public issue. Following Habermas (1996), these theorists place less emphasis on the deep divisions between comprehensive worldviews and more on the innately public quality of political acts in general. According to them, if the deliberative aspiration amounts to anything at all, at its core must be the notion that democracy is a forum for arriving at public agreements rather than a market for the exchange of private preferences (Elster 1997). The requirement of public reasons can be seen in this context as merely one of a number of rules of engagement that underscore the inclusiveness, decisiveness, and reciprocity of any discourse that purports to be genuinely democratic (Gutmann and Thompson 1996).

But difference democrats attack the idea of public reason per se. Their complaints might usefully be grouped under two headings: inequality and discrimination.

Deliberative practices are, in the view of difference democrats, doomed to reproduce the very inequalities that their designers sought to remedy in the first place (Forester 1999). Through a combination of disinterest, hostility toward politics, and lack of personal resources, groups that have been disadvantaged in the aggregative past will continue to be disadvantaged in the deliberative future. Even when historically disadvantaged citizens are willing and able to deliberate, lack of information, resources, and expertise will disadvantage them relative to the members of dominant social and economic groups. Moreover, existing patterns of status and hierarchy unavoidably shape patterns of speaking and listening. The reason giving of which deliberative theorists are so fond is indicted as a manipulative and ultimately coercive artifice by which existing patterns of privilege are maintained (Sanders 1997).

A second category of criticisms has to do with the proposition that the deliberative process does not merely reproduce patterns of political dominance but also discriminates actively against political perspectives held by minorities within a given population. Some attribute this effect to a lack of cognitive capacity of the sort necessary to engage effectively in reasoned debate. It is unrealistic, they claim, to expect rational deliberation from the average citizen (Mouffe 1996), much less the historically disadvantaged. In addition, to the extent that deliberative practices disfavor the passionate and sometimes-disruptive appeals that minorities use to advance their interests (Sanders 1997), those interests will fail to be reflected in any results that deliberation might generate. The consequences of deliberative failure may be more severe for minorities, exacerbating the existing sense of political powerlessness among the marginalized (Button and Mattson 1999). What all this amounts to is an argument that deliberative democracy provides new tools of domination for better-educated, better-funded, and already-engaged citizens to use to work their will on minorities.

What is to be made of these apparently serious complaints about deliberative democracy? For one, it should be said that neither the danger of reproducing privilege nor risk of reinforcing discrimination has escaped the notice of deliberation's advocates. Every criticism we have discussed has been echoed by deliberative democrats, and often in more forceful terms than those used by difference democrats. No one has spoken at greater length or with more conviction about the risks of elite domination along with the importance of inclusivity than deliberative theorists (Bohman 1996; Dryzek 2000; Gutmann and Thompson 1996). Some deliberative practitioners have elevated questions of representativeness nearly to the point of an obsession (Fishkin 1997, 2009).

Second, some of the most significant advances in both human rights (Lo 2005) as well as environmental protection (Perlman 2009) have come by way of administrative adjudications and court cases in which strict rules of evidence apply, and inflammatory or self-serving justifications are routinely ignored or even punished. Difference democrats would have us believe that if the logic of administrative review and litigation became a more prominent part of other political processes, the results would not be similarly positive. They offer no real justification for that fear.

Third, the empirical premises underlying the complaints of difference democrats with respect to public reason are simply not borne out by deliberative experience. The accusation that deliberative practices reinforce inequity is not supported by empirical analysis of the relationship between socioeconomic status and the experience of deliberative participants. Although group biases do exist, discursive efficacy by marginalized groups is significant in survey results with regard to both levels of participation and self-reports concerning deliberative experiences. Furthermore, a high level of diversity distinguishes those forums where participants are seen as most actively engaged (Jacobs, Cook, and Carpini 2009). In terms of the supposed inability of women and people of color to deliberate with the same rigor and efficacy as white males, experience with legal juries (our most extensively studied kind of deliberation) reveal that this claim is as groundless as it is insulting (Vidmar and Hans 2007). In fact, these precise groups have the most to gain from the attitude adjustment that the deliberative experience offers for all who participate in it (Gastil et al. 2010).

Persuasion and Democracy: The Real Deliberative Turn

A somewhat-broader and rather-inchoate criticism of deliberative democracy questions the place of deliberation in democratic practice by problematizing what might be called democratic rationality. This cluster of criticisms is not unique to difference democrats, and each difference democrat cannot be accused of subscribing to all its elements. But we will discuss the issue broadly in order to better and more fairly situate difference democrats within this critical discourse. What this cluster of criticisms amounts to is a claim that deliberative practice, even if it allows minorities to voice their concerns and make themselves understood, places insurmountable obstacles between them and the objective of actually persuading others. This criticism encompasses several elements.

It is sometimes argued that because its aim is to produce a more "rational" form of democracy, deliberative practice is so demanding of people's time and energy that they will decline in large numbers to participate (Hibbing and Theiss-Morse 2002). The resulting self-selection bias is likely to be particularly harmful to people whose experiences of social disaffection and political disenfranchisement make them problematic participants in public deliberation in any event (Williams 2000). Critics also argue that the problem-oriented and research-driven forms of discourse generally thought to be characteristic of deliberative practices have erected a barrier of technical jargon that is difficult for disadvantaged cultural groups to breach. An example offered is the technical language associated with water pollution that was alleged to have disadvantaged Native Americans who participated in a Portland, Oregon, citizens' forum (Button and Mattson 1999). A further count in the indictment of deliberation is its too infrequently influential role in determining political outcomes. Here, difference democrats would have trouble finding deliberative democrats who disagree. But the claim that the inefficacy of deliberation is especially harmful to minorities is arguable. The proposition is that the failure of deliberation actually to change minds decreases political participation most severely where difference is marked and oppositional views are likely to be aired, thereby promoting deliberation at the expense of nondeliberative forms of participation and activism (Sanders 1997; Mutz 2006). Thus, members of oppositional groups within a society are, if not actually co-opted, at least lulled into a state of quiescence as they are gently led by the "mild voice of reason" (Bessette 1997) away from potentially valuable strategies of confrontation into polite and perpetual conversation.

So this cluster of criticisms amounts to an assertion by difference democrats that deliberation is too demanding, confusing, and frustrating for women and minorities to master. Without pausing to consider what kind of advocates for difference that difference democrats have actually turned out to be, it is incumbent on deliberative democrats to respond to what would be serious criticisms if they were valid. Happily for human beings generally, there is good reason to doubt that they are. In the first instance, and as we have seen in other regards, the concerns of difference democrats have already occurred to deliberative democrats who have invested considerable effort in responding to them. Advocates of deliberation have discussed at great length the necessity of and various means for assuring that groups of deliberating citizens are not unrepresentative in any ways that matter for the issues at hand. It is important, however, to distinguish between two levels of representation: "speaking for" and "acting for."

When one is concerned primarily with representation as speaking for, or "communicative action" (Habermas 1987b), and the quality of that action from a cognitive point of view, it is of primary importance to achieve completeness of expression. What is being "represented" is not interests or groups but rather discourses (Dryzek 2001, 2006; Dryzek and Niemeyer 2008). It is not critical that all interested individuals and opinion groups be represented in the precise proportions that they occur in society. The critical concern is that everything worth saying eventually gets said and said capably. Better demographic representation is only one method for satisfying this requirement (and not necessarily the best, inasmuch as without an extremely large body of representatives, it still might exclude small minorities with distinctive perspectives). A better method would be repeated trials of the same substantive issue, allowing more opportunities for diverse perspectives to show themselves (Fishkin 2009). Perhaps more effective still would be a combination of representative and enclave deliberation. The latter would consist of deliberation of an issue by groups intentionally chosen to overrepresent a perspective suspected of having been overlooked by more typical deliberative practices. Participants in such enclave deliberation would then be "seeded" in more representative deliberations in order to ensure that the minority perspective is completely expressed. Producing this deliberative seed stock would be an ideal role for the organizations of civil society, which represent a vast and relatively untapped resource of opinion diversity, and many of which are populated by women and minorities who have already overcome some of the barriers to political participation that may exist in a given society (Jacobs, Cook, and Carpini 2009).

When we turn our attention to representation as acting for, though, a different set of concerns comes into view. Speaking for others in contexts where binding decisions are to be arrived at carries special burdens usually explored under the heading of "legitimacy." Setting aside the dubious proposition that good results confer "outcome legitimacy" on a decision ex post facto, what might we say about deliberative democracy that would lead us to believe that its products are more legitimate than those of normal legislation? The conventional answer to this problem is to invoke some variation of the principal–agent model (Parkinson 2006). It is worthwhile for theorists to remind themselves from time to time that conventional answers often come to be conventional because they are the best ones available. In this context, the question of legitimacy might be conceived of as a measure of the closeness of the relationship between principal and agent. Seen in this way, no theorists have been more sensitive to the problem of legitimacy than deliberative democrats. Indeed, the increasingly attenuated relationship between constituents and their elected officials has been one of the primary motivations of the deliberative movement generally (Baber and Bartlett 2005).

The deliberative solution to the growing gulf between the represented and their representatives is (in part) to infuse processes of rule making with well-structured, inclusive public participation. In those forums, policy experts are required to make themselves understood to citizen representatives who are interested in the policy problems at hand, but whose knowledge of those concerns is that of a layperson. Ideally, they should bring to the decision-making process "non-participants' values, wishes, and experiences," and then transmit back to their principals "the reasons for and against those points of view" in a recursive communicative process (Parkinson 2006, 153) that both improves the quality of representation and enhances the policy value of technical expertise. The extent to which representatives are willing and able to do this could be taken to be one measure of the legitimacy of the policies that they ultimately adopt (Baber and Bartlett 2005). This would seem to be exactly the kind of practice that would satisfy the calls of difference democrats for representation as relationship (Young 2000). If they are not satisfied with the way that deliberative democrats have responded to the problem of legitimacy, they should describe more inclusive mechanisms of participation at a level of specificity sufficient to allow for the testing of efficacy and ease of use. Or they should provide evidence that the diversity of opinion they seek to advance will be better served by recourse to the institutions of aggregative democracy that have been used heretofore.

Regarding the claim that deliberative democracy confronts women and minorities with burdens of participation that they find too confusing, that problem simply has not manifested itself in any consistent way in practice. For every instance of Native Americans who report being confused by the jargon of water quality, there are multiple examples of the same people mastering the intricacies of law and economics sufficiently to win the right to establish gaming businesses, and then make them pay off handsomely. The problem of communication between technical specialists and laypersons recurs constantly in the deliberative experience, but frustrating as it is, does not burden women and minorities more than others. It is not uncommon for experts and laypersons to talk past one another in deliberations. This deliberative dysfunction can generally be traced to incompatible problem definitions, inadequate respect for the agency of others, and deliberative processes that allow insufficient time and direct contact for those issues to be debated (Parkinson 2006). There is a solution to this problem that works tolerably well for all. It is for moderators of deliberation to qualify experts carefully, and prudently define and delimit their role. Judiciaries have extensive experience with this sort of problem, and have developed doctrines and procedures that allowed juries to resolve disputes over highly complex questions of both law and fact. Research comparing jury verdicts with those of judges who heard the same cases suggests that laypersons are fully capable of navigating complex, technical patterns of evidence and arriving at judgments that compare favorably with judicial opinions (Vidmar and Hans 2007). In fact, recent jury research indicates that whereas mundane technical complexity might dull engagement in some cases, by contrast, deliberative complexity more often enhances juror engagement (Gastil et al. 2010).

Finally, we have the claim that the deliberative experience is frustrating because of its frequent failure to affect the course of public policy, and that this failure is particularly discouraging to women and minorities who have suffered from a sense of inefficacy in the past. In a sense, this complaint combines the previous assertions that deliberation is difficult and confusing into a "pendent claim" that historically disadvantaged parties should be exempted from deliberative democracy's demands lest they suffer the harm of new political disappointments.[1] The problem with pendent claims, however, is that they must be closely related to the original one and are generally no stronger substantively than that claim. The arguments of difference democrats suffer on both counts. Although women and minorities have, unquestionably, suffered political frustrations to a disproportionate degree, it cannot reasonably be argued that deliberative democracy run amok is the cause. Elitism and discrimination in aggregative democratic practices (not to mention fundamentally undemocratic practices) are at fault, and these are some of the ills that the adoption of consensus as a political objective and public reasoning as a political methodology are intended to remedy. In fact, difference democrats are attempting here to do what lawyers frequently try to do with pendent claims. They are trying to draw parties into the case despite the fact that they contributed nothing to the injury complained of (Perdue 1990).

Moreover, the claims that deliberative democracy is too demanding and confusing for women and minorities to master do not provide the pendent claim of frustration with a strong foundation in any event. Advocates of minority perspectives have proven themselves quite capable of representing those perspectives in adequately open and inclusive deliberative forums. There is certainly evidence to suggest that the public airing of differences is supportive of the broader search for commonalities. Researchers have noted a significant correlation between deliberative facilitators' efforts to "help the group come to an agreement" and the commitment of the forum to the "airing of differences" (Jacobs, Cook, and Carpini 2009, 76). The persons that difference democrats most worry about have reported satisfactory experiences with shouldering what might be called the "burdens of deliberation." They are already participating in the search for political consensus based on public reasoning. In particular, they are participating successfully in addressing precisely those environmental problems that arise from what might be characterized as a violation of the rights of the person. The discourse of environmental justice can be usefully contrasted with the relatively less successful discourse of environmental activists (largely white and middle to upper class) whose primary concern is to acquit the rights of nonhuman occupants of the natural world—a contrast with implications for deliberative democratic environmentalism.[2]

Difference, Environmental Justice, and Animal Rights

From its earliest expressions, the environmental justice discourse (a set of overlapping discourses, not to be confused with the environmental justice movement, nor the ill-bounded collection of networks and organizations that comprise it) has been composed of several interwoven themes that set it apart. Using the definition favored by the US Environmental Protection Agency, environmental justice is simply the fair treatment and meaningful involvement of all people, regardless of race, color, national origin, or income, with respect to the development, implementation, and enforcement of environmental laws, regulations, and policies. To suggest that we should settle for anything less than this should offend the democratic sensibilities of anyone. At the time when early allegations of environmental racism were first being heard, however, it was far from clear that environmentalists and civil rights activists would eventually find common ground.

When the environmental justice movement emerged in the early 1980s, it was fueled by a mounting frustration among minority, immigrant, and indigenous communities with the ill effects of hazardous and polluting industries located predominantly in their neighborhoods. The activism to which this frustration gave birth adopted a civil rights and social justice approach to environmental justice, and grew organically from hundreds, even thousands, of local struggles, events, and various other social movements. What arose from this inchoate activism has been depicted as a network of discourse, constructed from the bottom up, that unites differently situated communities and individuals as they confront shared environmental hazards (Schlosberg 1999).

Despite its obvious potential to redraw the map of environmental politics, the initial prospects for environmental justice to become a fully integrated element of environmentalism were not bright. Early in their history, traditional environmental groups worked to keep the environmental movement apart from other social movements, concerned that any alliances that they might form would dilute their focus on environmental issues as well as hamper their ability to attract and retain members. Furthermore, these older environmental groups typically emphasized landscape protection and the protection of endangered species over issues of pollution prevention affecting primarily inner cities. Minority groups and indigenous peoples were rarely represented on the membership rolls of the early environmental organizations (Ringquist 2003). Against these odds, the development of an environmental rights discourse from the raw material of environmental injustice might have seemed improbable. Environmental justice nevertheless has become precisely such a discourse.

In modern societies, characterized by relatively free and healthy public spheres along with reasonably independent judiciaries, the rights of individuals and groups (regardless of theories regarding the provenance of those rights) are constantly evolving and being redefined. Nowhere has this process shown more dynamism in recent years than in the area of environmental rights. Prior to the advent of environmentalism, businesses the world over treated air and water as free goods—available either for appropriation or as sinks for industrial pollution. Until the 1960s, this tacit assertion of environmental rights went largely uncontested (Rhodes 2003). It was the success of the environmental justice discourse in further problematizing these assumed rights that opened the door to a fruitful partnership with mainstream environmental organizations. Stepping through that door required more, though. Without ignoring what mainstream environmental groups needed to do to exploit this opportunity, much was required of the environmental justice discourse for it to live up to its potential.

From its earliest expressions, the environmental justice discourse has been composed of several interwoven themes that set it apart. In comparison with other strains of environmentalism, it "integrates both social and ecological concerns more readily and pays particular attention to questions of distributive justice, community empowerment, and democratic accountability. It does not treat the problem of oppression and social exploitation as separable from the rape and exploitation of the natural world. Instead, it argues that human societies and the natural environment are intricately linked and that the health of one depends on the health of the other" (Taylor 1999, 57). The environmental justice discourse maintains a focus on both the human–nonhuman interface and interactions between humans, and has done so in an especially pliable way.

When early research led to suggestions that perverse distributions of environmental risks might be as much a function of class as of race (Burch 1976), the environmental justice discourse grew to encompass this idea. One can really appreciate the weight of this choice when one reflects on the fact that (as a general matter) in most places, it is illegal to discriminate against people on the basis of race, yet perfectly legal to discriminate against the poor. Environmental justice activists would have had this perfect excuse to cling to their original discourse of environmental racism. Still, environmental justice activists recognized that "the only manner in which the material interests of the working class and the oppressed people of color can be safeguarded is through their incorporation into the decision making processes of the major social, political, and economic institutions that impact their lives and the environment in which they live" (Faber 1998, 9).

Hence, they recognized that a key component of any workable system of ecological democracy is a greater emphasis on participatory democracy. As environmental justice activists moved into positions in various levels of government, and as corporate polluters had to engage with the governmental bodies that were being set up, environmental justice began to look more and more like a governance network. But "social movement activism remained highly visible and contestatory. So the result was networked governance that featured both empowered space and public space at a critical distance" (Dryzek 2010, 131). This dynamic balance is difficult to attain and maintain. It nonetheless is the hallmark of an emancipatory social movement that it achieves a reasonable level of political maturity by accepting the burdens of persuasion. Environmental justice is a movement that has "changed the content of public discourse on environmental affairs, most importantly by establishing the very idea of environmental justice as a public concern" (Dryzek 2006, 58). It contrasts markedly in this regard with the discourse associated with another rights-oriented branch of environmental radicalism: animal rights (Eckersley 1992, 42–45). The comparison tells us much about the importance of undertaking the burden of deliberation that some difference democrats ask permission to bypass.

The animal rights–animal liberation discourse (like environmental justice, it is really a set of overlapping discourses) faces an uphill battle in meeting the burdens of deliberation. It is not even clear that animal rights activists want to meet those burdens. For example, the Animal Liberation Front engages in its peculiar forms of direct action not to convince anyone of the inherent rights of animals but rather as a form of cost levying designed to change its opponents behavior by inflicting economic losses on them (Humphrey 2007). The point is not just to persuade but also to coerce. Civil rights movements have engaged in similar direct actions (generally in the form of boycotts) that have not convinced businesspeople to become more egalitarian but instead have altered their behavior by damaging their bottom line. Civil rights movements, however, have combined campaigns of direct action and concern for redressing individual grievances with efforts to address systemic problems of discrimination through legislation. This is a burden of persuasion that animal rights activists have rarely shouldered. With a few exceptions (like the use of animals in experiments), animal rights activists have sought to influence the views of others mainly through a campaign of person-by-person emotional appeal designed to convince people to abandon habits of millennia (such as eating meat and wearing clothing of animal origin). One of the many problems with this approach is its contingent character. The results that it produces depend too much on the circumstances of each encounter between the strategy and the world in which it operates.

For those who share a concern about the fate of individual nonhuman animal lives, it is not entirely apparent what concrete forms a principled commitment to that cause would take. What rule(s) of general application can they reasonably expect to achieve that would advance their objectives? A place to perhaps start would be the protection of animals as members of a species. But most animal rights activists regard endangered species protection as nothing more than people trying to maximize the yield of some of their "resources" in ways that do nothing to change the status of those resources from objects to rights bearers.[3]

Reconciling Diversity and Deliberation: Avoiding the Cost of Being Right

The environmental justice discourse has "been successful in reframing environmental issues related to risk, social justice, and so extending deliberative democratic control over these issues. Its discursive contests have been with more entrenched environmentalist discourses that conceptualize risk in terms of their collective and common character, as well as with industrialist discourses that deny the severity of risk or subordinate risk to the pursuit of material prosperity" (Dryzek 2000, 77). Environmental justice activists have also succeeded in creating a policy network, the most concrete manifestations of which are Executive Order 12898 (1973) and the creation of the Office of Environmental Justice within the US Environmental Protection Agency (ibid.). The salience of this new issue network is clearly visible, too, in its ability to influence the human rights discourse at the global level.

In a series of resolutions, the United Nations Human Rights Council and the former United Nations Commission on Human Rights have drawn attention to the relationship between a safe, healthy environment and the enjoyment of human rights. The Human Rights Council, in its resolution 7/23 of March 2008 and resolution 10/4 of March 2009, focused specifically on human rights and climate change, noting that effects related to climate change have a range of direct and indirect implications for the effective enjoyment of human rights. These actions have identified three primary dimensions of the relationship between human rights and environmental protection:

• the environment as a prerequisite for the enjoyment of human rights (implying that states' human rights obligations should include the duty to ensure the level of environmental protection necessary to allow the full exercise of protected rights)

• certain human rights, especially access to information, participation in decision making, and access to justice in environmental matters, as essential to good environmental decision making (implying that human rights must be implemented in order to ensure environmental protection)

• the right to a safe, healthy, and ecologically balanced environment as a human right in itself

These expressions of environmental justice as an emergent policy network are of such a character as to lead some to criticize the movement for promoting "an exclusively anthropocentric discourse," given that its concern with nature is "limited to examining how ecological degradation affects the human community" (Brulle 2000, 221). This stands in stark contrast to the animal rights movement, which has been offered as the most "extreme example" of environmentalism's regrettable tendency to concentrate on "things, not people" (Rhodes 2003, 90). It might also serve to explain why the animal rights discourse has not given rise to a discrete policy network. If one dismisses the work of animal welfare (humane treatment) advocates, as animal rights activists are prone to do, there is little of a concrete nature to which proponents of animal rights can point as a positive result of their efforts. Although its most strident defenders might deny that this is any shortcoming, the failure of animal rights advocates to institutionalize their discourse invites an unfavorable comparison to the successes of environmental justice proponents.

The environmental justice discourse "offers (at least) two different, but complementary paths toward transformation. First, it is a *vocabulary for political opportunity, mobilization, and action*, predominately at the local level.... It is also a *policy principle*: that no public action should disproportionately disadvantage any particular social group" (Agyeman and Evans 2006, 201; emphasis in the original). To the extent that the animal rights movement (and other variants of radical environmentalism) forgo such a Janus-faced potential for politics-policy advantage, opportunities for transforming environmentalism are lost. The failure to form policy networks around radical environmental narratives is particularly unfortunate "from the point of view of democratic contestations of discourses in the public sphere" because "to the degree they engage truly diverse participants, networks just have to work according to principles of equity, openness, respect, and reciprocity" (Dryzek 2010, 39). These cardinal virtues of deliberative democratic practice have long been characteristic of environmental justice activism and its network form of organization, which has become the paradigmatic case for deliberation across difference (Schlosberg 1998).

The opportunity for democratizing environmentalism more generally is also lost when radical environmentalisms are not institutionalized. This loss runs both directions because "the goal of social and environmental justice cannot be achieved unless the environmental movement itself becomes more democratic. ... By practicing ecological democracy organizationally, becoming more open and inclusive, movements for environmental justice could serve to unite the environmental movement firmly with other movements for social justice that normally do not identify with ecological issues" (Faber 1998, 9–10). Both improved environmental protection and increased social justice are at stake. Also hanging in the balance, ironically enough, is the fate of the diversity that difference democrats value so highly. "Difference democrats invoke the image of the gentleman's club in criticizing the excessively civil image of deliberation. If they have replaced the gentleman's club with the consciousness raising group, that is not good enough" (Dryzek 2000, 74–75). In service of what they declare to be their own objectives, difference democrats should aspire to create precisely the same sort of policy network that environmental justice activism has produced because "deliberation across variety is a necessary, not a contingent feature" of these networks—within which the diversity of participants virtually guarantees that there can be "few taken-for-granted truths" of the sort that frustrate difference democrats in other social contexts (ibid., 135).

To lend greater precision to his use of the concept of a policy network, Dryzek resorts to a definition employed by Eva Sørensen and Jacob Torfing. On their account, a policy network is (1) a relatively stable horizontal articulation of interdependent but operationally autonomous actors (2) interacting through negotiation that (3) takes place within a normative, cognitive, and imaginary framework, that (4) is self-regulating within limits set by external agencies, and that (5) contributes to the production of public purpose (Sørensen and Torfing 2008). This network form can be found across the entire range of identifiable policy issues, and its component structures extend their reach from the local and regional levels to the global arena. They have become so ubiquitous and are by now so well understood that Dryzek (2010, 121) argues, "Governance networks now join markets and hierarchies as a recognized mode of interaction in the delivery of public outcomes." On the assumption that difference democrats do, in fact, wish to affect the delivery of public outcomes, what must they do to achieve that end?

Habermas (1984, 1987b) portrays markets and bureaucracies as rationalized social systems that have been differentiated from the lifeworld by the development of steering media—money and power. Applying Sørensen and Torfing's definition of a policy network, these steering media empower (1) the interdependent but operationally autonomous actors, and (3) establish the normative, cognitive, and imaginary framework within which (2) their interactions take place. In the case of markets, for example, the actors are producers and customers, and the framework within which their exchange interactions occur is the objectified mythology of the marketplace. The notorious invisible hand (4) sets the institutional limits within which (5) the public purpose of maximized need satisfaction is produced.

So clearly, governance networks have all the characteristic features of a rationalized social system as Habermas has described them. If then, like markets and bureaucracies, they have a steering mechanism, it is necessary to identify the nature of the steering media that is at work within that system. Although both money and power are undoubtedly all-purpose resources in governance networks, they cannot be used to differentiate that system from the communicatively organized lifeworld. Money cannot establish the nature of the relationships within the system (which do not rely on exchange) nor establish the conceptual framework of the system (which operates in the boundary areas outside markets and bureaucracies). Power can neither identify the actors (who are self-selected and voluntary participants) nor impose the structural characteristics of the system (which are horizontal rather than hierarchical).

Alternatively, might we imagine (and recommend) deliberation as the steering mechanism for the emerging social system comprised of governance networks? In order to answer that question, it is important to understand what a steering medium must look like if it is to obviate the "expenditure and risk" associated with consensus-forming processes while enhancing the prospects for "purposive-rational action" (Habermas 1987b, 263). Following Talcott Parsons, Habermas argues that steering media must possess certain structural features and qualitative properties. Structurally, steering media must apply to a narrow class of standardized situations defined by clear interest positions covered by a generalized value. The medium must allow one party to steer the response of another in a yes–no interaction where both actors are able to adopt an instrumental view of the choices at hand (ibid., 264). Qualitatively, units of the medium must be measurable, exchangeable, and storable (ibid., 265). When a medium possesses these features, it can be used to detach a cluster of interactions from the processes of "consensus formation in ordinary language" that allow "cultural transmission and socialization as well as social integration to come about" in the broader contexts of human experience (ibid., 266). With such a medium in hand, parties are able to engage in a process of asserting claims and redeeming them within a subsystem that has been differentiated from the functions of cultural reproduction, which become for that subsystem the "environment" (ibid., 267).

It should be apparent, then, that deliberation per se does not and cannot satisfy the requirements of a steering medium. It can be applied to a vast array of situations involving often-inchoate interest positions grounded in competing values. But it does not (necessarily) involve yes–no choices that can be interpreted in entirely instrumental ways. Neither is deliberation itself measurable, exchangeable, or storable (those ideas cannot even be applied to deliberation in sensible ways). Because these characteristics are absent from deliberation, it cannot be used to differentiate the subsystem of governance networks from processes of consensus formation in ordinary language. Deliberation, as a concept, simply is not sufficiently well focused and exclusive to serve as a steering medium in the sense that Habermas uses that term.

More appropriate to the role of steering medium in the system of governance networks is the concept of evidence. Because this term is likely to set off alarm bells with difference democrats, it is important to appreciate how well the concept of evidence satisfies the requirements of a steering medium.

In the context of judicial proceedings, evidence is simply probative material, legally received, by which a tribunal may be lawfully persuaded of the truth or falsity of a fact at issue (Leonard 1962). Material is probative if it speaks to the likely validity or falsity of one party's argument as a factual premise. It can be legally received by a tribunal if its use does not violate the rights of either party, expressed as generalized values. Evidence is legally used if doing so does not exceed the authority or jurisdiction of the tribunal, thus legitimately steering the tribunal's choice. A putative fact is at issue if it is a necessary component of the argument presented by one party to the dispute at hand, framing a yes–no choice, and has not been stipulated by the parties or noticed by the tribunal, thereby adding instrumental value to the decision process. Moreover, evidence is measureable by an ordinal scale, ranging from "substantial evidence" to "evidence beyond a reasonable doubt" (with preponderance of evidence along with clear and convincing evidence as intermediate quantities). Evidence is identified (in part) by its exchange under rules understood in advance. Evidence is routinely stored in court records, the value of which is confirmed with every act of appellate review.

The fact that evidence is also a nearly perfect candidate for the role of steering medium in a governance network system does not mean that difference democrats will inevitably warm to the idea. Indeed, they may be more likely to add the pivotal role that evidence plays in the governance subsystem to their list of reasons for turning their backs on anything that smacks of deliberation. But if they chose to do so, they cannot reasonably argue that they had no alternative. Historically disadvantaged groups have shown a clear capacity to turn evidence-based, deliberative procedures to their benefit. They are able to do so by converting their distinctive discourses and personal perspectives into evidence by demonstrating its probative value—specifically, its ability to cast doubt on the factual assertions of historically dominant groups and interests. In the particular case of environmental justice advocates, this process of problematizing existing factual narratives has even succeeded in altering the generalized values that guide the exchange of evidence by creating a new understanding of the parties' rights. In this manner, environmental justice actors have introduced new yes–no choices that connect with preexisting environmental disagreements, often tipping the balance in ways that the broader environmental and civil rights movements have found to be highly instrumental.

The contrast between the environmental justice and animal rights discourses should serve as a cautionary tale both to environmentalists of all stripes and difference democrats. Global environmental governance advances markedly when systems of governance networks are adopted as alternatives to markets and bureaucracies. Crafting and nurturing particular policy networks will require accepting the burdens of persuasion that come with those deliberative processes that assume a central role in network governance. Globally as well as locally, environmentalists must decide that it is more valuable to achieve collective will formation based on an overlapping consensus of reasonable views than it is to hold out for more comprehensive agreement based on what they regard as the right reasons. This, too, is the price that difference democrats will be asked to pay if the views they espouse are to find a place in the systems of environmental governance networks.

Choosing to become an element of the environment of this newly differentiated social system may impose a still-higher cost—the cost of being right, which entails the costs of embracing both the obligations of deliberation and obligations that make possible environmental justice.

5

Environmental Justice and the Globalization of Obligation and Normative Consensus

Justice is the first virtue of social institutions, as truth is of systems of thought.
—John Rawls

Men hoist the banner of the ideal, and then march in the direction that concrete conditions suggest and reward.
—John Dewey

The many and varied discourses surrounding the idea of environmental justice would seem to share at least one essential quality. They all are about obligation. The nature of this obligation can be, and has been, debated along a number of dimensions. Who are the parties to the obligation? From what source or sources does the obligation arise? Is the obligation entirely procedural, or can some of its substance be specified? Are there practical limits to the extent of the obligation, and if so, what are they? Various responses to these questions have been combined to create a family of different but related notions about what environmental justice is and how it can be achieved. Before we can usefully explore the challenges posed by environmental justice for a globalization of environmental common law, a better understanding of these questions and the possible responses to them is necessary. As Dewey might put it, if we are to become more just (and true), we will need a banner to follow.

Parties to the Obligation

When the idea of environmental justice is invoked, who are the parties to the referenced obligation? Who is the obligee and who the obligor? The very terminology we employ influences the direction of our inquiry. When we speak of the parties to an obligation, we are at least suggesting that an obligation is analogous to a duty owed under the provisions of a contract. For instance, it has been argued that environmental justice has been done when (generally speaking) people get what they deserve or what is due them. The idea is that people should receive their fair share of the scarce things that they want, including environmental resources and amenities (Wenz 1988, 114–117). Quasi-contractual obligations of this sort fit most naturally (although not exclusively) within a scenario featuring parties who are individuals. This is more clearly evident when we ask whether a contractual obligation is divisible or indivisible. If I contract to pay you a sum of money for work you perform, you may not assign one-half of the amount to another individual, so as to create an obligation on my part to that person. Either the third party must be an original signatory to the contract or a separate agreement creating this new obligation is required.

To characterize environmental justice in this way will strike many people as unproblematic. It tells us, in a relatively simple way, what environmental justice is. It is a state of affairs in which all individuals meet their obligations to fairly distribute environmental risks and resources among themselves under the terms of some agreement. This distribution does not necessarily treat everyone equally. It simply guarantees to each and all that which they have accepted and requires of them that which they have offered. Yet it is possible to adopt a different perspective on the subject. This view of the matter regards instances of environmental injustice not as failures to meet the obligations that exist between individuals but rather as the imposition of environmental losses on one individual or group of individuals by another. Here we must distinguish two situations.

In the first situation, you enjoy a share of environmental resources that is less than the share of those resources enjoyed by others. This could be because you value those resources less than others and have traded them for something you value more. Or it could be because you lack the personal qualities that would allow you to secure more of those resources through your dealings with others. So here your environmental disadvantage is a result either of your personal preferences, skills, or bad luck. In any case, though, it could be argued that no obligation to correct the disadvantage would run to others.

Imagine now a second situation. Again you enjoy a smaller share of environmental resources than do others. But in this case, the reason for your disadvantage seems to have nothing to do with you as an individual. Assume that you value environmental resources at least as much as the average person and are no less capable of realizing your individual preferences than are others. Yet you live in a community where environmental hazards are more common and severe than they are elsewhere. Finally, imagine that another noticeable characteristic of your community is its minority composition. Your neighbors and you are also less well off financially than average, and females head households in your community to a greater degree than is typical in society as a whole.

Now we have drawn the contours of a problem of environmental injustice that is more familiar to an environmentalist than the problems that arise between contracting individuals. Here the parties to any obligations that we might describe are likely to be groups of individuals whose members think of themselves (at least in part) as belonging to those groups, and tend to understand both their rights and disadvantages in collective terms. The existence of such group-based conceptions of environmental justice is central to our concerns because much of the dynamism of the environmental justice discourse can be traced to the intersection of race, gender, and class groupings (Camacho 1998). In this scenario, the obligee of an environmental justice obligation is a group and the obligor is likely to be thought of collectively as well.

Sources of Obligation

One source of the obligation to do environmental justice involves either natural or corporate individuals, arising under agreements that antedate any particular dispute. In fact, this is the conventional understanding of contractual obligation generally. It is a two-stage obligation. First, there is the primary personal right antecedent to the wrong, and afterward, a secondary right consequent on a wrong. An example may help to illustrate both the difference being described here and importance of depicting it. Assume that you own a red convertible, which you agree to sell to someone for a thousand dollars. Assume further that you change your mind about the deal. The primary obligation in this instance is the underlying agreement to exchange things of value and secondary obligation is a consequence of someone else's rights that arise on your breach of the agreement. The primary obligation may be incontestable. Still, you could concede the first obligation and resist the second.

Imagine that you belatedly discovered that red convertibles are worth far more than a thousand dollars. You now regret your hasty decision and wish to evade the consequences of it. In this case, we may wish to simply enforce the original agreement precisely, transferring title in exchange for the money promised. Lawyers call this remedy "specific performance." Specific performance would be especially appropriate, of course, if the high cost of a red convertible results from the unfortunate fact that yours is the only one left on the road.

Alternatively, imagine that you have changed your mind because your spouse has objected to the deal. Imagine that this particular car has sentimental value, the precise nature of which we need not explore. Now we may wish to grant some other form of relief. We may find an essentially similar car on the open market, and you may be held responsible for the difference between that other car's price and the purchase price to which you had agreed. If that car can also be purchased for a thousand dollars, little or nothing may be recovered from you. This remedy leaves the purchaser no worse off than would specific performance and protects the continued existence of your family unit.

It should be obvious from this portrait that imagining obligation as a two-stage contractual phenomenon offers significant potential advantages for both the contracting parties (who enjoy multiple options for satisfying their goals) and society at large (which avoids a certain number of angry divorces). These advantages are gained not by frustrating anyone's reasonable expectations but instead simply by disentangling issues of rights and remedies. Consider, however, a second potential source of obligation. This is the *obligatio ex maleficio*, the obligation founded on a wrong. Here, someone might be obligated to you in some way because of an invasion of a right that you enjoy as a person. This might be your right to the exclusive possession of some object that someone takes from you or your right to be left alone that someone's behavior violates in some especially egregious way.

Regardless of the specific circumstances, obligations of this sort have a unitary quality and arise in a unilateral way based on something other than an explicit agreement between the two of you. Moreover, it is difficult to conceive of a remedy for the failure to meet these kinds of obligations that does not involve returning a possession or ceasing to annoy you. The obligations we refer to when we discuss environmental justice are often of this general sort. In these instances, we are not simply concerned with an inappropriate distribution of environmental risks and resources. We are concerned that the distribution of environmental goods is being determined by forces that abridge our rights as persons. The distribution is not merely unequal; it is discriminatory. The distribution is not only disadvantageous; it is oppressive. The distribution does not just violate human rules; it violates human beings.

Procedure versus Substance

The fact that our concern for the violation of obligations might also be a concern for the violation of persons suggests that at least with respect to a certain kind of obligation, it will be hard to distinguish between procedural and substantive justice. Where obligations are of a contractual sort, our ability to distinguish between primary and secondary obligations allows us to examine two distinct aspects of doing justice. First, we can question the original agreement that gave rise to the primary obligation. Were the parties fully competent to enter into it? Was the agreement founded on some form of deceit or fraud? Was the agreement itself oppressive or coercive in some way? Is the agreement an example of a broader category of agreements that we wish to disallow for reasons of the public good (e.g., meretricious contracts)? All these questions are important in their own right, and are available to us for examination because the right underlying the obligation is not considered any way absolute or essential. Having been created by humans, the right can also be abjured by humans when the circumstances indicate that to do otherwise would increase rather than reduce injustice.

A second level of analysis is available to us in evaluating contractual obligations. We can acknowledge the existence of the primary right, but problematize the secondary right to have the agreement authoritatively enforced. Does a violation of the right require that the party in breach be held to requirement for specific performance, or would some form of damages suffice? If damages are the appropriate remedy, are nominal ones sufficient, or has there been real and substantial harm done that requires significant compensation? Further, is the breach of such a serious nature that punitive damages (beyond the actual losses incurred) are necessary to punish the obligor or discourage similar behavior in the future on the part of others?

With respect to both primary and secondary obligations, our ability to analyze the distinct stages of doing justice allows us to also consider the complex problem of relating procedural and substantive justice. As we evaluate the primary obligation, we work our way down a checklist of reasons why the underlying agreement might be voided. Each step, from the competency of the parties through problems of fraud and coercion to issues of public policy, focuses our attention on a parade of different values, and requires us to decide which procedural requirements and analytic approaches are most conducive to realizing those values. The same can be said of our efforts to think through the issue of secondary rights. What procedure will allow a court to choose between specific performance and compensatory damages (to determine whether your reluctance to complete the sale of your red convertible is an effort to realize a financial gain or avoid a personal loss)? If damages are to be awarded, how direct must the underlying harm be, and how can we tell that the losses have been adequately compensated? What would, under any given set of circumstances, constitute excessive damages? When would the situation require criminal damages, and how could we tell that the threshold had been crossed?

Conducting such an analysis of contractual obligations is complicated enough. When the obligation that has been violated arises directly from rights possessed by people as people (*jus in rem*), these same issues of procedure and substance arise, but our ability to disentangle them is reduced by the "unitary" character of the obligation. The "goods" secured to us by such rights often have a certain nonfungible quality about them. We find it hard to imagine an accurate or adequate exchange involving such values (perhaps explaining why they have struck some people as constituting inalienable rights). This accounts for both our reluctance to accept monetary damages in compensation for racial or ethnic affronts and our difficulty in saying precisely why we feel that reluctance.

Matters are more complicated still when the right abridged is thought of as a group right requiring a group remedy. Hence, proponents of affirmative action view that remedy as the only reasonable response to the wrongs of which they complain, yet have difficulty making that view understood to others who recognize the grievances involved only at the level of actual damages to individual persons done by other persons. Consider the case of a proposed manufacturing facility to be located in a minority community. The objection can be to the imposition of the environmental risk itself, or the forced choice between the possibility of environmental harm versus opportunities for employment in the context of a history of economic disadvantage. Frequently, of course, the objection sounds at both levels—complicating the difficulty involved in arriving at a procedure that will achieve just results. The case of an individual manufacturing plant in a particular minority community can be viewed as merely one instantiation of a broader historical pattern that requires disadvantaged groups to choose between equal protection from environmental hazard and equal opportunity for economic advancement.

Thus, we can see that as the field of discourse moves from rights that are individual and contractual to those that are collective and unitary, our ability to separate issues of substance and procedure is reduced to the point that the distinction itself loses much of its analytic as well as practical utility. We can also see that there is something of a conceptual and practical mismatch between claims and obligations of this sort and the quasi-contractual techniques of regime formation and implementation that characterize international law.

The Limits of Obligation

What are the practical limits to obligation, and implications of those limits for issues of environmental justice? When we conceive of environmental justice as a matter of contractual obligation, we inherit all the complexities implicit in contract law generally. But is this necessarily a bad thing? If we assume that legal rules are largely a reflection of the underlying social conditions to which they relate, we may want the complexity of law to keep pace with that of society. When the law does this, it actually expands the scope of human possibilities by allowing us to harness social, economic, and technological change to our purposes. Along with this advantage, however, comes increased transaction costs and the new risks created by increasing uncertainty about how complex legal rules will be enforced.

The severity of these costs depends on our incentives and capacities to comply with the demands of environmental justice, our values and intelligence, and the reliability of our social control mechanisms in general (Schuck 2000). Indeed, many of our "second-generation" contractual arrangements can be regarded as efforts to simplify social complexity along with the intricate systems of legal rules it spawns. For example, parties to contracts may attempt to circumvent some transaction costs through agreements that run parallel to the primary obligation they seek to establish. Liquidated damages clauses and agreements to use alternative dispute resolution can be understood in this context. In the public arena, parties in certain industrial sectors may engage in negotiated rule making—a proceeding in which participants attempt to reach a consensus on the requirements of a regulatory policy and include an agreement not to challenge the negotiated rule in court (which we discuss in greater depth in chapter 8).

The notion that the complexity of law is a product of social complexity suggests that there may be considerable practical value in having an "extralegal" realm of human endeavor, the organizing principle of which is something other than obligation. After all, the law does not forbid everything that is bad, and not everything that is good is legally required. That this is true has less to do with our inability to be comprehensive in ordering our principles and preferences than with our awareness that the judicialization of human activity, like nearly everything else, has a point of diminishing returns. This is evident when one considers the broad sweep of the history of the English common law. For roughly the first three centuries of its development, it comprised a relatively narrow range of land law cases, criminal justice, and constitution building. This stage of development witnessed the proliferation of increasingly specific, indeed arcane, writs designed to address specific problems as they arose. But beginning in the late thirteenth century, this relatively isolated tradition of law branched out to cast its shadow over the contours of a fast-changing social terrain. This expansion nevertheless was accompanied by an emerging modesty about what law could accomplish. As it matured, the common law "learned" to leave some problems unresolved for debate in future centuries and concentrate on the immediate melioration of a limited range of social functions. The democratic deficit of judge-made law, increasing complexity of the challenges that law encountered, and growing fluidity and diversity of society itself all argued that the law should often stay its hand (Cantor 1997). By the time of the founding of the United States, this modesty had matured into (among other things) the doctrine of limited government.

A society wherein many desirable outcomes are left to social processes not directly guided by systems of legal obligation is obviously dependent on the existence of and voluntary compliance with an extensive system of social norms. This is both true as a practical matter and important as a theoretical perspective. We have already noted that advocates of environmental injustice face the dual challenge (as do proponents of affirmative action) of directing the attention of others to their grievances and explaining why the rights that they assert merit special treatment. It is not simply that the victims of environmental injustice have suffered a disadvantage. It is also that they have had that disadvantage imposed on them for reasons that leave them deprived *and* diminished. To fully address their grievance requires not merely that they be compensated but also that the social and political institutions that produced their grievance be reformed in ways that both protect their rights and honor them as rights holders. For a remedy of this intricate and subtle character to command popular support, and then finally succeed in practice, it is necessary to develop new, shared understandings of the relationship between legal institutions and the forces of civil society. Although legal procedures and institutions may guide this process of development, they are not capable of producing the necessary understandings sui juris any more than the common law of a millennium ago could summon modernity single-handed.

Three Imperatives

An adequate understanding of the obligations involved in the idea of environmental justice leads to three general observations. Achieving environmental justice is an exercise in the management of complexity, managing complexity in the realm of law requires limiting the scope and reach of law, and when a society's institutions and processes are largely extralegal, a relatively sophisticated understanding of the normative relationship between the institutions of law and civil society is necessary. These three insights provide the foundation for discussing three "democratic imperatives" that confront advocates of environmental justice and the impact of globalization on those imperatives. First, there is the imperative to protect and empower social diversity in such a way that the environmental concerns of all are attended. Second, there is the imperative to establish a system of constitutional essentials of sufficient strength to protect those environmental interests that rise to the level of fundamental rights. Third, there is the imperative to create a set of cultural institutions and social processes that can generate the normative consensus necessary for the perpetuation of a regime of environmental regulation that is democratic in character as well as effective in practice. Understanding these imperatives in some conceptual detail is important because the conditions created by globalization render them even more challenging.

Managing Social Complexity

Beginning with the problem of managing social complexity as it relates to the goal of achieving environmental justice, it is increasingly evident that our ability to achieve justice through reasonably democratic means is constrained in significant ways by cultural pluralism, the existence of large social inequities, the economic and technological intricacies of modern societies, and community biases and ideologies that discourage political change (Bohman 1996). These complexities are clearly magnified by globalization, which is breaking down conventional boundaries between the communities of humankind. By breaching those boundaries, globalization creates a diverse and highly interdependent social ecology that presents us with seemingly insoluble problems of agricultural production, technological change, political decentralization, and the development of new social relations (Bookchin 1999).

Understood in this way, globalization has a second effect that increases social complexity and reduces our ability to manage its consequences. Globalization, whatever else it implies, necessarily involves modernization. The societies that exist in a thoroughly modern world have been described as "postmetaphysical" (Habermas 1992) or "disenchanted" (Bennett 2001). The essential characteristic of these societies is that they are dominated by instrumental reason. Their residents are alienated from one another by the absence of any shared ethical commitments beyond the behavioral codes of worker and consumer. They are people adept at imposing on themselves the language of self-discipline, regulation, and subjugation to the power of organization (Cawley and Chaloupka 1997). In short, they are people unlikely to hear the pleas for justice that are expressions of social solidarity, or imagine themselves as owing obligations for which they did not specifically and personally contract.

A third consequence of globalization is a reduction in the ability of nation-states to deal with the increasing levels of social complexity and alienation associated with modernity. As the movement of capital, migration of labor, and decentralization of production more closely links economic systems, the ability of any single government to develop effective regulatory policy (much less engage in industrial planning) becomes severely limited. As the regulatory reach of nations declines, the scope and complexity of private sector activity increases dramatically. A new world order, in essence, is emerging as entirely new layers of exchange relationships are negotiated, new markets open, and product lines diversify (Slaughter 2004). As the forces of modernity advance, the ability of nation-states to deal with the environmental consequences of that new order retreats.

Initially after the collapse of communism, the triumph of modernity was widely seen as an entirely positive development. Structural adjustments in the world economy, trade liberalization, and the spread of the free market would eventually relieve global poverty, encourage the development of democratic institutions, and promote new international agreements that would protect human rights along with the environment (Stewart-Harawira 2005). But since those halcyon days, the persistence of global disorder has become apparent, the inevitability of economic progress has been cast in doubt, and environmental degradation has come to be recognized as a threat to the international system itself (Jayasuriya 2005). This has revealed what may be an inherent weakness in international law.

As the international legal system has expanded into new fields, such as environmental protection, the group of parties expected to comply with its mandates has grown both larger and more varied. This group has come to include entities that are both individual and collective, both public and private, whose relationships multiply and diversify faster than new rules can be created to manage them (Lindblom 2005). As a result, nation-states have adopted a strategy of political retrenchment. In the environmental arena, they have promoted a series of state-centric international agreements that attempt to isolate environmental "problems" and apply to them the managerial expertise of international regulatory bureaucracies.

They have eschewed the idea of an international environmental court with the jurisdiction to resolve specific environmental disputes in a way that would allow for the accumulation over time of a body of legal precedence that might play the same role on the global stage that the common law does domestically (Schoenbaum 2006). In so doing, they have replicated in the environmental arena the domination of hegemonic powers evident in the global economy (Gearey 2005), and yet again marginalized indigenous populations whose national representatives are commonly indifferent to their needs or incapable of representing them effectively as their agents in international negotiation (Stewart-Harawira 2005).

So we return to the first political-legal imperative mentioned above— the imperative to protect and empower social diversity in such a way that the environmental concerns of all are attended. The widely discussed democratic deficit in international negotiation plays an especially prominent and pernicious role here. Not only are historically disadvantaged populations poorly represented among the public and private groups that populate the international stage, they also are routinely ignored by the national governments that should represent their interests as parties to international agreements. In part, this is simply the result of political and economic weakness performing the same role in environmental policy that it plays elsewhere. But there is more to it than that.

When parties to the formation of international environmental obligations are not engaged in concrete disputes, they couch their positions in abstract terms. Their dialogue aspires to embrace the totality of an often-complicated set of concrete issues and they try to imagine all the circumstances to which their formulations of policy might ultimately be applied. It is little wonder, then, that international environmental agreements usually require such long periods of gestation and still suffer from low birth weight. In spite of a worldwide movement for environmental protection, the response has been anemic. "Institutions are weak, legal and political regimes are 'soft,' and compliance and enforcement are sporadic" (Schoenbaum 2006, 248).

Contrast this picture of fecklessness with the continuing importance of the Trail Smelter case. This case, heard by a special arbitral tribunal, was the first involving the adjudication of an international pollution dispute. In 1941, the tribunal handed down a ruling that declared the general proposition that no state has the right to use or permit the use of its territory in such a manner as to cause injury in or to the territory of another state when the case is of serious consequence, and the injury is established by clear and convincing evidence (Schoenbaum 2006). Here was a declaration of legal principle of such clarity and force as to warm the hearts of lawyers everywhere. It is a principle derived from the careful adjudication of a specific case, argued by the best available parties—those actually involved in the dispute. The problem, of course, is that having established its right based on the wrong done to it, the "plaintiff" had no court of continuing jurisdiction to appeal to in subsequent years.

But the Trail Smelter case demonstrates convincingly that there is nothing about international tribunals that renders them incapable of hearing concrete disputes and arriving at sound dispositions of them that provide the normative content of an international environmental jurisprudence. The flaw in Trail Smelter is not internal to the case. It is that the case itself stands virtually alone. The potential of the case is obvious, and its limitations are equally so. The regular and routine adjudication of such disputes eventually would yield a body of legal precedent that would serve not only as a guide for the future but also as a deterrent to repeated environmental offenses and, ultimately, a legitimating force in support of genuine international jurisdiction over genuinely international issues. Without an appropriate forum, however, that body of precedent is never developed and the isolated decrees of special tribunals have no home for the future. The inherent complexity and pluralism of the world community can be captured by ongoing processes of adjudication only if such forums are created.

Constitutional Essentials and Fundamental Rights

The continuing significance of the Trail Smelter case results, at least in part, from the relative simplicity of its underlying rationale. The case provides no analytic framework for assessing the strength of competing environmental claims or deciding what remedies would be appropriate for any wrongs that those claims might demonstrate. It simply asserts that states should not allow their territory to be used in ways that create environmental damage within the territories of other states. Although the parties to the case were individuals and businesses (rather than national governments), the obligations that arose from the litigation ran to the governmental representatives of those parties. The operative principle is that states owe the same duties to individuals outside their borders that they owe to their own citizens when it comes to the environmental impacts generated by industrial activity tolerated within their national territory. What a state would not allow its citizens to do to one another, it also must not allow its citizens to do to foreign nationals. The International Court of Justice now recognizes this *harm prevention* (or *good neighborliness*) *principle* as a customary principle of international law (Schoenbaum 2006). Moreover, the idea of harm prevention has also been "codified" in the soft law of Principle 21 of the 1972 Stockholm Declaration and Principle 2 of the 1992 Rio Declaration.

If Trail Smelter establishes something like a fundamental right to be protected by a foreign government from environmental harms originating within that government's territory, what sort of constitutional essential does that right imply? In his treatment of the obligations owed by different peoples to one another, Rawls distinguished between well-ordered societies (which practice nonaggression toward other societies and govern themselves in light of a shared conception of the good) and others that are not well ordered. Members of well-ordered societies, in Rawls's (1999) view, owe members of other such societies a duty of toleration. This right does not imply an obligation to address the issues of distributive justice (with which Rawls was centrally concerned) as they may arise between societies. It is an entirely political concept, limited in scope to the commitment of a people to refrain from using political power to repress the reasonable doctrines that may be affirmed by political communities not their own (ibid., 16n18). This idea is similar to Immanuel Kant's ([1794] 1994) description of "hospitality" as a cosmopolitan right. Like hospitality, toleration is a boundary obligation that all human beings owe to one another. It is not an obligation of accommodation or support. These rights and obligations exist at the boundaries of the polity, delimiting our civic space by managing the relations among members and strangers. Characterized by Seyla Benhabib (2006b, 22) as cosmopolitan rights, they occupy the space "between human rights and civil and political rights, between the rights of humanity in our person and the rights that accrue to us insofar as we are citizens of specific republics."

To think of tolerance (or hospitality) as a cosmopolitan right involves certain compromises. It obviously limits the field of issues across which these rights can be invoked. To return to the Trail Smelter example, for a citizen of one country to invoke the principle of that case against an alien polluter, it is necessary to argue that the imposition of the environmental harm amounted to the repression of a reasonable (though not shared) concept of the good. It is also necessary to downplay the importance of nation-states. Rawls (1999) does this by conceiving his normative structure as a law of "peoples," and thus, focuses our attention on the moral character of a political community and reasonably just (or decent) nature of its self-understanding. Government, as the political organization of a liberal people, is not the author of its own powers. Just as domestic political arrangements respond to shifts of democratic will, "changes that occur in the powers of sovereignty from one period to another arise from those changes that occur in people's ideas of right and just domestic government" (ibid., 27n23). Reducing the emphasis on the role of nation-states in this way inevitably marginalizes the process of establishing mutual obligations through international negotiations. International agreements are thereby legitimate only to the extent that they reflect the understandings of mutual obligation that already exist between the members of well-ordered societies. They serve as codifications of previously existing obligations rather than the source of new obligations.

Construing cosmopolitan rights in this manner involves a second compromise—one that would fundamentally alter our understanding of the contours of national sovereignty. If one conceives of obligations between peoples as a set of principles founded on mutual recognition of the legitimacy (reasonableness) of ways of life, then a national government's refusal to respect those obligations would be more than a failure of international law. In the Trail Smelter case, for example, a failure by the Canadian government to address the damage caused by the industrial activities of its citizens to the interests of US loggers and ranchers would involve more than a breach of obligation between peoples. It would constitute a failure to respect the determination of the Canadian people to exist as a well-ordered society within the global community of well-ordered societies. Even though material benefits might accrue to individual Canadians from a breach of that obligation, the right of all Canadians as a self-governing people to determine their place in the global order would be abridged. Beyond simply establishing a right of standing for US citizens in Canadian courts, this view of cosmopolitan rights would create a substantive cause of action that would allow Canadian citizens separately to assert their right to see that their transnational obligations were respected by their own institutions of government.

We are already past the point that nation-states can exercise unrestrained power, either internally or externally. States no longer enjoy absolute immunity in domestic courts against actions in contract and tort. Furthermore, states that sponsor terrorism may now be sued for damages, and the ILC has formulated broad rules for international state responsibility for other actions that breach international law (Schoenbaum 2006). It is only a short step from these developments to the recognition of a body of human rights (both individual and based in group identity) that provide for access to domestic courts for foreign nationals, legal recourse for citizens when their own governments fail in their international obligations, and sanctions for national governments that defy the normative consensus shared by the members of the world's well-ordered societies. How easily this last step can actually be taken, though, will depend on our ability to give form and substance to the evanescent notion of a normative consensus among the members of well-ordered societies.

Globalization and Normative Consensus

The idea of a normative consensus will strike many as improbable. For some, it is nearly an oxymoron. It is at least arguable that modern societies are so deeply divided (both internally and from one another) over questions of value that nothing like a normative consensus is possible (Bohman 1996). Indeed, continuing to insist on achieving consensus in the face of deep normative conflict might not only be impractical; it also would actually run the risk of suppressing the pluralism and diversity that democratic government is founded to protect (Bohman 1994). On the international stage, a similar dynamic might turn cosmopolitan universalism from its hopeful path as a gentle civilizer of nations (Koskenniemi 2001) toward a darker future as the conceptual foundation for a repressive, imperialistic new world order (Stewart-Harawira 2005).

If this is the disease that the pursuit of normative consensus causes, globalization might actually offer a possible cure. Just as Kant shied away from the creation of a global republic, contemporary scholars of globalization have been careful to distinguish between the growth of institutions of global governance and the advent of international government. One of the clearest explications of this matter has been provided by Anne-Marie Slaughter, who has been careful to point out that transnational networks of policy specialists have developed along a path quite separate from that taken by the so far rudimentary efforts to create international legislatures. Legislators (as opposed to regulators) are concerned with the enunciation of basic political norms and therefore powerfully constrained by the deep divisions over fundamental values that characterize the international political culture (Slaughter 2004).

Another form of inoculation against the pathological potential of consensus is found in different perspective on globalization. Far from producing a "universal civilization," globalization may be the cause of a revival of religious and ethnic specificity. The current historically exceptional levels of civilizational and societal interdependence along with the resulting perception of the world as increasingly a single place is exacerbating social as well as ethnic self-consciousness. So globalization may not produce a normatively homogeneous world order but rather a clash of civilizations that places any form of consensus further out of reach than it had been before (Huntington 1996). Perhaps normative consensus is not only unattainable and undesirable in domestic politics; it is also actually a fictive creature that globalization is destined to render as extinct in our imaginations as it is in social reality.

If our discussion of normative consensus so far is all that bears saying, then the search for international environmental justice (or anything remotely like it) would seem destined to fail. But there may be more to consider if we back away from the grand project of building a universal world civilization and think instead of matters at a more human scale. If common law is not seen as a grand historical tradition that merely declares what has been true from time immemorial, then it must be the result of centuries or millennia of gradual construction by judges who have given expression to the fundamental principles of the societies in which they have lived (Barak 2006). Unless we are to believe that these judges have been a breed apart, possessed of abilities that other mere mortals lacked, then it stands to reason that their insights are within the grasp of citizens generally.

Perhaps an example of this idea would be useful. There is an ongoing disagreement over how to resolve claims for personal damages that result from events clearly the fault of the defendant, yet to which the plaintiff also contributed. The two contending approaches are comparative and contributory negligence. Under a rule of comparative negligence, the damages awarded are reduced by a factor that represents the jury's estimation of the plaintiffs' contribution to the injury. So in a case where the damages caused are $1,000 and the plaintiffs are 15 percent at fault for their own injury, the defendant will be made to pay $850 to the plaintiffs. Under contributory negligence (in its strictest form), the plaintiffs in a case of this character would recover nothing because they contributed to the injury.

Much has been written on the logic of these two approaches to personal damages, and there is at least something to be said for each approach. But the question that concerns us is whether either approach represents something like a normative consensus. There are numerous ways that one might investigate this query. A public opinion poll could simply ask people their preferences. Or a careful analysis of a large number of actual jury cases and their results might be possible. Both these approaches are beset with problems. As a consequence, judicial scholars have instead developed mock jury experiments that present "jurors" with hypothetical cases that they are asked to decide. Mock jury experiments, in this instance, indicate that when given no instructions on the matter either way, jurors discount damage awards consistent with their estimates of the degree of the plaintiff's fault (Feigenson, Park, and Salovey 1997). There is a clear preference for comparative over contributory negligence, which may explain the fact that contributory negligence is now found only in a minority of US states, and has been modified significantly even in those to mitigate the harshness of its results.

If this brief description of the evolution of the comparative–contributory negligence problem is at all representative of how common law has evolved, then a much more hopeful view of the issue of normative consensus is possible. The stability and durability of the common law as a legal tradition suggests both that it reflects existing social norms, *and* responds to those norms as they change or as new information about them emerges in practice. This is not to say either that there is near unanimity underlying every common law doctrine or the principles of common law reflect existing social consensus with complete accuracy. It is only to suggest that the deliberative process that juries employ along with the legal mechanisms that aggregate and interpret jury actions constitute social mechanisms that are more effective as well as representative than they are sometimes credited with being—they constitute, in effect, a kind of slow-motion democracy. How much does this modest claim help in our search for a global normative consensus on problems of environmental justice?

One of the most nettlesome problems of international environmental justice has been the deadlock over global climate change. The dispute can be summarized, in normative terms, with relative ease. Generally speaking, the Kyoto Protocol imposed a system of greenhouse gas reduction that required more of industrialized nations (which have caused a disproportionate share of the global warming problem) than countries of the developing world. The main articulated US objection was that the necessary reductions should be produced by a "fair-shares" regime requiring roughly the same proportionate contribution from all nations that are significant contributors (Singer 2002). How might we explore the question of whether or not there is an underlying normative consensus in support of one view or the other?

Consistent with the example of damage awards discussed above, we might simply take a worldwide public opinion poll or comparable polls in a large number of countries. Happily enough, a number of different researchers have already done so. The problem is that since the lay public everywhere has thought little about solutions to global warming, the results vary considerably depending on the precise nature of the questions asked, so the comparability of the results is extremely limited. In fact, an analysis of more than seventy surveys administered over a span of twenty years concludes that matters are so confused, the entire question has been reduced to an ideological Rorschach test (Nisbet and Myers 2007).

Whereas public opinion surveys are unreliable, an analysis of existing jury verdicts on the principle underlying the Kyoto Protocol is impossible. There is much to be said for research in comparative law, but the methods of that discipline require an existing body of litigation to examine. International agreements do not produce much, if any, litigation. One might search out analogous systems of obligation in domestic legal traditions—systems requiring a differential contribution to the mitigation of a problem from various parties based on their degree of responsibility for the problem. The trouble with searching for analogies to the question at hand is that the legal categories constituting the comparativist approach are related to issues of international governance in subtle and ambiguous ways (Kennedy 1997). To draw conclusions about the relationship between issues framed in the categories of a given system of domestic law and the underlying normative questions of an international environmental agreement is highly problematic.

A third option—and the most intuitively attractive—is to create a mock jury experiment in which the hypothetical case is designed specifically to capture the fundamental normative question at the heart of the disagreement over the Kyoto Protocol and prospective successor protocols. The factual characteristics of the hypothetical would, of course, be altered in a manner that concealed the real-world correlate without sacrificing the normative verisimilitude of the experiment (an example can be found in appendix B, scenario 1). If repeated trials of the experiment (in a variety of countries with diverse legal traditions) produced reasonably consistent results, a powerful argument in support of an otherwise-contested norm of international governance would have been created.

A Jurisgenerative Process

An experimental technique can be used to document the dimensions of transnational normative consensus on issues of environmental justice. Assuming (not unreasonably) that merely describing the elements of this normative consensus will be insufficient to change the behavior of recalcitrant nation-states, what more will the cause of environmental justice require of us in an age of globalization?

By itself, the development of common law doctrines was insufficient to summon modernity. A transnational common law, limited to normative precepts, would be similarly ineffectual. For legal precepts developed in this way to influence the course of events, they must become the focus of "jurisgenerative politics" (Benhabib 2006a). If they are to work in the world, these normative principles will have to draw their meaning and power from "social activity that is not subject to the strictures that characterize formal law-making." A jurisgenerative politics is a process whereby a people engages in iterative acts of "reappropriating and reinterpreting" the guiding norms as well as principles that they share, thereby showing themselves to be "not only the *subject* but also the *author of the laws*" (ibid., 49; emphasis in the original).

When one considers the processes of jury deliberation, judicial ruling, restatement, and codification that characterize the origin and development of the precepts of the common law, it is not difficult to interpret that process as a form of jurisgenerative politics that both broadens and blurs our conventional understanding of positive law. If a parallel is pursued in the arena of international environmental law, the implications are clear. The restatement and codification processes that have helped to structure as well as clarify the development of common law (making it accessible to judges as genuinely useful precedent) will also need to be replicated at the international level. Fortunately, the institutional framework for that step already exists in the form of the ILC (Baber and Bartlett 2009a). It will also be necessary for international tribunals to begin to recognize the products of this jurisgenerative international politics as legitimate precedents available to them in adjudicating the claims that come before their courts. Legal precepts of this sort certainly cannot be regarded as positive international law. Neither can they properly be called customary law, inasmuch as they capture the sense of justice shared by citizens instead of the historical practices of states. But a fully developed jurisgenerative process of identifying and systematizing environmental norms, such as juristic democracy, would allow advocates of environmental justice across the globe to overcome the difficulties generally encountered in trying to identify domestic legal concepts with sufficient consistency and clarity to qualify them as "general principles" of international environmental law (Lutz 1976).

Such a fully developed jurisgenerative process will require an experimental program to determine where a normative consensus on problems of international environmental justice exists and where the lack of consensus indicates the need for a more carefully focused debate. That determination will be dependent on the merits of having small groups of deliberating citizens (i.e., juries) serve as agents of democracy.

6

The Citizen Jury as a Deliberative Forum: Juries as Instruments of Democracy

The juristic form of deliberative democracy obviously shares many more commonalities with deliberative polling and the use of policy juries to choose among competing policy proposals than it does with the use of community-based stakeholder groups to develop concrete plans for policy implementation. For that reason, criticisms concerning the representation of discrete interests and the structure of governing institutions are of less concern than they might otherwise be. But it is still possible to press criticisms of this approach to deliberation (as well as deliberative polling) in at least three areas: this form of democratic participation is too subject to the irrational elements of human nature; on the contrary, it is excessively rational inasmuch as it either ignores or actually represses views grounded in diverse personal perspectives; and citizen juries produce substantively inferior results when compared with other (more elite) forms of decision making.

Were we to attempt an assessment of these criticisms based on our limited experience with deliberative democracy over the past two decades or so, our results would not be particularly robust. Still, each of these complaints also has been leveled at the use of petit juries to resolve real-world civil and criminal cases in the judiciary.[1] The research base that has been created in evaluating those criticisms is extensive indeed. In this chapter, we tap that empirical literature in order to assess the criticisms most commonly leveled against forms of deliberative democracy that employ disinterested "juries" to adjudicate disagreements or choose among alternative policy proposals.

Jury Deliberation Is Too Irrational

A jury too often has at least one member who's more ready to hang the panel than the traitor.
—Abraham Lincoln

The argument that a jury-based form of deliberative democracy is prone to irrational results can most sensibly be interpreted to mean that deliberation magnifies (or does too little to challenge) poorly reasoned biases that jurors bring with them to the deliberation. Lincoln worried that pretrial prejudices would too frequently prevent a jury from reaching a verdict, especially in notorious cases. Yet over the course of time, this has not been the jury system's biggest problem. Hung juries, after all, generally result in retrials. Of far greater concern is the fact that numerous studies on pretrial publicity and the psychology of prejudice indicate that juror bias can undermine the initial assumption of innocence, distort the evaluation of evidence through selective attention, influence the initial distribution of verdict preferences, distort the deliberative process itself, and spread the taint of prejudice from one juror to another (Vidmar and Hans 2007). The danger is not that juries will be unable to reach verdicts because of bias but instead that they will be far too ready to do so.

Even those who are generally supportive of the aims of deliberative democracy have expressed concerns on this score. Sunstein has, over the years, returned repeatedly to the problems associated with group polarization. The mechanisms at work are varied. Often, juries approach a particular case with a preexisting and shared sense of outrage. People who begin deliberations with a significant level of outrage tend to become still more outraged as a result of group discussion (Sunstein 2009). This pattern can be discerned even in deliberations not characterized by shared moral outrage. Group polarization has been found to occur even when the question involves some obscure empirical fact, such as how far below sea level Sodom (on the Dead Sea) lies (Turner 1987). This result supports Sunstein's view that group polarization is mainly a function of information sharing. Most people, most of the time, listen to the arguments made by others and gravitate toward them if they are persuasive (Sunstein 2006).

There is, of course, nothing inherently troubling in the notion that persuasive arguments tend to persuade. But arguments may prevail for reasons other than their intrinsic merits. One such reason is that people on juries are subject to social influences. They want to be perceived positively by others, and if a particular view dominates at the outset of deliberations, those less sure of their perspectives will be swayed by the desire for approval. Moreover, there is frequently an information cascade at work—a well-documented tendency for juries to move, gradually at first but with building momentum, in the direction of the initial majority view (Sunstein 2003). As the process proceeds, statements by jurors referring to evidence that supports the majority view become more numerous and social pressure on the minority to conform increases, systematically distorting the deliberative process (Devine et al. 2001).

Some pretrial prejudices are clearly widespread and generalized rather than tied to the facts of a single case. For instance, mock jury experiments show that given the same underlying facts, such as in a toxic waste case, jurors believed that a corporation was more likely than an individual defendant to have known beforehand about the hazard. Jurors also were more likely to view a corporation as recklesss and more likely to find a corporation negligent (Hans and Ermann 1989). Matters potentially are worse when jurors' prior beliefs about the law and its relationship to the case at hand make it difficult for them to follow instructions given to them by a convening authority (Smith 1991), further tainting the deliberative process from a procedural point of view.

Courts have a number of potential remedies for the problem of bias resulting from jurors' pretrial knowledge of a case. One is a change of venue. This approach offers the benefit of removing any bias resulting from local publicity without resorting to the removal of jurors who follow the local news closely. But the expense and inconvenience of a change of venue makes it an unattractive option. Likewise, jury sequestration has fallen out of favor, not only because of its expense, but also because it has a differential effect on the composition of juries and runs the risk of alienating the jurors. The preferred solution is questioning prospective jurors about their possible biases during the jury selection process. The objective is to select jurors who either have not been tainted by the publicity or are able to set that information aside.

The problems with this approach are obvious. It is not at all apparent how choosing jurors who are either illiterate or indifferent to the events that surround them advances the cause of justice. In addition, biases and prejudices are not easily detected. "Some jurors, probably the minority, consciously and purposefully lie—whether to get on or off the jury. More often, the right questions aren't asked, or jurors fail to disclose pertinent information. Still others may not recognize their own biases" (Vidmar and Hans 2007, 91). Questioning about possible biases has been shown to produce "minimization behavior" among potential jurors. Under questioning, many people will either deny knowledge of the case or provide socially acceptable answers regarding their own objectivity (ibid., especially 114–117).

Finally, bias resulting from pretrial knowledge of the case is not the only worry when it comes to potentially irrational jury behavior. Human beings harbor all sorts of persistent and generalized prejudices that can be revealed when confronted with the facts of a court case. These kinds of biases can often cut both ways. Valerie Hans (2000) has documented antiplaintiff biases that jurors frequently bring with them to a trial—biases that are likely to translate into antiplaintiff tendencies in the jury room. Alternatively, there is also significant evidence to suggest that when the defendant is a corporation, it faces a higher level of expectations from jurors, who view it as better situated to avoid doing harm and more likely to do great harm if it is negligent. This anticorporate bias alters the way that jurors both perceive the evidence and interpret the applicable legal standards, to the distinct advantage of the individual plaintiff suing the corporate entity (Vidmar and Hans 2007). So the antiplaintiff bias has its anticorporate flip side. These sorts of biases also are, of course, targeted when questioning prospective jurors. But that technique, as with the case of pretrial publicity, is still subject to the limitations of minimizing behavior by jurors who see what answers are expected of them by the reaction to the answers of those questioned before them. In any real-world court case, competing attorneys conduct the juror questioning seeking to minimize one sort of bias and maximize another.

Happily for the deliberative democrat, the use of citizen juries allows for more sophisticated techniques to mitigate or even avoid the bias problem. Deliberative exercises commonly use preliminary surveys to constitute a "jury pool" representative of the population in the respects most relevant to the deliberation at hand. It should be remembered that Sunstein's analysis of the problem of group polarization and critique of deliberative techniques in general deals with deliberating groups that display a homogeneous attitude on a given question. Researchers in deliberative democracy enjoy the luxury of being able to compose their panels of citizens who represent the entire range of opinion on the subject at hand or allow random selection to produce a variation of jury profiles over a large number of experimental trials (Fishkin and Farrar 2005). The same experiment can be run repeatedly, with entirely different jury pools, subject only to the limitations of the researcher's patience and resources. Whatever approach conveners choose, they have the opportunity to build as much diversity of opinion into the experimental population as seems desirable given the nature of their research question. They can do so secure in the knowledge that diverse trial juries have been shown to be both better fact finders than homogeneous panels, and the kind of forum in which invidious prejudices are less likely to be advanced and more likely to be challenged (Ellsworth 1989).

Jury Deliberation Is Too Rational

Do not your juries give their verdict
As if they felt the cause, not heard it?
—Samuel Butler

Yet another complaint about juries is that they obscure valuable perspectives based in gender and sociocultural differences, forcing a level of rationality onto political questions that is inappropriate to their nature. A leading voice in this discourse is that of Chantal Mouffe (1999), who argues that deliberative democracy is dominated by a rationalistic framework that renders it both unresponsive to the concerns of historically underrepresented groups and interests, and unaware of its own blind spots. Stanley Fish (1999) has sharpened this attack, asserting that deliberative democracy is just one more liberal ploy to seize the moral high ground, defined by values such as reasonableness, reciprocity, objectivity, impartiality, and fairness. All these values, he contends, are simply devices of deliberate exclusion.

Other similar claims are cast in broader, less conspiratorial terms. As reviewed in chapter 4, difference democrats maintain that deliberative democracy leaves too little room for nondeliberative political activities: educating, organizing, mobilizing, demonstrating, lobbying, campaigning, fund-raising, and ruling. An emphasis on deliberation betrays an antipolitical bias and reduces the political world to a jury room in which people are deprived of too much of their own identities to be good citizens (Waltzer 1999). Studies of the group dynamic that prevails within the jury room would seem to reinforce these worries. They show that within the confines of the jury, men talk more than women, as do people with more education and higher-status occupations (Hawkins 1962).

There are at least two responses to concerns of this sort. The first is external to the conceptual framework of deliberative democracy. Critics of deliberation would be hard pressed to find one of its advocates suggesting that deliberative practices replace any, much less all, of the other forms of political activity. Were they to find such a person, the vast majority of deliberative democrats would readily join them in their criticism. To suggest that deliberative democracy presents itself as an institutional substitute for any or all other types of political activity is to set up a straw person. Indeed, many advocates of deliberative democracy argue that it can be most successfully pursued outside government altogether, within that generalized public sphere on which Habermas pins so much hope.

A second response to deliberation's critics is internal. Within the bounds of the deliberative experience, our choice is obviously between diversity and homogeneity. Deliberation's critics do not recommend that deliberative bodies avoid diversity of membership. They simply betray a lack of confidence in what diversity can accomplish. But experience with trial courts is illuminating in this area. It suggests that deliberation in a diverse environment can be quite effective. As an example, consider the question of the death penalty. The racial and gender composition of death penalty juries is significantly related to whether or not a defendant receives a death sentence. In the United States, the highest probability of a death sentence being imposed is in cases where a black defendant is convicted of killing a white victim. Moreover, data gathered from fourteen states indicates that the results in these cases are significantly influenced by the jurors' race. The death sentence is three times as likely in black-on-white murder cases if there are five or more white males on the jury. On the other hand, a sentence of life imprisonment is twice as likely if there is at least one black male on the jury (Bowers, Steiner, and Sandys 2001).

In more general terms, research shows that jury diversity is positively related to both the deliberative process and deliberative outcomes. Diverse juries deliberate for longer periods of time. They discuss a wider range of issues and are more accurate in their statements about factual aspects of the case before them. Of particular interest, whites on diverse juries are more careful and systematic than whites on homogeneous juries, making fewer factual errors and raising more different issues for discussion (Sommers 2006). As one researcher has put it, "White people worry about being racist when they are reminded of it, but when it's all white people, it just doesn't occur to them to remember their egalitarian values" (Mize 1999, 12). So whether or not women and minorities on juries succeed in commanding their own share of deliberative time, their mere presence affects the behavior of others and the outcome of cases. This fact perhaps contributes to the further result that having a diverse jury lends added political legitimacy to the verdict. Unfortunately, the legitimizing effect of a jury's diversity is most readily apparent when absent, as the case of the 1991 police beating of Rodney King in Los Angeles demonstrated so vividly and tragically (Vidmar and Hans 2007).

Neither the external nor internal defense of deliberative juries should be taken to suggest that all is well, and that we have no need to worry about the representativeness of either trial or citizen juries. The relative advantage of male, middle-aged, dominant-social-group professionals in deliberative contexts is undeniably too well documented. Even in the case of the trial jury, where the only alternative to a heterogeneous jury is a homogeneous one, it may be insufficient to place all our confidence in diversity. If jury members come to think of themselves as representative in a demographic sense, they may concentrate more on their imagined constituents than their responsibility to engage in a robust, intelligent debate (Abramson 1994). Even if this distortion does not occur, we are still confronted with the problem of the difficulties faced by minority and female jurors when serving as isolated individuals or in small numbers.

The deliberative democrat has two responses to this problem that are not available to the trial court. First, as already noted, the number of specific kinds of individuals on citizen juries is subject to the determination of the researcher. In fact, one side benefit of deliberative democratic experiments is that they provide us with additional opportunities to put the findings of jury research to the test in more controlled circumstances. A second response is that deliberative democracy is a reflexive practice. It is capable of recognizing the extent to which it contributes to the creation of its own environment. In this connection, Sunstein (2009) observes that perhaps not all instances of group polarization are created equal. We may have reason to create, as part of our ongoing deliberative practice, forums in which group polarization is particularly likely. What Sunstein has in mind is the use of citizen juries composed of those individuals whose perspectives and opinions have been historically neglected, in order to cultivate, refine, and strengthen those discourses using all the same influences that produce group polarization in juries populated by members of dominant social groups. The advantage of such enclave deliberation is that it "promotes the development of positions that would otherwise be invisible, silenced, or squelched in general debate" (Sunstein 2009, 152). Indeed, liberation movements in the United States and around the world can be understood as the manifestation of just such enclave deliberations. The advantage has not been just that the movements' levels of enthusiasm have been heightened but that their arguments have been sharpened as well. To paraphrase a popular aphorism about democracy, there may be nothing wrong with deliberation that more deliberation cannot cure.

Juries Produce Inferior Results

I was married by a judge. I should have demanded a jury.
—Groucho Marx

A final criticism we assess is the complaint that juries produce results inferior to those arrived at by experts. To some degree, deliberative democrats let themselves in for this criticism. Some deliberative theorists couch their discussions, from time to time, in the context of multimember courts. This is always tempting, because (similar to juries) there is a significant body of empirical research on appellate courts that deliberative democrats can appropriate for their own purposes. But having tasted the fruit, deliberative democrats are left with the rind. Thus it is that Daniel Bell (1999) contends that deliberation is an elite activity, for which elite institutional arrangements should be developed. The majority of deliberative democrats, however, are reluctant to give up democracy for the sake of deliberation or even admit that the two are in serious tension with one another.

The literature on trial juries allows us to explore this conundrum. The obvious alternative to trial by jury is trial by judge. The empirical differences between the two are readily accessible to the scholar. At the outset, it must be observed that trial by jury is thought by many to be on the critical list. But if it is, it is because jury trials have been supplanted by means of alternative dispute resolution, the expense of formal litigation has escalated, and the caseloads of the courts have exploded. The decline in the popularity of jury trials is far more a response to the exigencies of expense and delay than to any frustration with the lack of deliberative qualities among today's jurors.

Yet there are more troubling signs for the institution of the jury. Research indicates that jurors sometimes have difficulty with science-based evidence (Vidmar and Diamond 2001). When it comes to statistical evidence specifically, jurors have trouble of two sorts. First, jurors (like journalists) often have problems drawing valid conclusion from statistical probabilities. This issue arises frequently, for example, in cases where DNA evidence is of importance (Kay and Sensabaugh 2000). Second, jurors often give either too much or too little weight to statistical evidence in relation to other forms (Thompson and Schumann 1987). The cognitive challenges faced by jurors do not end there.

In a legal system, juries struggle with the complexity of law to a greater extent than they do with either complex procedures or scientific evidence. The prevalence of legal jargon in the courtroom as well as the law's tendency to use familiar words in unfamiliar and unexpected ways are two of the more obvious causes. Recent and ongoing efforts to develop more refined and less impenetrable jury instructions are of some help. There is clear evidence that jurors' attempts to follow the law are sincere and nearly universal. But still, they are not as successful in disentangling the complexities of the law as they are at understanding the bodies of evidence with which they are confronted (Vidmar and Hans 2007). So how large is the impact of these difficulties?

One way to gauge the success of juries is to compare jurors' results to those of the presumed experts—namely, trial court judges. In a study of over seventy-five hundred civil and criminal jury trials, Harry Kalven Jr. and Hans Zeisel (1966) found a high level of judge/jury agreement, approaching 80 percent in criminal cases, with a strong pattern of jury leniency in instances of disagreement. Of particular interest, the hypothesis that juries differed from judges because they failed to understand complicated evidentiary matters was not supported by the data. Variables such as community attitudes about the issues involved in the litigation, juror disagreement with the law itself, and a juror preference for a higher standard of proof were more frequently indicated as reasons for their disagreements with the judges. Assuming for the sake of argument that judges are always correct in their determinations, this study suggests that jurors are right about four times out of every five, and that when they are "wrong," it is because they decline to see a case the way the judge does, not because they make factual mistakes.

More recent research offers additional support for the work of trial juries. Many of the problems related to evidentiary and procedural complexity can be ameliorated by the use of preinstruction from the judge and allowing jurors to take notes during the proceedings. Verdicts after deliberation are more likely to be correct from a purely legal point of view than were initial judgments that individual jurors have made in pre-deliberation surveys or test votes (Bordens and Horowitz 1989). A study of jury awards in malpractice cases shows that the magnitude of awards correlates positively to the severity of the injuries (Bovbjerg, Sloan, and Blumstein 1989).

More generally, jurors interviewed after trials using expert witness testimony appeared to have employed entirely reasonable techniques in assigning weight to that evidence. They attached value for clarity, educational value, and apparent expertness in much the same way that judges do. Conversely, they discounted experts who were full-time witnesses or appeared to be biased (Ivkovic and Hans 2003). Contrary to the imagined "white coat" syndrome, jurors are often demanding and skeptical in their evaluation of expert evidence (Champagne, Schuman, and Whitaker 1992).

In short, there is little to suggest that juries do a measurably worse job of processing evidence than do judges. To abandon jury trials in search of greater accuracy would be ill advised. In fact, in the context of a civil trial, an adequately representative jury is no less accurate in processing information than a judge. A jury reflects community expectations about duty and responsibility better than could a judge, who almost by definition is a member of the socioeconomic elite and typically jaded from hearing case after case over the course of a long career. Being more immediately and intimately in touch with the prevailing social norms as well as central concerns of the community, jurors are better suited to evaluate the conduct of plaintiffs and defendants against those important standards (Vidmar and Hans 2007). In criminal cases, it is arguably the juror, who must return to the community with the victim and (eventually) defendant, who is best situated to determine what constitutes reasonable doubt. To whatever degree community standards and values are important in civil and criminal trials, they are obviously more so in the case of the policy questions addressed by deliberative democratic experiments. In that arena, political legitimacy of the sort conferred by jury trials on the resolution of civil and criminal disputes is not just a valuable side benefit; it is the crucial difference between policies that deserve to be respected as democratic and those that do not.

The Verdict?

I consider trial by jury as the only anchor ever yet imagined by man, by which a government can be held to the principles of its Constitution.
—Thomas Jefferson

A jury is a group of twelve people of average ignorance.
—Herbert Spencer

So where does all this empirical research leave us? Are juries our best proof against abusive government, as Jefferson believed? Or are they easily manipulated tools of the powerful and privileged, as Spencer's dismissive remark might suggest? More to the point, as they are applied to the concerns of deliberative democratic theorists, are juries a plausible mechanism for determining the content of general social norms along with their relationship to fundamental principles of law (juristic democracy) and the preference structures of individuals and groups of citizens relating to more concrete matters of public policy (deliberative polling and policy juries)?

It is probably appropriate at this juncture to admit to a fundamental truth that some have used to dismiss democracy, of whatever variety, as unworkable. Most of the knowledge possessed by ordinary citizens is a relatively haphazard structure and cannot meet even the most basic epistemological criteria for its justification. For most people, most of the time, a street-level epistemology makes far more sense as a source of the ordinary knowledge needed to navigate daily life than would any system of formal knowledge. But street-level epistemology yields a subjective account of the world, not a public one. It is not concerned with what counts as knowledge in the sciences, a legislature, or a court of law. Instead, it deals with what we all know without being entirely sure of how we know it: that we "know more than we can tell" (Hardin 2000; Polanyi [1966] 2009).

Based on informal knowledge of this sort, jurors build and employ mental constructs, schemes, and scripts, premised on personal experience filtered by the prevailing culture and their immediate social environment, to explain the world around them, and relate the case or controversy before them to that world. These constructs include notions about physical and social causality as well as assumptions about what is typical and atypical in the human experience (Feigenson 2000). These constructs are exceedingly diverse and not always consistent with one another. But their prevalence offers one explanation for the apparent contradiction between two pieces of empirical evidence that we encountered earlier.

Women and members of minority groups are at a disadvantage in the jury room. In general, they speak less than others. Their views often enjoy less influence than those of dominant-social-group males in high-status occupations. On the other hand, the presence of just one black juror on a death penalty jury in the case of a black-on-white murder is sufficient to halve the probability that the death sentence will be imposed. We can account for this apparent contradiction, as observed earlier, by pointing out that the introduction of a person of color (or a woman) reminds others of an entire complex of street-level knowledge, having to do with discrimination and disadvantage, that they had already possessed, but to which they had not been paying attention. It also may cause persons to recognize the existence of experience-based knowledge that they themselves do not and perhaps cannot have. This is a case of an irrational (or perhaps nonrational) response by jurors that leads them to use a more rational decision process. It is also a potent response to the critics of deliberative democracy who worry about the influence of bias as a source of either irrationality or exclusionary hyperrationality.

Another useful way to think of jury deliberations in both courts and deliberative experiments is that they are competitions among a set of narratives. Each juror imposes a narrative structure on the trial evidence, using her own knowledge about analogous issues and events as well as generic information about what is required to make a complete account of events in the real world. Each of these narratives constitutes a plausible, coherent story explaining what has occurred and what is at stake in the instant case. Evidence is filtered through these narrative structures, with inconsistent trial evidence likely to be ignored or scrutinized and rejected (Pennington and Hastie 1991). This perspective allows us to develop a more sophisticated notion of the kind of diversity that deliberative democracy requires to succeed.

Diversity in any jury is more critical at the level of discourses than at that of demography. Mouffe (1999) asserts that democratic discourses should be grounded in the participants' core identities rather than some idealized personality that they must don to participate in a deliberation imagined as a political philosophy seminar. Focusing deliberation on the more concrete, specific needs of individuals (either the parties to a dispute or groups of citizens) allows deliberators to deploy the narratives that best express their own identities and perspectives without engaging the most deeply held commitments of others in what is likely to be a divisive contest of irreconcilable first principles. Deliberation about the concrete does so without forcing jurors to serve as surrogates for a gender they may wish to de-emphasize in their lives or cultural identity they may even wish to escape through assimilation (Baber 2008). Moreover, this understanding of deliberation, unlike Mouffe's account of democracy, suggests an important way that collective decision making capable of actually resolving pressing social problems can be organized and carried out (Dryzek 2006). Juries regularly come up with concrete solutions by combining critical engagement and collective decision making.

Critics of deliberative democracy who have chosen diversity and multiculturalism as their field of battle perhaps can be forgiven for having done so, as there is much in the deliberative literature that invites the attack. In particular, Rawls's account of public reason trained a generation of theorists, both deliberative democrats and their critics, to think of deliberation as a search for consensus, understood as agreement for the *right* reasons (Baber and Bartlett 2005). But this preoccupation with agreement on both outcomes and cardinal reasons for outcomes puts a greater burden on deliberation than it really needs to bear. Sunstein describes politics in diverse societies as a search for incompletely theorized agreements. The objective is to "make it possible to obtain agreement where agreement is necessary, and to make it unnecessary to obtain agreement where agreement is impossible" (Sunstein 1996, 8). The merit of this understanding of democracy is, of course, that it allows people to decide what to *do* when they disagree about what to *think*. Following this line of thinking, Amartya Sen (2009) has suggested that we move away from a Rawlsian unitary understanding of public reason in favor of a public reason that admits of plural reasons, grounded in partial orderings of available alternatives instead of agreement on general rules founded in universal principles.

This perspective on deliberation also provides a new perspective on certain elements of political history. In the early years of colonial development in New England, juries were more than just groups of citizens gathered to serve as the referee in a particular dispute. Juries were viewed as central instruments of governance, applying social norms to both criminal and civil matters great and small. They enjoyed far greater power than does a contemporary legal jury to find matters of both fact and law (Nelson 1975). More important, both grand and petit juries had the latitude to bring in special as well as partial verdicts at their own discretion, owing to the Puritan reluctance to force persons to act against their own consciences (Vidmar and Hans 2007). It can hardly be a coincidence that this high-water mark in the jury's role in the United States occurred in the same area of the country also known for its use of the town hall meeting to address every manner of public policy.

It is certainly true that the political franchise's exclusiveness as well as restrictions on jury service make eighteenth-century New England an odd poster child for democracy. But the robust character of the New England jury at this time and its uncommon solicitude toward the personal commitments of individual jurors is of a piece with the town hall meeting perspective that citizens should stand on an equal footing and occupy an equal space in the public square so that each can give hee account of the issues at hand (Bryan 2004). In each case, an essential requirement of both practical success and political legitimacy was to bracket (often tacitly) foundational beliefs and core identities, and concentrate on specific policy problems and individual disputes. Agreement on cardinal reasons was not required in the town hall. Indeed, to insist on it would likely have been viewed as unneighborly. In this environment, democratic self-governance as a concern of all was recognized as the privileged territory of none. This approach allowed communities to achieve broad participation without suffering the consequences attendant to battles over first principles.

A similar advantage is available to practitioners of deliberative democracy who use deliberative polling to tap public opinion on the choices between competing policy paradigms, or employ techniques such as juristic democracy to identify the underlying normative commitments people use to resolve particular disputes and that sometimes (over extended periods of time) enter into jurisprudence in the guise of general principles of law. These theorists can aspire to extend the reach of democracy because they seek only to build democratic governance one incompletely theorized agreement at a time. Their populist approach might well have been inspired by an observation of the paradox-loving Englishman G. K. Chesterton (1910, 86–87):

Our civilization has decided, and very justly decided, that determining the guilt or innocence of men is a thing too important to be trusted to trained men.... When it wants a library catalogued, or the solar system discovered, or any trifle of that kind, it uses up its specialists. But when it wishes anything done which is really serious, it collects twelve of the ordinary men standing round.

Of course, this inspiration comes with an implicit warning built right into it. Chesterton's remark only serves to legitimate the use of citizen juries once they are shorn of their gender specificity—a contemporary twist that might well have amused him.

7

Slow-Motion Democracy: Synthetic and Progressive Development of the Structure of Rationalization

Anyone interested in what citizen juries can contribute to environmental governance and action must worry about several conceptual as well as methodological problems that all deliberative democratic theorists and experimenters confront. These questions include:

• How do we define and relate the roles of those who deliberate environmental quandaries, and those who convene such deliberations?

• What part do (or should) substantive experts play in processes of environmental deliberation?

• What do we mean when we call environmental arguments rational or public?

• How do we conceive of the relationship between deliberation and decision?

As with jury deliberation itself, an allied discipline, law, has dealt with many of the conceptual and methodological problems of postjury aggregation, synthesis, and rationalization. Restatement is a potentially useful mechanism for aggregating the considered opinions of deliberating citizens in ways that allow us to progressively develop legal structures that can contribute to the rationalization of the human relationship to the environment. Like content analysis in political science, restatement begins with a range of theoretically relevant subjects—in this case, reasons that the law can recognize as permissible justifications for a specific kind of judicial outcome. But beyond documenting how frequently as well as in what ways concepts and ideas identified a priori by researchers occur in a given text or narrative (as in content analysis), the objective of restatement is synthetic and progressive. The idea is to craft a comprehensive, precise statement of the underlying legal rationale for a certain category of decisions and explore the potential paths along which we might expect (or want) that rationalization structure to develop, taking advantage of the similarities and contrasts between legal restatement and its distant relative content analysis as it is practiced in the social sciences. Responses to the questions posed above, derived from reflecting on that process, offer a guide to the further development of juristic democracy in global environmental governance.

Content Analysis and Restatement: The Dynamic Duo?

Content analysis, as it is practiced in the humanities and social sciences, is a method of analyzing the text of various forms of communication. It involves summarizing as well as the qualitative and quantitative analysis of messages. It relies on the classical values of scientific methodology: attention to objectivity, intersubjectivity, a priori design, reliability, validity, generalizability, replicability, and hypothesis testing (Neuendorf 2002). The underlying assumption is that the words and phrases that happen most often and prominently in any communication reflect the core concerns of the message being conveyed. Word frequencies in print material, time counts in radio and television, keyword-in-context routines, and synonym and homonym analysis are common quantitative techniques. Qualitatively, content analysis can involve any methodology by which the communication content is categorized and classified. Yet the focus of content analysis and its methodological characteristics in any given instance depend on the researcher's purpose.

Practitioners of content analysis generally pursue one of a number of research purposes. By concentrating on the source of communication, the encoding process used, and why the communication under examination was initiated and structured in the way that it was, a researcher can draw inferences about the antecedent conditions and intentions of the communication. By attending to the channel of communication used, substantive content of the communication, and nature of the target audience, it is possible to describe and draw inferences about the fundamental characteristics of the communication in question. By examining the decoding process used by the target audience, it is possible to reach conclusions about the consequences of communication (Holsti 1969).

Regardless of the particular focus of the research, certain common methodological concerns arise. Content analytic research can be categorized as employing either prescriptive or open methods. Prescriptive analysis uses a closely defined set of communication parameters and categories designed a priori by the researcher. Open analysis, on the other hand, employs more qualitative (some would say impressionistic) techniques to tease the dominant messages, subject matter, and appropriate analytic categories from the text itself (McKeone 1995). Each approach gives rise to particular problems. To the extent that a research design is prescriptive, it confronts an obvious challenge of validity—does it understand an instance of communication in a way that does justice to the intentions and understandings of the parties to that communication? If an open analysis design is used, questions of reliability arise—are data being coded in ways that are consistent, both within and across coders' work (Krippendorf 2004)? In either case, it is reasonable to wonder whether an analyst has been sufficiently attentive to the potential difference between a communication's *manifest* meaning (its actual wording) and *latent* meaning (what the communicator intended), or its *imbedded* meaning (its conscious or unconscious meaning embedded in a whole discourse).

A feature of content analysis that offers a basis for optimism regarding its usefulness to advocates of democracy is the phenomenon of mimetic convergence. A feature of the long-term articulation of partisan competitions is that discursive articulations of multiple parties, through frequent repetition, combine to frame issues in ways that represent more than a mere conflict over the representation of interests. This recursive process of recomposition and rearticulation builds a shared construction of the choices as well as controversies confronting the polity. Over time, political actors reorient their arguments and thematic selections to this constructed political reality in search of political advantage (Lipset and Rokkan 1967). A content analytic examination of this process—identifying the sources of these constructs, revealing the intentions of their authors, and describing the consequences of their acceptance—offers the opportunity for citizen empowerment to replace elite manipulation.

Restatement of the law is a method of legal analysis used, most prominently in the United States by the ALI. The institute's series of legal restatements are sets of treatises intended to inform judges and lawyers about the general principles of the common law as it is found in the

United States. Each restatement volume is a summary and codification of the case law in a given area (torts, contracts, property, etc.). Although restatements are not themselves binding law, they are widely recognized as a highly persuasive legal authority because legal specialists (professors, judges, and practicing attorneys), with special expertise in the area of law concerned, develop them. They are intended to represent the consensus of the US legal community as to what the law is and, to some degree, what it should become. This combination of the descriptive and prescriptive strikes some as problematic, but it is conceptually consistent within the context of a legal system governed by the doctrine of stare decisis—as mentioned earlier, the principle that judges should respect the precedent established by prior decisions and attend to the precedent that their own decisions establish. This principle clearly implies that existing legal doctrine establishes a presumptively legitimate pattern for its further development and application, though that conclusion is far from incontestable.

Each topical section of a restatement contains a principle of so-called black letter law, a section of comments and illustrations, and reporters' notes supplying a detailed discussion of all the cases that went into the legal principle summarized in that section. The intention is to provide not only a legal rule but also the considerations that support the rule along with the concrete circumstances that give rise to those considerations. In this way, the restatement reduces the existing case law to a problem-specific general rule, and offers guidance regarding the application of that rule and its probable limits. This kind of information allows practicing attorneys to anticipate the reaction that judges will have to the arguments they can potentially advance on their clients' behalf. It allows judges to decide cases consistent with authoritatively summarized precedent or, in cases of first impression, an informed judgment about the direction that the law is developing.

Criticisms of the restatement movement in general as well as particular restatement volumes are legion (Adams 2007). It is neither practical nor desirable to survey that entire discourse here, but we do call out certain elements of that criticism for the perspective offered regarding the methodological approach used by the ALI in its restatement projects.

At the outset, restatement largely avoids the reliability critiques leveled at content analysis. Restatements are a committee product, with drafts of each section being subjected to exhaustive review and criticism by teams of specialists led by uniformly distinguished reporters. Validity is another matter, however. On that score, the restatements have been criticized for going beyond merely reporting what the law is and asserting what the law (in the ALI's opinion) believes the law should be. This may be a greater threat to the validity of conclusions based on the restatements now than it has been in the past because it is more common in subsequent editions than in the first.

Over time, the restatements have become both more normative and more susceptible to overt interest group influence (Adams 2004). Normativity is not entirely undesirable, especially inasmuch as progressive development of the law has always been an objective of the restatement movement. Given that fact, the eventual attention of organized interests was inevitable. The solution to both potential problems is, of course, transparency. Moreover, one must consider the argument that it is no less inappropriate for the ALI to consider how to accommodate the past to the present and future than it is for common law courts to do the same thing (Wechsler 1969). The prevalence of judicial elections and level of attention given them by voters where they do occur provide little support for a contention that progressive development of the law by individual judges in chambers is more legitimate than the same process carried out by groups of professional specialists (including judges) operating in public.

A more common criticism of the restatements is that they are inherently conservative. The dominant variant of this theme is that the restatement movement was a rearguard action against the advent of legal realism. This view is lent credence by the fact that both legal realists and the movement's advocates were heard advancing it at the time that the ALI launched the restatement project. The institute also seems to have tacitly admitted the validity of this criticism by declaring its intention to make the second series of restatements as dynamic as the common law they purport to represent (Adams 2007). Indeed, one might offer this pattern of call and response as evidence that the ALI has achieved a level of pragmatic progressive reform (Hull 1990) that could not have been reached either by common law courts resolving specific disputes or legislators whose policy pronouncements arise from the competition of special interests rather than the issues presented by concrete cases. Finally, restatement is but one element in a broader process that ultimately leads to the development of contending components of model statutes and eventual codification through legislative action (Posner 1999, especially 303–309). Viewed in this light, restatement is less a threat to democratic legitimacy than it is a stem on democratic government's least dangerous branch (Bickel 1986).

Content Analysis and Legal Restatement: An Arena of Application

So both content analysis and legal restatement have a potential role to play in the development of democratic norms. But the question remains: To what should we apply these analytic tools? Content analysis is commonly applied to the stuff of mass communications. In the political realm, this often means the rhetoric of parties and political campaigns. Legal restatements, on the other hand, are analytic summaries of legal opinions issued by judges in specific proceedings. Both political campaigns and legal decisions have clear, if frequently indirect, implications for the formation of democratic norms. Political rhetoric is frequently distorted by strategic (as opposed to normative) considerations that make it hazardous to draw direct conclusions about the meaning of assertions or their support within the polity. A legal opinion, in contrast, is relatively unambiguous—at least on its face. A winner is declared, and a reason for the victory is given. The complexity arises from our attempts to make inferences about how the case at hand will (or should) affect the outcomes of future cases.

The formation of democratic will, as a multistaged process, is related to both these phenomena. It involves assertions that come from particular sources and are encoded in particular ways. Those claims have specific characteristics. They are designed to channel selected content to target audiences. Furthermore, the assertions are decoded in specific ways that affect how the messages are understood and acted on. Content analysis is well suited to understanding these features of democratic will formation. What it does less well is interpret the practices involved in resolving concrete disputes. The fact that one party to a contest prevails, generally to only some extent with respect to only some aspects of the dispute, is evidence that one assertion (or cluster of them) has prevailed over another in some important way. What that claim originally meant and the reasons that it was structured in the way that it was are no longer as significant as an analysis of the institutional response it prompted, how that response can be explained and justified, and what that response means for subsequent assertions about similar disputes.

The parts that content analysis and legal restatement play in research on democratic will formation can be described with greater clarity. The assertions underlying the positions of each hypothetical litigant are developed from actual arguments advanced in support of contending regulatory regimes. To put each regime to a fair test of its democratic legitimacy requires that the contentions presented to deliberators accurately represent the positions of the actual advocates of those regimes. Reproduction of those rationales must do justice to the intentions, content, targeting, and expectations of those who are the real-world advocates of our hypothetical litigants' positions. Legal restatement then provides the means for summarizing the results of these deliberations, characterizing the justifications given for those results, and suggesting how a set of general rules might be structured that would replicate those outcomes if it were applied to actually occurring regulatory problems.

The challenges to anyone wishing to pursue this kind of research or norm identification are myriad. Chief among these is, obviously, that of representativeness. If the participant pool is insufficiently diverse, the results of the experiment will be open to insurmountable problems of reliability. Many of the deliberative dysfunctions that have been identified (i.e., groupthink) are particular dangers in insufficiently heterogeneous deliberative groups. Even when the problem of representation has been adequately addressed, however, there remain conceptual and methodological questions—those questions posed at the beginning of this chapter. How do we define and relate the roles of those who deliberate environmental quandaries, and those who convene such deliberations? What part do (or should) substantive experts play in processes of environmental deliberation? What do we mean when we call environmental arguments rational or public? How do we conceive of the relationship between deliberation and decision? These are questions about how one aggregates deliberatively informed opinion in ways that preserve their democratic provenance and enhance the legitimacy of the regulatory regimes founded on them. Having provided a critical appraisal of both content analysis and restatement as complementary techniques for aggregating as well as interpreting participants' views in democratic deliberation, these are the questions to which we now turn.

Problems of Aggregation: Juristic Deliberative Solutions

All deliberative democratic theorists are confronted with the problem of how to define and relate the roles of those who deliberate problems of public policy along with those who convene such deliberations. The technique of asking participants to deliberate hypothetical legal disputes suggests a particular answer to this question. Participants are most similar to the members of a trial jury. Panel members are presented with detailed set of facts about a concrete but wholly hypothetical situation. Each of the fictional parties to the dispute has petitioned for its preferred outcome and provided arguments in support of its position. Members of the deliberative panel are then asked to choose between the positions of the parties or craft a resolution of their own, and provide a statement of the reasons for their decision.

The role of the deliberative participants is to declare a winner in a discursive contest that has been presented to them in the form of a trial. As summarized in chapter 6, research on juries suggests that people of average backgrounds perform this task quite well. The role of the convener of a juristic deliberation, like that of the trial judge, is to supervise a process through which the facts and arguments of the "case" are presented to the jury. In adversarial systems, like that of the United States, this generally amounts to playing the part of umpire in the contest between attorneys who elicit facts from witnesses and present the arguments of their parties. In juristic deliberation, though, the framer of the scenarios and petitions serves as an interpreter to the jury of both the facts and arguments of the parties. The framer does this by constructing a set of "facts" that capture the salient features of a real-world regulatory dilemma. The framer also builds the arguments of the parties to the hypothetical dispute from the political assertions of interests and individuals who advocate alternative approaches to regulating the problematic circumstances at hand. These functions are more nearly like the judge's role in an inquisitorial system of litigation. Ultimately, someone, possibly the framer of a series of juristic deliberations, will also perform a role similar to that of the ALI in crafting its restatements.

With regard to what part substantive experts might (or should) play in processes of environmental deliberation, two distinct roles immediately suggest themselves. First, the conveners of the deliberation fill an obvious role as experts in the process of deliberation and decision itself. It can hardly be doubted that deliberative exercises can be structured in ways that distort the results. As an example, participants may initially be provided a form on which they are asked to render their decision and offer an explanation of it, without the form in any way indicating that a vote should be taken or a minority report is possible. If participants inform the convener that they are at a stalemate, a minority opinion form can be at the ready and provided. The intention is to encourage the most serious effort to arrive at a consensus possible, both for the sake of empowering minority views and in order to promote a thorough airing of views. An alternate perspective, however, would be that this pressure for consensus might actually work to silence minority views and disempower those who hold them, although research on juries in actual trial courts does not lend much support for this concern (Vidmar and Hans 2007). Nevertheless, transparency in the research process and peer review of its results are especially important in research of this sort. A generation of experience with content analysis in social scientific research suggests as much (Berelson 1952; Krippendorf 2004).

Second, policy experts are a potential source of information that can be given to participants in deliberative experiments in precisely the same way that expert witnesses offer guidance to trial juries. With respect to deliberations on regulatory matters, especially those involving environmental protection, this function is likely to be particularly valuable. Yet from a democratic perspective, the role of experts is likely to be especially troublesome. Still, again, both experience in the courtroom and systematic research on trial juries offer reassurance.

Research indicates that whereas jurors with higher levels of education more easily process expert testimony, even juries lacking such membership are able to differentiate between more and less reliable scientific evidence. Misunderstandings of such evidence appear more often to be the result of errors by lawyers and judges rather than the inadequacies of jurors (Lempert 1993). Moreover, where expert witnesses are selected in the context of an adversarial process, jurors are able to adopt a discerning attitude toward their evidence. Jurors do not uncritically accept expert testimony in those circumstances. Rather, they appear to employ commonsense techniques to evaluate evidence for its clarity and informational value (Ivkovic and Hans 2003). Finally, as noted earlier, multiple studies have concluded that there is little evidence of any white coat syndrome. Jurors generally make expert-specific decisions about who to believe based on a sensible set of considerations—including "the expert's qualifications, reasoning, factual familiarity, and impartiality" (Vidmar and Hans 2007, 179).

The implications of this research are clear. It may be both practical and economical for deliberative framers to distill the collective wisdom of substantive experts into a set of undisputed facts, but there is no necessity to do so. If circumstances and finances allow, participants in deliberative decision making can be provided direct expert evidence. Expert testimony can be offered in an adversarial manner by representatives of civil society organizations standing on opposing sides of a regulatory problem. Alternatively, a single expert witness (selected by the convener) can be tasked to supply deliberators with a summary of the received wisdom in a field of expertise as it relates to the regulatory problem at hand. In this context, the expert would function in the manner of a "special master" such as those sometimes appointed by US federal judges under authority of Rule 53 of the Federal Rules of Civil Procedure to assist them in cases especially dependent on technical or scientific detail (Baber and Bartlett 2005, 149–152). The appropriate discretion and impartiality of a convener in choosing among these alternatives can be best assured, as in other matters, by transparency and careful peer review of the results.

Almost inevitably, questions of method lead to matters of substance. Discussion of the roles of framers, conveners, and expert testimony suggests questions about the character of the deliberative results, the first of which is, What do we mean when we say that an environmental (or other regulatory) decision is rational or public? No two terms have been dearer to the hearts of deliberative democratic theorists. Yet it is difficult to invoke these two ideas in the same breath without causing some wag to point out that no public is capable of rationality in the first place. Much as democrats would like to deny it, there is substantial real-world experience (as well as considerable scholarship) underlying this derisive sort of humor. Finding public grounds for rational decisions therefore will require us to focus our use of these terms. We can start to do so by exploring the sociological concept of rationality as it pertains to the rationalization of society.

Few serious students of the development of human society would dispute the proposition that the rationalization of traditional lifeways is a central element of modernity and indispensable precondition for the development of democratic forms of governance. But there is considerable variation in the attitudes that various scholars have adopted toward the process. For his part, Weber approaches the question with the hallmark detachment of his work. Denying that rationalization represents anything like the triumph of "reason" over "intuition," Weber characterizes it as something external to the values and intentions of the person. The advent of rationalism is "not inherent in the creator of ideas or of 'works,' or in his inner experience; rather, the difference is rooted in the manner in which the ruled and led experience and externalize these ideas." The rationalization of society, Weber (1978, 1116–1117) observes, "proceeds in such a fashion that the broad masses of the led merely accept or adapt themselves to the external, technical resultants which are of practical significance for their interests ... whereas the substance of the creator's ideas remain irrelevant to them." Rationality is nothing more than a wave of technical improvement in social organization that sweeps over humanity without fundamentally disturbing its normative orientation—in Weber's (24–26, 339) terminology, its "value-rationality."

In Habermas's hands, however, the rationalization of society takes on a more ominous character. Habermas (1987b) sees the institutionalization of the instrumental rationality of bureaucracies and market forces proceeding in much the same way as does Weber, but attaches a far different normative significance to it. He contrasts technical rationality with the practical rationality that governs what he calls communicative action. Communicative action, as Habermas frames it, is concerned with ideas of social importance mediated through processes of communication in natural languages. By contrast, technical rationality governs systems of instrumentality—primarily those of capital accumulation and bureaucratic power that are concerned with ideas of instrumental importance only within those systems. For Habermas, then, the contrast between technical and practical rationality are matters of *both* form and substance. These modes of rationality do not coexist peacefully, each in its own domain. The "imperatives" of autonomous subsystems of modern society (capital and bureaucracy) make their way into the "lifeworld" of communicative action. They invade traditional life "from the outside—like colonial masters coming into a tribal society—and force a process of assimilation on it." The result, notes Habermas (355), is a "fragmented consciousness" that blocks personally and socially valuable insights along with the development of collective wisdom "by the mechanism of reification."

This dispute over the normative significance of rationality is of more than passing interest for deliberative democrats because it bears directly on the justifications one can offer for governance—understood as a set of relationships in which the legitimate public use of coercive force is one possible outcome of deliberation (Larmore 2008). Deliberative democrats have, generally speaking, responded to this problem by insisting that decisions that are public in this sense require the support of equally public reasons. For Rawls, this means that our collective arrangements must be supported by reasons not grounded in comprehensive doctrines (such as religions) but instead of a character that all citizens could potentially accept them. As Rawls (1993, 61) puts it,

Since many doctrines are seen to be reasonable, those who insist, when fundamental political questions are at stake, on what they take as true but others do not, seem to others to insist on their own beliefs.... They impose their own beliefs because, they say their beliefs are true and not because they are their beliefs. But this is a claim all equally could make; it is also a claim that cannot be made by anyone to citizens generally. So when we make such claims, others, who are themselves reasonable, must count us unreasonable.

Yet for Habermas, public reasons are somewhat different. Publicity, in his view, is not so much a characteristic of the reasons themselves as a quality of the reasoning that produces them. He develops a "discourse ethics" from an empirically based understanding of the praxis and conditions of democratic discourse itself. Habermas (2001, 97) holds that democracy is predicated on an ideal speech situation in which "communication is impeded neither by external contingent forces nor, more importantly, by constraints arising from the structure of communication itself." This situation produces a genuinely deliberative politics as a result of the dynamic interplay between "democratically institutionalized" practices of collective will formation" and a free-flowing process of "informal opinion-formation" in civil society (Habermas 1996, 308). A useful way to characterize this distinctive viewpoint is that whereas Rawls has adopted the observer perspective toward public reasons, Habermas predicates the public quality of political reasoning on the perspectives, values, and intentions of the participants in democratic deliberation themselves

(McCarthy 1994). Public reason is not an independent standard one aspires to meet. Rather, it is a consensus that deliberating citizens come to in a process of mutual reciprocity.

When we employ these contending perspectives on rationality and publicity to evaluate juristic deliberation as it has already been described, a number of useful observations are possible. First, the deliberating citizens in a juristic democracy exercise are, by their very nature, impartial. Their own material interests are not involved in the dispute (which, after all, is hypothetical), and any philosophical or religious points of view they might hold are relevant only to the extent that they can be expressed in sufficiently public terms to gain their fellow jurists' assent. Second, any narrowing of perspective that might result from the unavoidable limit to the deliberative diversity imposed by a "jury" structure is mitigated by both the transparency of the research and influence of peer review imposed by the social scientific method. Third, the danger of elite influence over the deliberative process can be substantially ameliorated by inclusion of a broad range of civil society perspectives, either in the pleadings of the hypothetical parties or by the use of *amicus* briefs solicited by the deliberation conveners. In this way, the richness and variety of informal opinion formation (so valued by Habermas and avoided by Rawls) can be incorporated into democratic deliberation in a manageable form. Fourth, the close relationship between rationality and publicity is conceptual rather than coincidental. To see more clearly why this is the case, consider the example of rationality review in constitutional law. Courts have consistently interpreted both the due process and equal protection clauses of the US Constitution to require that the government act rationally. By this is meant simply that public measures must be at least minimally related to the promotion of some public value—which is understood as a value that impartially advances the interests of all (Sunstein 1993).

The second substantive question raised by the deliberative methodology described here is, How do we conceive of the ultimate relationship between deliberation and decision? This issue is well known among deliberative theorists as the problem of deliberative uptake. A useful structure for exploring this question, with respect to virtually any deliberative exercise, is provided by Goodin and Dryzek (2006), who identify the following eight ways that deliberative minipublics might affect the course of collective decision making in governance.

For one, a minipublic might actually make public policy. The limiting case occurs when a minipublic is formally empowered as part of a decision-making process. This arrangement is usually difficult to imagine, but somewhat less so with respect to juristic deliberation. A conceptual parent technique would entail the adjudication of hypothetical cases by actual administrative courts when the judge(s) can see the need for guidance to a regulated industry, but cannot analyze the issues at a level of generality sufficient to engage in rule making (Davis 1969a, 1969b). An administrative court facing a similar need to promulgate regulatory policy, yet also wishing to provide policy with democratic provenance, might well adopt that approach. More generally, administrative authorities who seek to formalize decentralized and informal regulatory arrangements that have grown up from local practice (Ostrom 1990) might wish to assemble a series of minipublics drawn from the communities whose practices the new policy is expected to subsume and have them deliberate a hypothetical (or series of hypotheticals) crafted to resolve the issues at hand.

Second, the much more frequent case happens when a minipublic offers recommendations in an existing political process. These recommendations are "taken up" with no formal guarantee that they will be taken any further by any macropolitical institution. Legislative bodies or administrative courts with rule-making authority might wish to commission juristic deliberations of minipublics in order to gain insight into the views of average citizens who have had the opportunity to examine the relative merits of competing policy prescriptions in some depth and the context of a concrete (though hypothetical) dispute. This might be particularly useful to IGO officials, who are unlikely to have an intimate knowledge of the wide range of political, social, and cultural groups that their decisions will affect.

Third, organizations sponsoring citizen dialogues of one sort or another can have as one of their major goals simply to provide information. NGOs, for example, often have a significant interest in the actions of government officials. Traditional lobbying techniques certainly have a place in the pursuit of those interests. But governmental officials may be more likely to pay attention to the results of deliberative exercises by minipublics (even when they are sponsored by interested groups) than toward nakedly self-interested appeals of a more conventional sort. The relatively low cost of sponsoring minipublic deliberations offers organizations that represent the poor and historically underrepresented populations an opportunity to level the political playing field to some degree.

Fourth, minipublics can shape public policy by market testing potential policy solutions. There are instances of commercial ventures benefiting in just this way from commissioned minipublics (Goodin and Dryzek 2006). This possibility might be especially attractive to the professional staffs charged with the progressive development of international conventions. The ability to anticipate the reception of specific policy regimes, say, could improve the feasibility of proposed protocols to the UNFCCC. In knowing that the citizenry is unopposed to the concept of common but differentiated responsibility, elected officials might allow for the development of a set of formal rules that apply to more of the world's nations, instead of ones so crosscut with specific exceptions that they nearly consumed the rules themselves. This would allow advocates of the potential protocols to "market" them as universal in a formal sense, even though they might force changes on only a relative handful of nations in practice.

Fifth, minipublics can help supply symbolic legitimation for public policies in whose process of production they have had a role. This much goes nearly without saying, although this quality of minipublics is a double-edged sword from the democrat's point of view. Like any other form of social scientific research, juristic deliberation is subject to manipulation by special interests. But for this form of minipublic to have much influence over policy processes it must, by definition, be public. The relative ease and economy with which competing organizations can replicate juristic deliberative exercises makes this form of collective will formation inherently difficult to counterfeit without being contradicted in highly damaging ways.

Sixth, minipublics can provide confidence- or constituency-building benefits by promoting "empowerment" in the psychological or sociological rather than strictly political sense. Participants in juristic deliberation exercises, like those in other deliberative minipublics, routinely report positive reactions to the process of deliberation itself. This result closely tracks the widely reported positive effect of service on actual trial juries (Vidmar and Hans 2007), even where juries fail to reach verdicts. The inescapable conclusion is that the deliberative experience does not have to produce tangible results to have a positive impact on participants. Being taken seriously and being listened to by others is an inherently valuable experience.

Seventh, participatory, consultative mechanisms also sometimes serve as a means of public oversight, forcing official accountability. Whenever the policy actions of public officials can be rerendered as possible resolutions of concrete disputes, those policies can be subjected to the test of *considered* public opinion (as opposed to mass survey oversimplification) by the use of juristic deliberation.

Eighth, minipublics offer a possible solution to the problem of co-optation in public participation. The discursive component of minipublics and their relatively unstructured character makes their proceedings especially hard to predict or control, and hence unsuited to elite co-optation. In the case of juristic deliberation, the low cost and relative simplicity of the methodology allows for nearly infinite replication in nearly infinite variation.

Social Science as a Source of International Environmental Law

We have sought to unite content analysis and legal restatement in an analytic framework for the interpretation of discourses aimed at the resolution of concrete disputes with significant implications for global governance, especially regarding environmental protection. That analytic framework can be applied in a specific form of policy research through the use of a particular type of minipublic: juristic deliberation. This deliberative approach can offer responses to several of the most persistent questions confronting advocates of deliberative democracy.

Content analysis is a social scientific technique, and social scientists are, first and foremost, members of academic disciplines. For this reason, the incentive structures within which they live their professional lives differ markedly from those of government officials, either elected or appointed. For any of their efforts to bear fruit, social scientists must eventually submit their work to review by their peers. This process, even though it operates imperfectly, tends to advance certain values. One is transparency. It is difficult to get one's research published if it one's procedures or results are obscure. Furthermore, empirical findings are of far greater value (both personally and to the discipline) if they are subject to replication. This further encourages transparency as well as simplicity of design and care in implementation. Ideally, these characteristics of social scientific research make its results fairly reliable even if they are nearly always tentative to some extent. Public officials charged with the development and implementation of regulatory regimes thus proceed at their peril if they ignore social scientific findings that cast doubt on the assumptions underlying their rule structures.

Social scientists, whatever their professional merits, remain mere mortals. They are as susceptible as anyone to both conscious and unconscious forms of bias. The various features of scientific methods guard against this kind of bias to a considerable degree. Deliberative designs of the sort that we propose add another layer of protection. A diverse set of disinterested deliberators is likely to frustrate most efforts to build particular outcomes into an experimental design. It should be noted that most of the deliberative dysfunctions that have been noted in the literature arise from deliberations among individuals who are homogeneous in ways relevant to the outcomes. Even if principal investigators fail to avoid this pitfall (for whatever reason), others seeking either to replicate or challenge their results are likely to be their undoing.

It is vitally important that deliberation offers opportunities for the widest possible variety of discourses to find expression, and content analysis married to restatement is a way of ensuring that. Even the most diverse juristic deliberation is unlikely to contain within its participant group the entire range of potentially meaningful discourses regarding the issue under consideration. The parties to a hypothetical dispute therefore serve as the conduit for the complexities of the real world to enter into the deliberation. In the hands of an unscrupulous or lazy political manipulator, it is certainly possible for these parties to become nothing more than a Greek chorus, chanting in a homogeneous way the framer's own message as a mere commentary on the dramatic action of the jury. The democrat will take great pains to ensure representation for all the political themes and interests that bear on the policy problem of concern. The results will suffer at the hands of peers—both citizen and social science peers—if not.

8

Deliberatively Democratic Administrative Discretion in Global Environmental Governance

Where law ends, tyranny begins.
—William Pitt

Where law ends, discretion begins.
—Kenneth Culp Davis

Administrative power should not reproduce itself on its own terms ... but only from the conversion of communicative power.
—Jürgen Habermas

In the opening sentences of his classic work on discretionary justice, Davis (1969a) argues that Pitt has overlooked a significant range of possibilities—that the exercise of discretion by bureaucrats may mean either beneficence or tyranny, either justice or injustice, either reasonableness or arbitrariness. It is easy to find differences of opinion concerning which end of these continua discretion tends. For Theodore Lowi (1979), the growing inclination of legislatures to pass broadly worded (often-vague) statutes and rely on administrative agencies to fill in the details poses a critical risk for liberal government. Alternatively, the US National Performance Review cited the inability of administrators to deviate from strict operating procedures and agency rules as one of the major factors contributing to modern government's inability to either serve the public interest effectively or even satisfy the demands of individual citizens (Gore 1993). But it is not difficult to find agreement about two other matters related to administrative discretion: discretion is an unavoidable characteristic of modern regulatory governance, and administrative discretion must be subject to popular restraint if it is to remain the servant of democracy rather than becoming one of democracy's primary rivals. These characteristics, readily observable at the nation-state level, become both more pressing and problematic when one enters the arena of global governance. Ultimately, however, whether administrative discretion is viewed with ardor, acceptance, or alarm depends less on the level of government of concern than on how one evaluates these two propositions.

The Inevitability of Administrative Discretion

The major premise underlying the idea that administrative discretion is unavoidable is the proposition that no legislature (or citizenry by the way of direct democracy) has the insight or vision necessary to regulate all the details of administration or render in the form of unconditional commands the rules necessary to express the state's will (Goodnow 1905). Even if the cognitive assets necessary to achieve that level of specificity in legislation existed in a legislature, any procedure that required legislators to debate such minute details would raise the decision costs in the legislative process to a level sufficient to derail any legislative initiative (Landis 1938). Moreover, there are reasons to believe that it would be undesirable. Detailed standards and controls imposed early in the process of developing any regulatory regime may do more to obscure than reveal the intent of the legislature, and may constrain administrators' ability to develop a program that will ultimately achieve that intent (Sofaer 1972). Not only that, but any regulatory regime would rely on a foundation of technical and scientific expertise that would shift as well as grow more quickly than any legislature could respond. Only a specialized administrative agency can command the resources to initiate and sustain the pursuit of so elusive a form of the public interest. Finally, administrative discretion makes it possible for regulatory regimes to individualize the application of governmental power over private interests. This permits regulators, if they are so inclined, to adjust the demands of the law to varying circumstances, and avoid most of the unjust, otherwise-undesirable results of standardized restraints and particularized requirements (Freund 1928).

The arguments for the unavoidability of administrative discretion are thus both political and functional. Our institutions and the individuals who populate them are both unable and unwilling to legislate with greater specificity. Furthermore, our governing processes would work less well

if we tried to legislate with greater precision, and we would be less satisfied with the results in any event. This last observation serves as a useful
bridge to the second point of consensus regarding administrative discretion—that it must be subjected to some measure of democratic control
if it is to be tolerable in a system of popular government. Administrative
discretion can be a useful tool, but "like an ax, it can be a weapon for
mayhem or murder" (Davis 1969a, 25). So vivid a simile should serve to
remind us that when we allow legislators to stop short of saying precisely
what they mean, we also allow them to escape much of the moral and
political heavy lifting that goes into establishing behavioral norms in a
complex society.

Living with Administrative Discretion

What one chooses to do about administrative discretion depends in large
measure on what one takes it to be and what interest one assumes it
threatens. If the emphasis is placed on the inability of legislatures to be
more specific than they usually are, then administrative discretion appears
to be a shortcoming in our effort to achieve what is often characterized
as the rule of law. If, however, this specifically *legal* perspective is taken
to suggest that the objective of law is to leave no indeterminate space for
details that must be filled in by administrators, then we have been sent
on a wild-goose chase. Even those who generally identified as political
conservatives are frequently willing to admit that the notion of the rule
of law as the mechanical application of rules that require no interpretation, no fleshing out, is a profoundly silly idea (Posner 2008). If taken to
be an empirical proposition, it can only refer to a halcyon past that never
was. If it is a normative prescription, it summons a legalistic (even rigidly
authoritarian) future that we all should hope never materializes.

Yet a more modest and sensible rule of law critique of administrative
discretion is available. On this view, law should attempt to give guidance
to private individuals, administrators, and judges through clear, abstract
rules laid down in advance of their actual application (Sunstein 1996).
The point of the exercise is not to reduce discretion to zero. It instead is
to lend a higher degree of predictability to the exercise of that discretion
by describing (in general terms) the patterns that it should follow. This
process is not presumed to be the legislature's exclusive domain. It is the

heart of both the modern reliance on administrative rule making and general preference for rule making over adjudication as a means for defining the restraints as well as obligations that governance places on individuals.

The only clear alternative to rule making (if one dismisses chaos as an option) is the case-by-case adjudication of administrative issues—the creation of law at its point of application. The long-term trend is to avoid this alternative. Rule making is preferred because the promulgation of rules enhances efficiency. It provides a widely deployable standard for decision, and leaves a documentary record that aids in both interpretation of that standard and long-term policy development. Rule making also reduces the likelihood of arbitrary treatment of individuals and enhances the general sense of fairness in the administrative process. Rules go beyond protecting the interests of individuals. They encourage a regularity, predictability, and transparency in the operation of administrative agencies that allows elected officials along with citizens generally to more easily understand administrative action and hold administrators accountable (Cooper 2007).

Beyond rule of law perspectives on administrative discretion, it is possible to approach the subject from a managerial point of view. This approach emphasizes the role that discretion plays in allowing administrative decisions to more effectively utilize our technical, scientific, and social scientific (especially economic) understanding of the empirical content of regulation. The role of expertise, in whatever discipline it is based, has long been a subject of debate in the policy sciences, where it is recognized that human activities are normally organized by one of three different techniques: markets, politics, and expert analysis (Munger 2000). Both markets and politics are the subject of extensive literatures. But we have a much thinner foundation for our discussion of expertise.

Expertise has been taken to refer to either a knowledge claim based on the expert's membership in a specially trained group that can contribute valuable advice to administrative decision makers, or the claim to a form of tacit knowledge that allows an expert to puzzle out the underlying dynamics of a problem by combining both systematic knowledge and personal intuition along with experience in a unique perspective that permits the expert to assert personally authoritative knowledge claims (Baber and Bartlett 2005). It matters a great deal what one takes expertise to be. If we adopt a "group knowledge" perspective, then we may deprive ourselves of the most flexible and creative perspectives on our problem because of the inherently cautious, conservative character of scholarly practice (Munger 2000). But expertise grounded in "tacit knowledge" is problematic for a different reason. Tacit knowledge, even when it appears to be objective and factual, may be subject to resistance because of the personal quality of the perspective that it legitimizes. Citizens, policymakers, and even other experts may reject this form of expertise because of their attitudes about its source, or because of the challenge it presents to their own tacit knowledge (Stone 2002).

A solution to the problems of integrating expertise into the practice of administrative rule making is the use of the public hearing. Ideally, administrative hearings allow all interested parties to challenge each other's knowledge claims in an open process of rational give and take. In the United States, administrative hearings have evolved rules of procedure that are more permissive than those found in judicial hearings. Decisions about who may participate and what kind of information may be introduced are made with the idea of maximum feasible participation in mind. As a general matter, most of the evidence proffered in administrative hearings is accepted because to do otherwise increases the risk of having the ultimate ruling overturned (Cooper 2007). This tends to be true in both administrative rule making and administrative adjudication. The potential burden of holding open the agency door to all comers has been ameliorated in the rule-making process by the frequent (in the United States, nearly universal) resort to informal rule making—also known as notice-and-comment rule making. Notice-and-comment rule making retains the broadly adversarial qualities typical of both adjudication and formal rule making. It nonetheless is far less restrictive on the issue of who may participate in the process and how extensively the agency must justify its exercise of discretion. As a general matter, to have standing in notice-and-comment rule making, one need only have an opinion (what it takes to gain actual influence is another matter).

A third perspective on administrative discretion is neither specifically legal nor narrowly functional. Instead, it is an unapologetically political argument that administrative discretion has strong antidemocratic tendencies. As an extension of interest group liberalism, administrative discretion is unavoidably suspect on this score. It has no internal mechanism to ensure that worthy arguments are heard, especially when their advocates lack the resources and special access of well-organized interest groups. One recent development in the United States, designed in part to address this problem, is the negotiated rule-making process.

Negotiated rule making evolved against the backdrop of an increasing tendency for US agency actions to be challenged in court (O'Leary 1993). It involves the creation of a committee (of twenty to twenty-five persons) whose membership is determined by a facilitator to represent all the relevant stakeholders in a given rule-making situation. The committee is then led by a second facilitator in a process designed to reach a consensus on the contours that the ultimate rule should take. The product of the committee's work becomes (with agency approval) a notice of proposed rule making, which is then subject to the normal hearing and decision process.

Negotiated rule making works best where the number of interests affected by the rule is manageable in size and reasonably well organized to begin with. There has to be at least some clarity as to the issues involved, and those concerns must be ripe for decision. The parties involved must have sufficiently complex interests that they can be effectively traded off against one another without requiring any group or individual to surrender something of fundamental importance to them (Cameron et al. 1990). The agency itself must be prepared to live with the committee's decision. Although within an agency's right to do so, walking away from the consensus of a stakeholder committee can be a political disaster—further limiting the range of application for negotiated rule making. It therefore should be obvious that negotiated rule making is no panacea. Although it has the potential to be more inclusive and representative than other approaches to the use of administrative discretion, there is no guarantee. Even assuming that a given issue has only two sides (a heroic assumption to be sure), there will often be a large number of different groups that adopt each position. These groups may have little in common with one another, other than a shared position on the issue at hand. If all are included, how are their different priorities traded off against one another? If some are to be excluded, how will that choice be made and defended? In the United States, exclusion from the process will be hard to challenge because it may not be a reviewable "final action" of the agency. An excluded party may find it difficult to contest the final rule because showing a nexus between its exclusion and the violation of a legal right in which it has a concrete interest will usually be quite difficult to prove (Cooper

2007). Thus negotiated rule making appears to have the same potential to exclude disadvantaged or historically marginalized interests that plagues other forms of rule making.

These potential flaws in negotiated rule making are not unique to that approach, however. They are imported, as it were, from the basic characteristics of notice-and-comment rule making. Situating a rule-making process designed to be more open and responsive into the bleak choice between an excessively demanding procedure (formal rule making), on the one hand, and an informal process susceptible to only the most limited judicial review (notice and comment), on the other, was problematic from the start. In response to this problem (and many others), the US judiciary developed a third alternative in a series of cases. Intermediate between formal rule making and the notice-and-comment process, this approach is referred to as hybrid rule making.

The general thrust of hybrid rule making is to allow administrative agencies to continue using the flexible, open procedures of notice-and-comment rule making, but to require them to generate a more substantial record in support of their exercise of discretion that demonstrates the thoroughness of their analysis and completeness of their attention to the stakeholders' arguments (Williams 1975). Under the approach, agency decisions are required to state the basis and purpose of the rule as well as the data and methodology on which the agency relied. Furthermore, the agency is required to show that adequate notice was given to all potentially interested parties, sufficient time to respond was allowed, challenges to agency data were entertained, and the agency examined and responded to all relevant public input (Pederson 1975). Although this approach originally emerged from the judiciary, it was reinforced and expanded (particularly with respect to opportunities for public participation) by a series of executive orders issued by presidents Jimmy Carter, Ronald Reagan, and Bill Clinton (Kerwin 1994).

It is at least arguable that all the inventors of hybrid rule making have done is to require of administrative agencies in practice what the US Administrative Procedures Act already required of them in theory. When the more demanding record of decision requirements of hybrid rule making meets the consensus standard of negotiated rule making, new potential for democratic responsiveness is created—although many questions remain. Can negotiated rule making really be sufficiently representative and inclusive, given the complexity of modern society? Can a committee meeting over a protracted period of time be genuinely open in a democratic sense? Will the notice-and-comment process that follows the development of a consensus add anything to the outcome, and should it? Will a regulatory agency genuinely conform itself to the stakeholder committee's will, both when the rule is adopted and the time comes to apply it to concrete circumstances (Cooper 2007)?

Making Discretion Safe for Democracy and the Environment

Identifying a distinctive legal, managerial, and political perspective on administrative discretion does more than provide us with a general analytic framework for organizing ideas and concerns on the subject. It also suggests a developmental trend in administrative law. Administrative law first drew serious attention as a result of the recognition that in contemporary representative democracies, reliance on administrative discretion is a practical necessity. Where there is an independent constituency as well as distinctive legislative role for both the legislature and executive, there usually are high transaction costs. Even though it gives rise to significant legal issues, leaving the details of lawmaking to administrators lowers those costs (Posner 1999).

An emerging political consensus that government had a responsibility to deal with the social consequences of industrialization made the reliance on administrative discretion increasingly useful as a means for integrating scientific and technical expertise into the governing process (Hofstadter 1955). In spite of their legally problematic provenance, informal and discretionary procedures came to be regarded as the lifeblood of the administrative process, allowing government to achieve a level of speed, flexibility, cost-effectiveness, continuity, and expertise that would otherwise be impossible (Woll 1963).

The 1960s and 1970s ushered in a period of social turmoil that roiled every major institution and function of government globally. Social unrest, upsurges in crime, and unpopular wars all conspired to deprive governments of popular confidence and support precisely when they were required to manage the challenges of a transition from industrialism to the information age, and respond to the demands of new social movements for greater transparency and responsiveness in both politics and administration. These pressures manifested themselves in a variety of administrative law initiatives. There were packages of statutes designed to foster openness in government. There were efforts to provide for greater levels of public participation in administrative rule making. There were the constitutionally dubious experiments with the idea of reserving a "legislative veto" over the exercise of administrative discretion so that the peoples' elected representatives could more easily protect their interests (Cooper 2007).

When placed against this historical backdrop, the general preference for rule making over the adjudication of particular cases, development of negotiated regulation, and advent of hybrid rule making as an alternative to formal and notice-and-comment rule making all appear as signposts on the road to a more effective, fully democratic role for administrative discretion in modern governance. The questions, of course, are, How far along that road do we have left to go, and are we headed in the right direction? Acknowledging that administrative discretion was widespread and unavoidable, Davis (1969a) maintained that it was open to abuse because administrative proceedings were insufficient and those who objected to the results faced excessive burdens in their efforts to get judicial review of agency actions. He characterized the system of administrative discretion as being in a state of "rudderless drift" (ibid., 189). But he expressed confidence that an incremental process of reform would eventually lead administrators themselves to adopt the necessary remedies. Davis foresaw that administrators would cease interposing technical obstacles in cases where citizens sought judicial review of their decisions. Perhaps more important, he also expected administrators ultimately to expand their use of rule making in order to lend greater transparency and predictability to their exercise of discretion. If agencies failed to take these steps, Davis suggested that courts could effectively encourage them to do so.

Needless to say, his optimism about administrators' openness to the idea of curbing their own discretion provoked considerable debate. Even those who agreed with his assessment of the problems were dubious of the proposition that the necessary reforms would not eventually have to be forced on administrators by the judiciary (Jaffe 1969; Wright 1972). In particular, doubt was expressed that administrators would come to choose rule making (the preferred form of discretion) over case-by-case adjudication (Sofaer 1972). Davis acknowledged that administrators would be tempted to resolve discretionary issues on an ad hoc basis. But rather than attribute this tendency to sinister intent, he saw it as a result of administrators' lack of confidence in their own ability to fashion rules that would not produce "unforeseen and unwanted consequences" (Davis 1969a, 59). Administrators, he asserted, are reluctant to issue abstract generalizations until they are confident that their understanding of the issues at hand will allow them to include all the necessary qualifications and limitations. Yet Davis had a proposal to deal with this administrative reluctance to make rules.

Davis observed that both our statutes and administrative rules have always taken the form of abstract generalizations, but there is no reason why they must. A rule, he argued, can be limited to one or more hypothetical cases, and can contain no generalization at all. What Davis imagined was that an agency could enlarge its capacity to serve the interests of affected parties if, instead of generalizing in a rule, it issued rules that contained a hypothetical set of facts, a statement of the problem raised by the facts, and a statement of the agency's answer to the problem and reasons for it. In so doing, the agency is able to extend the advantages of rule making (clarity, predictability, and reviewability) into areas where generalizations are not yet possible, but where an appropriate exercise of administrative discretion is capable of answering the questions that the agency is prepared to answer while avoiding questions it is not yet prepared to answer. An agency that issues rules in the form of hypotheticals in addition to ones in the form of generalizations and adjudication would be far better equipped to serve the public interest than one that limited itself to only the latter two of these techniques (ibid.).

It should be noted that Davis's notion about rules in the form of hypotheticals is not meant to resolve all the problems associated with the exercise of administrative discretion. Where administrators have only administrative discretion (rather than an unambiguous legislative requirement) at their command, and where their understanding of the social and economic facts underlying a problem are uncertain, rule making via hypotheticals gives them an opportunity to provide guidance to interested parties without risking the inefficiency and unfairness that often attends case-by-case adjudication. But this technique, at least in the form that Davis presents it, holds out little hope for a form of administrative discretion that is more responsive and accountable from a democratic perspective.

Discretion as an Opportunity for Democratic Deliberation

In trying to imagine a reform of the use of administrative discretion that would address the political challenges we face, it is useful to recall negotiated regulation and hybrid rule making. The objective of both is to maintain the flexibility and potential for openness that characterizes notice-and-comment rule making, while gaining more of the procedural protections that characterize formal rule making. A key assumption, clearly, is that whereas open and participatory rule-making processes have considerable value from both a managerial and political perspective, a backup plan for the protection of individual rights through litigation remains a valuable form of political insurance.

In fitting Davis's suggestion for administrative rule making as the adjudication of hypotheticals into the context of negotiated regulation and hybrid rule making, one is immediately struck by the fact that both are still dependent on judges (administrative judges along with those in the judicial branch) to acquit the rights and protect the interests of citizens. It is also apparent that the citizens who are allowed into the process are still a particular sort: representatives of interest groups. Their orientations to the questions of regulatory discretion are determined by their particular stakes in those issues. Moreover, they have won their roles in the administrative process as a consequence of their privileged positions in the political system within which that process is taking place. This is not to say that negotiated regulation, hybrid rule making, and rule making through hypotheticals are not (or would not be) improvements in the control of administrative discretion. It is only to say that their advantages are most apparent from the legal and managerial perspectives.

From a more thoroughly political vantage point, it is clear that what is lacking is not *popular* participation but rather fully *public* participation. The distinction, obviously, is between those outside government who have a direct stake in the issue at hand and those outside government who have only that interest in the issue that all other citizens have. The resolution of a concern by a committee of stakeholders may be reasonably stable. It may be immediately defensible as a reasonable modus vivendi. If it is the result of a process of hybrid rule making, there may be a record of the decision sufficient to subsequently allow a court to evaluate whether the action has harmed the interests of persons not party to the discretionary process. But none of these advantages (over unrestrained exercises of discretion) are sufficient to satisfy the demands of democratic legitimacy. These demands have become more acute as the decline of the notion of divinely ordained natural law has left common law grounded, apparently, in nothing more credible than either fiat or the judiciary's democratic character. Many US states have made the judiciary elective, yet their experience indicates that plunging judicial service into the swamp of electoral politics only makes the problem of legitimacy worse (Posner 1990).

Habermas offers a critical point of departure for analyzing the problem of democratic legitimacy as it relates to the exercise of administrative discretion. He suggests that legitimacy is *interactional*, the result of a social bargain of sorts, observing that in the course of social interaction, we cannot expect the other to "obey a norm that she would not also recognize as legitimate" (Habermas 2001, 101). So the crucial quality of a legitimate norm (if our analysis goes no further) is simply that others take it, for whatever reason, to be legitimate.

In an earlier work, though, Habermas (1979, 186) implies a *cognitive* standard, suggesting that a democratic society is "a self-controlled learning process" constantly in search of "arrangements which can ground the presumption that the basic institutions of the society and the basic political decisions would meet the unforced agreement of all those involved, if they could participate, as free and equal, in discursive will formation." The key here is not that there is actual participation on the part of anyone in particular. Neither does the substantive fairness of the decisions actually taken seem to be the crux of the matter. Rather, it is that a special kind of learning has taken place, and if everyone involved had experienced the same learning, everyone would recognize one set of institutions and decisions as the appropriate outcome. The standard is cognitive instead of procedural because it does not imagine a decision process that all agree to in advance as likely to produce the best (or merely better than average) outcomes. The agreement that results in discursive will formation is not about the correctness of the procedure; it is about a particular sense in which the decision itself is correct.

Elsewhere, Habermas (1998) situates the legitimacy of discretionary action in a broader *institutional* context related to the validity of law. The "validity" of a legal norm depends on the state's ability to "simultaneously guarantee factual enforcement and legitimate enactment" of the law. This implies that the state assures each of its citizens "the legality of behavior in the sense of average compliance" as well as behavioral norms of sufficient legitimacy that it is always "possible to comply with the norm out of respect for the law" (ibid., 255). Matters are not left to the vagaries of social interaction; they are tethered to a master norm of respect for "the law" grounded (in some as yet unspecified way) in its legitimacy. Perhaps this move has not advanced us much in our understanding of the notion of legitimacy, but it has achieved one thing of importance. It has pulled government into the equation as the guarantor of both average compliance *and* normative legitimacy. Government is not only an essential party to the "social interaction" but also the classroom in which the "learning process" takes place that leads to normative acceptance of the law. According to Habermas (1996, 135; emphasis in the original), "The law receives its full normative sense neither through its legal *form* per se, not through an a priori moral *content*, but through a *procedure* of lawmaking that begets legitimacy."

The significance of this view is that it allows us to focus on the institutional practices that legitimate discretionary actions of government by grounding them in legitimately enacted law (ibid.). Habermas's general formulation describes a law as legitimate if it "could be rationally accepted by all citizens in a discursive process of opinion- and will-formation" (135). Habermas allows that the professionalism of the competent implementation of law through acts of agency discretion plays an important role in legitimating administration in a constitutional democracy. But positive results, in themselves, are insufficient to legitimate administration. Ultimately, legitimately generated law must "determine the direction in which political power circulates" if administration is to be fully legitimized (187). Democratic legitimacy requires that administrative discretion be exercised competently, yet "only under normative premises not at its disposal" and on the basis of "communicatively generated power" (188). Power of this kind does not emanate from either the marketplace or the negative rights of the private individual but instead from the positive rights of political participation and the communication of citizens oriented toward mutual understanding (Habermas 2001).

Habermas develops his theories of communication in especially rich ways. His notion of an ideal speech situation is at the heart of this work. It captures a circumstance in which all interested parties participate equally in a social discourse and only the force of the better argument determines the outcome. In order to make something more than a regulative norm for personal behavior out of the ideal speech situation, Habermas grounds the concept though the use of two crucial assumptions. The first is that normative claims have cognitive meaning, and that careful observation of the use of normative language will allow us to join in communicative action (action aimed at understanding) through which we can discover what is true and good (Elliot 1994). In the ideal speech situation, language achieves a world-disclosing capacity that can transcend the structural constraints of communication in everyday life (Habermas 1987a). This provides a nexus between communicative action and the formation of political and legal norms. Only practices that permit genuinely undistorted and uncoerced communication are capable of generating legitimate restraints on individual conduct because only those practices can reveal an intersubjectively reliable reality to us.

The second assumption undergirding Habermas's concept of the ideal speech situation is that internal dialogues are insufficient as a basis for our participation in the process of deliberating the content of political and legal norms. It shifts our attention away from what *each* of us might will (without internal contradiction) to be a universal law and focuses us instead on what *all* of us in agreement might will to be a universal norm (McCarthy 1978). This is the sense in which Habermas (1998) characterizes discourse ethics as a method of rational justification. When structured in this way, the practice of argumentation sets in motion "a *cooperative* competition" for the better argument, and in such a situation, "the orientation to the goal of a communicatively reached agreement unites the participants from the outset" (ibid., 44, emphasis in the original). Thus, the rational acceptability of political and legal norms is the result of a deliberative process, the fundamental characteristics of which we are now able to describe. The most important of these are that nobody who could make a "relevant contribution" is excluded, all participants have an "equal opportunity to contribute," all are required to "mean what they say," and no form of coercion compels participants to adopt stances based on considerations other than "the rational force of the better reason" (44). Only in such a discursive process of opinion and will formation can citizens exercise the positive right of political self-legislation (Habermas 1996).

The Next Step: Deliberative Rule Making

One response to the expanding discretionary power of the modern state has been to build new forms of participation and arenas for deliberation into the decision-making process of administration itself, so as to avoid the dangers of the administrative discretion tethered only to normative premises of its own devising (ibid.). But to constrain acts of discretion, normative premises must be "formulated with sufficient abstraction and not just independently of their varying institutional forms" (191). This is to say that the norms must not simply be the work of some actor other than the agency whose discretion is to be limited but also that they must be "abstract" in that they are not derivative of the case in which the discretion is to be exercised. Yet the "semantic concept of a general norm" prejudges too much by straying into the realm of "discourses and negotiations in which the legislature's will is formed" (191). So the norms that an administrative agency's participatory and deliberative processes might generate to constrain its discretion must be abstract, but not general. They must be generated in a form that speaks directly to, though is not distorted by, the discretionary objectives and interests of the agency.

The implications for the administrative practices discussed above are reasonably clear. Davis's rule making by the adjudication of hypotheticals is suited to the development of norms that are abstract, but not general. The process relies on what administrative agencies do well. It allows the administrator to identify the most relevant characteristics of frequent parties to actual disputes that the agency must resolve, structure a hypothetical scenario capturing those characteristics and contestations, and then apply to them the agency's expertise in order to arrive at what would be an adjudicatory conclusion were the case a real one, but is, in this instance, a rule that applies prospectively to cases of that sort (and that sort only). The flaw in Davis's formulation is that the deliberator is the administrator or perhaps an administrative law judge. This fails to produce a norm for the exercise of discretion independent of the administrator's interests. Insofar as the implementation of programmatic goals in modern government requires administrators to perform tasks that require a further development of the law than the legislature has so far achieved, the legitimation basis of existing administrative structures will not suffice (Habermas 1996, 193).

The process of negotiated regulation offers a solution to this short-coming. Replacing the single administrator as deliberator with a group of citizens, such as a stakeholder committee, produces a constraint on the exercise of administrative discretion that is independent of the administrator. In the case of rule making by the adjudication of hypotheticals, we have no stakeholders because no real-world dispute is yet at hand. This is, however, more a strength of the approach than a weakness. When stakeholder committees are used to resolve actual disputes in concrete circumstances, the results are always open to criticism due to the fact that parties have been allowed to serve as judges in their own cause. Using citizens drawn together in another way, as juries similar to those employed in trial courts, allows for the aggregation of perspectives that serves the cognitive objectives of democratic deliberation without surrendering the impartiality of administrative adjudication. This institutionally captures the distinction that Habermas (ibid., 273) alludes to when he observes that there is "a structural difference between the communicative power that political communication brings forth in the shape of discursively formed majority opinions and the administrative power available to government apparatus." In the last analysis, it is only the former that can genuinely legitimate the later.

Hybrid rule making supplies an appropriate framework within which to situate the use of policy juries to formulate administrative rules through the adjudication of hypotheticals. Hybrid rule making shifts the focus of our attention from the rule-making outcome to the record of deliberation that generated it. The original purpose of this shift, of course, was to enhance the ability of courts to review agency use of administrative discretion, thereby better protecting individual citizens whose interests might be overlooked by the agency or overwhelmed by the organized groups that dominate conventional agency procedures. That function would remain, and remain important, in a regime of rule making through the adjudication of hypotheticals. But a wider process of approximating justice in the use of administrative discretion would be set in motion.

Justice is always administered outside courts more than it is inside them. Particularly when we shift our thinking from justice to injustice, our institutional focus shifts with it. The largest cluster of injustice in any society resides not in the courts of law, nor even in the administrative courts where the use of administrative discretion is reviewed by administrative law judges. The greatest injustice occurs in the theater of the mundane, where actors who are not judges exercise discretionary power, without the kinds of procedural protections that courts customarily employ, in ways that are largely unreviewable (Davis et al. 1976). Administrative discretion in particular is largely unreviewable for three reasons. One is that the parties involved frequently lack the resources or even basic knowledge of their rights required to challenge an administrator whose actions have frustrated their interests. Another reason is that when administrative actions number in the millions each year, and the matters that can be taken up by existing institutions of administrative and judicial review may number only in the hundreds or thousands, often there simply is no opportunity to be heard. Yet significantly and perversely, many (if not most) of the exercises of administrative discretion that aggrieve individual citizens are in their nature unreviewable because they are decisions to refrain from exercising discretion. Generally speaking, decisions of that kind (nondecisions) are unreviewable both as a matter of law and because they would usually leave no record for a reviewing authority to examine.

When a policy jury adjudicates a hypothetical and issues its ruling, a rule for cases of that sort is pronounced. If the hypothetical has been properly structured, and the reasons for the ruling have been elicited, an administrative law judge or court of law would be quite capable of evaluating the ruling for its logical consistency, reasonableness as a matter of policy, compatibility with other existing legal norms, and legality within the statutory boundaries of the agency whose discretion the rule is intended to guide. Legal scholars would be capable of collecting rulings of this sort and subjecting them to the same kind of analysis that produced the restatements of law discussed in chapter 7. Ultimately, this kind of ruling can become the raw material for the creation of model codes eventually allowing for the codification of laws with a uniquely democratic provenance (Baber and Bartlett 2009a). The deliberative discourse described here would thus take place in an arena that is administrative, employs procedures that are judicial, and produces results that are legislative.

Lest this offend the well-developed sense of the importance to democracy of the separation of powers, we should recall Habermas's (1996, 192; emphasis in the original) observation that "the division of powers and responsibilities among authorities that respectively make, apply, and implement laws follows from the *distribution of the possibilities for access to different sorts of reasons* and to the corresponding forms of communication that determine how these reasons are dealt with." The purpose, clearly, is not to render less effective the work of government but rather to render more effective citizens' control over government. A stress on the distinctions between the legislature, judiciary, and administration promotes an "overly concrete understanding led astray by inherited forms of institutionalization." If a system of separated powers is to achieve its full democratic potential, "the logic of the separation of powers must then be realized in new structures" that promote citizen participation along with communicative action "by introducing quasi-judicial and parliamentary procedures" (ibid., 193) directly into the institutions where most interactions between citizens and their governments take place, and where democratic self-legislation will likely occur—if it does.

Implications for Global Environmental Governance

From the perspective developed above, it is possible to extend and enhance our understanding of the role played by bureaucratic discretion in environmental governance at the transnational level. Slaughter (2004) famously identified regulators as the new diplomats. As members of the executive branches of various nation-states as well as technical staffs of IGOs, regulatory bureaucrats are especially well positioned to form the transnational policy networks that have become a primary focus of research in international relations. This attention is the result of several convergent factors: changes in the organization and activities of national financial regulators, the emergence of a new multilayered regulatory system among the countries in the Organisation for Economic Co-operation and Development, the development of the European Union as a concentrated site for multilevel governance, the emergence of a system of transatlantic economic cooperation, and a growing awareness of the significance of transgovernmental networks in determining the manner and degree to which governments comply with international rules (ibid., 42–44).

These factors explain not only why regulators are coming to occupy the leading role in international governance but also why legislators find themselves lagging behind. In democratic systems, legislators are directly tied to territorially defined policies by the representative nature of their function. "Remaining resolutely 'national,' or even parochial, is their job" (ibid., 105). Also, the high turnover rate among legislators gives them little incentive to invest in the long-term relationship building required for them to operate successfully as monitors of the performance of transnational bureaucratic regulators. Furthermore, almost by definition, legislators lack the kind of specialized training that would allow them to play a leadership role in regulatory decision making. The members of transnational regulatory networks are largely the product of relatively uniform professional training and socialization. They therefore are able to operate with simpler institutional processes often characterized by consensus decision making. Legislators are a far more diverse group of individuals accustomed to dealing with a highly diverse array of issues in more abstract ways in decision-making processes that tend to be highly differentiated and complex (105). It is no wonder, then, that when legislators are aggregated in regional or global assemblies, they tend to be ineffectual—precisely the kinds of bodies that "spread skepticism about international law or institutions of any kind" (106). Here we have a concise description of the circumstances that both make administrative discretion inevitable at the global level and produce the democratic deficit commonly associated with the problem of enforcing democratic accountability on regulatory bureaucrats. The scope of administrative discretion in international governance is especially broad in the environmental arena, where the external pressures for coordinated action bring to the fore regulatory actors and increase their independence (Delreux 2011).

Against this backdrop of bureaucratic forcefulness and legislative fecklessness, alarm about the dangers of an emergent global Leviathan might seem justified. Arbitrary rule by transnational technocrats—Eurocrats, according to the European popular media—is routinely offered as an example of the inevitable consequences of the democratic deficit in global governance. A closer look at the European example, though, shows just how overwrought these concerns are. First, the European Union does not tax, implement policy, or coerce its members, and spends little directly. In many areas, it does not even hold a legal monopoly of public authority. EU policymaking faces tight substantive, fiscal, administrative, legal, and procedural constraints built into the European Union's constitutional order. Even the more modest critique that absent supervision by directly elected officials, regulatory action in the European Union has become an elite-driven project that escapes democratic accountability, is exaggerated. There are multilevel constraints embedded in the European Union's constitutional order, arising from both democratic control over national governments and the growing strength of the European parliament. While it is arguable that the European parliament is still not as proactive as national legislatures tend to be, it is clearly the case that its endgame role in the EU legislative process has made its determinations far more difficult for the European Council to reject than to accept. Where neither indirect democratic control through national legislatures nor direct control by the European parliament is present (as where power is delegated to an EU level court, central bank, or other semiautonomous authority), the accompanying accountability mechanisms are not significantly inferior to those typical of most advanced industrial democracies (Moravcsik 2005). In short, existing democratic national orders are not that much better at constraining administrative discretion than the most fully developed transnational order.

Two other complaints about the democratic deficit that might accompany administrative discretion cannot so easily be dismissed. First, it has been asserted that EU decision making in general and its elitist reliance on bureaucratic regulatory networks in particular impose a neoliberal bias on national communities that have strong social democratic policy preferences (Scharpf 1999). The creation of decentralized (or perhaps decentered) market competition, it is feared, has created the incentive for a "race to the bottom" in both regulatory and social welfare policy at the nation-state level. In this view, a transnational collection of policy networks like the European Union lacks democratic legitimacy not for procedural reasons so much as substantive ones—its policies are systemically biased against particular interests consensually recognized as legitimate by the national communities from which members of those policy networks come. Critics of these perspectives have countered that there is little evidence to suggest that such a race to the bottom is actually occurring, and that in any event, such neoliberal bias as may exist at the transnational level is a product of policy developments at the national level—involving increasingly unfavorable demographic trends and changes in patterns of economic activity (Moravcsik 2005). Yet this defense clearly fails to take into account the political dynamics that played themselves out during the global recession, and ignores the extent to which national and international policy initiatives are probably codetermined by the influence of the regulatory elites that populate both transnational policy networks and national regulatory agencies.

A second democratic indictment of transnational regulatory networks is that they are part of a larger pattern (both national and international) of isolating decision making from popular political participation, and that the civic costs of this are simply too high (Weiler 1999). For example, it is argued that the development of the European Union has failed to promote transnational political parties, identities, and discourses that might render European political participation more meaningful, effective, and widespread. An opportunity thus has been missed to enhance the democratic legitimacy of transnational decision making by increasing the likelihood that its products reflect popular policy preferences.

Critics of this view have contended that unless it is based on "an ideal preference for democratic participation," it depends on "the questionable premise that a greater participation in European political institutions will generate a deeper sense of political community in Europe or, at the very least, greater popular support for the EU" (Moravcsik 2005, 235). Critics also maintain that suggestions for further democratizing the European Union, such as substituting a minimum guaranteed income for the European Union's complex of elite-designed price supports and structural funds, would increase political conflict and destabilize the institution itself (ibid., 237).

Leaving aside the dubious claim that an ideal preference for democratic participation is somehow an inappropriate guide for the project of modernity, popular participation does far more than promote some vague sense of political community. With respect to problems of environmental protection in particular, it is increasingly apparent that the democratic quality of regulatory decisions is a crucial element in their practical success. Democratic legitimacy, in short, is a key component of environmental sustainability (Baber and Bartlett 2005). Moreover, if widespread popular participation gives rise to political pressures of a genuinely democratic provenance, it is not at all clear why the unsettling result of those pressures should outweigh their inherent legitimacy. Why, to be blunt, should features of the European Union (or any other transnational order) that cannot withstand a genuinely democratic appraisal be insulated in ways that the nondemocratic features of national and subnational governments no longer are?

The problems posed by administrative discretion for global environmental governance are not so much institutional and procedural as they are normative and political. The popular image of a transnational Leviathan is hard to credit given the grudging manner in which nation-states share their competencies and responsibilities with networks of transnational regulators. Criticisms of the institutional procedures of regional organizations such the European Union tend to give those organizations insufficient credit for their subtlety as well as essential similarity to their national counterparts. Transnational policy networks are susceptible to the same Habermasian criticisms as national bureaucracies: in the absence of external normative limitations and political contestations, they tend toward predictably self-serving policies that privilege the already privileged and empower the already powerful. In the area of human rights protection, popular participation in the form of international citizens' tribunals have already proven themselves a counterbalance to that tendency—as a meaningful source of external normative and political pressure (Klinghoffer and Klinghoffer 2002). Similar "tribunals" can, as part of an integrated and participatory system of regime formation, offer similar advantages in the more prosaic field of global environmental governance.

9

Consensus, Consensual Federalism, and Juristic Democracy: A Governance System for Earth Systems

Lijphart (2008) argues that majoritarian democracy has become a Kuhnian paradigm, the flaws of which are blinding people to the potential advantages of other forms of democracy. Majoritarianism, in Lijphart's account, is more than a collection of institutions and practices. It is both a conceptual model and language of discourse through which we identify what is crucial in the political world, and constrain the way that world can be discussed. Like other conceptions of both nature and society, it serves to "shape the world to which it is applied" (Kuhn 2000, 219). As with other paradigms, majoritarianism is a discrete structure of "law, theory, application, and instrumentation" from which we construct "coherent traditions" of political practice (Kuhn 1970, 10). The dominance of majoritarianism is due, in part, to the fact that Anglo-American perspectives tend to dominate the practice of political science worldwide (ibid., 120). As with other paradigms, theoretical innovation is more likely to take place at the margins than at its core (Dogan and Pahre 1990). So it is perhaps not surprising that the most important frontal assault on the inconsistencies of majoritarianism were launched by a public choice theorist, William Riker, and the first modern theorist of consensus as a contending democratic paradigm was an economist, Arthur Lewis (Lijphart 2008, 121).

A similar circumstance exists with respect to the sovereignty of the Westphalian nation-state and its theoretical hegemony, which blinds theorists and practitioners alike to the potential of transnational governance (Baber and Bartlett 2009a). Nation-states, as it turns out, are commodious structures within which to work out the logic of majoritarianism. They are not, however, particularly good building blocks for a structure of global governance. They vary widely in the degree to which their international attitudes and actions represent the desires of their citizens in the form of fundamental international norms (Kuhnian laws). Moreover, nations and the positions that they adopt are difficult to aggregate into coherent policy models (forms of political theory and application), as the frequent futility of voting in the United Nations and collapse of the Kyoto process amply illustrate. As a result of this inability to engage in genuinely global political will formation (the joining of fundamental principle to theory and application), nation-states are limited in their ability to design policies to address global concerns. This both prevents global policy initiatives from developing and allows the failure of that effort to impose social costs on groups within global society that are least capable of bearing those costs (Baber and Bartlett 2009a). The democratic failings of global politics render the nations of the world incapable of crafting shared approaches to the implementation of policies (Kuhnian instrumentalities) that might advance their common interests through effective rule making.

The tenacity of these two paradigms, despite their increasingly evident flaws, has hamstrung theorists of both national and transnational governance, and contributed to the views that interest group liberalism is the best domestic system that we can reasonably aspire to and a serious democratic deficit in global politics is unavoidable. These two paradigms, in concert with one another, obstruct our ability to conceive of democratic forms of governance that entail more than merely giving effect to majority preferences (while providing some minimal level of protection to the rights of minorities) and can be scaled up to address transnational policy problems. These blind spots result in the difficulties of will formation, policy design, and policy implementation mentioned above.

Still, there are promising alternatives to the majoritarian and Westphalian paradigms. The work of deliberative democratic theorists offers a coherent approach to using nonmajoritarian, microdeliberative democratic techniques to develop international norms for global governance. Political actors whose primary concern is the protection of the environment are well situated to develop these forms of democratic practice because they deal with policy issues that are incontestably global in character and often grounded in empirical questions susceptible to intersubjectively reliable answers. Experience in this arena can then feed its insights back into the core concerns of security and economic development that dominate national politics as well as negotiations on the international stage. This process has the potential to improve our ability to engage in collective will formation based on shared *norms* of global governance, craft new *policy models* possessed of more genuinely democratic provenances, and approach the *implementation* of global policy in more thoroughly participatory ways (as initially outlined in chapter 2).

We do not wish to claim more for such processes than a critical reading of them would warrant. But a consociational-federal-consensual governance paradigm of democracy is far better suited to politics in the international arena than a majoritarian-unitary paradigm, and the dedicated democrat can advocate such an approach without apology. Furthermore, a consociational-federal-consensual paradigm of international democracy is institutionally adapted to the present conditions of global environmental politics—it makes virtues out of what appear to be (at least in the near term) necessities. Invocation of the concept of consensus triggers a range of doubts that are of special concern (which we explore in chapter 10). In the areas where current practice fails to satisfy the requirements of consociational federalism (direct constituent representation and judicial independence), it is relatively simple to craft mechanisms of deliberative democracy that offer the gradual development of solutions to those shortcomings and address doubts about consensus without demanding extensive procedural innovations or the creation of new transnational institutions. Positive results might not come quickly. Yet the relatively low cost of the effort and potential for a significant long-term payoff suggest that we get started.

Deliberative Formation of Global Governance Norms

The importance of formulating global environmental governance norms can be seen clearly in the special case of environmental justice issues. The parties to the obligations that comprise environmental justice can be either individuals or groups of individuals. Environmental justice claims are likely to be compound in nature—claims pressed by individuals based on wrongs that they alleged to have happened as a result of their membership in groups. Although it is possible to conceive of those obligations as quasi-contractual, it is more common that obligations of environmental justice will arise as an immediate result of some wrong that has been committed. A consequence of this tendency for the wrongs of environmental justice to be derivative of wrongful behavior rather than dependent on some prior agreement is the difficulty of separating procedure and substance in this class of disputes. So dealing effectively with problems of environmental justice will require a relatively sophisticated understanding of social and political institutions. This demand is complicated by the fact that environmental justice claims can be significantly affected by the forces of globalization. As a result, three democratic imperatives confront advocates of environmental justice. To pursue environmental justice in an age of globalization, it is critical to establish a system of normative essentials of sufficient strength to protect environmental interests that rise to the level of fundamental rights. It is also imperative to create a set of cultural institutions and social processes capable of generating the political consensus necessary to sustain a regime of environmental regulation that is both democratic in its political character and ecologically effective in practice. Finally, it is essential to protect and empower social diversity in such a way that the environmental concerns of all receive attention as environmental policies are implemented.

Citizen juries are quite able to reveal areas of transnational consensus on environmental values, usefully map areas of normative dissensus, and problematize forms of elite consensus whose democratic foundations are suspect. But assuming (not unreasonably) that merely describing the elements and limits of transnational normative consensus on environmental issues will be insufficient to change the behavior of recalcitrant nation-states, what more would the cause of environmental justice require of us in an age of globalization?

As discussed in chapter 5, for legal precepts developed in an incremental and bottom-up manner to influence the course of human events, they must become the focus of jurisgenerative politics—to reiterate, a process whereby a people engages in iterative acts of "reappropriating and reinterpreting" the guiding norms as well as principles that they share, thereby showing themselves to be "not only the *subject* but also the *author of the laws*" (Benhabib 2006a, 49; emphasis in the original). To affect the course of human events, legal precepts must be lived, not merely pronounced.

A fully developed jurisgenerative process of identifying and systematizing environmental norms would allow advocates of environmental protection across the globe to overcome the difficulties generally encountered in trying to identify domestic legal concepts with sufficient consistency and clarity to qualify them as "general principles" of international environmental law (Lutz 1976), the recognition and acceptance of which is well within the traditional practice of international tribunals. This advance would provide one point of institutional entry for direct deliberative participation of the world's citizens in the process of protecting their own environment. The discovery of a normative consensus on some basic principles of environmental protection will supply international environmental organizations with a new source of raw materials (of an unusually democratic character) to use in the process of building environmental regimes through codification and administrative rule-making processes. This can be done with considerable confidence about the value of the results. As summarized in chapter 6, rigorous empirical studies of jury performance suggest that when even highly complex problems are appropriately structured, groups of deliberating citizens are capable of arriving at reasonable resolutions that achieve high levels of consensus without losing the advantages of the diverse perspectives that they bring to those problems.

Toward a Paradigm of Consensual Federalism

In the overlap of and interactions between the majoritarian and Westphalian paradigms, politics is about majorities ruling nation-states. Any normative consensus that might exist transnationally has neither voice nor venue. Policy models can and should address only issues that arise in the national context and resonate with national populations. Whatever policy initiatives that result should have their effect through the actions of political agents (assuming a representative form of majoritarianism) at or below the national level.

From a democratic perspective, majoritarianism is tolerable where two basic conditions exist. First, majority and minority groups need to be closely enough balanced in terms of their political power that they alternate in office. Stated more generally, power disparities cannot be so significant that there is a permanent winner in the political game, or the permanent losers will withdraw (sometimes violently). Second, the polity needs to display a significant level of homogeneity. Under those circumstances, differences of political opinion vary within a relatively narrow range so that the difference between winning and losing is not intolerable (Lijphart 1984). In pluralistic polities, divided by "religious, ideological, linguistic, cultural, ethnic, or racial lines into virtually separate subsocieties," these two conditions are absent. Majority rule (the rule of the stronger), in the absence of those conditions, "is not only undemocratic but also dangerous" (ibid., 22).

Each of the functional dimensions of democratic governance, each set of institutional rules and practices, can be described as a variable ranging along a scale from majoritarian to consensual in character. So whereas there are many ways to run a democracy, all of their institutional characteristics can be organized into a two-dimensional conceptual map on which each form of democracy can be located (Lijphart 1999). Of the institutional variables that one might identify, those that concern us presently occur in two identifiable clusters—one related to consociationalism and the other to federalism.

At the domestic level, consociational democracy is characterized by the necessity of a grand coalition for the organization of executive governance and relatively high degree of cultural autonomy reserved for constituent groups. Secondary characteristics are proportionality in representative institutions and the existence of opportunities for minorities to exercise the power of veto. In varying degrees and combinations, these elements can be found in many countries that maintain democratic traditions in the face of a high level of pluralism (Lijphart 2008). They also describe reasonably well many existing international institutions and practices. International regime formation is a useful example. Legislative bargaining in majoritarian nations is designed only to produce minimum winning coalitions to meet the minimal requirements of legislative success. On the other hand, "institutional bargaining in international society normally operates under a consensus rule that gives participants an incentive to put together packages of provisions that will prove attractive to as many interests as possible" (Young 1994, 27). This process reflects the necessity of achieving a grand coalition among a large number of diverse actors whose cultural (and political) autonomy is assumed. Considered in this light, the demands of international regime negotiation that are sometimes regarded as systemic weaknesses (Susskind 1994) can be regarded as democratic adaptations to the diversity of perspectives and preferences impinging on global governance.

A second cluster of democratic variables that can take on antimajoritarian values has to do with what Lijphart (2008) portrays as the federal-unitary dimension of democracy. At the majoritarian-unitary extreme, these variables describe as system of centralized government, unicameral legislature, flexible and easily amended constitution, and absence of judicial review. At the consensual-federal extreme are systems of decentralized government, bicameral and differently constituted legislatures, rigid constitutions subject to amendment only by supermajorities, and independent courts with constitutional jurisdiction. Diverse national combinations of these elements can be observed. These characteristics are also loosely descriptive of the institutions of the global polity. The global polity is decentralized (almost to a fault), and its foundational documents are notoriously difficult to amend. There are, though, two notable qualifications that must be discussed. The closest thing to a legislature is not bicameral in any meaningful way, and the capacity of its judiciary to craft a tradition of judicial review is extremely limited.

When one considers the United Nations as an example of a legislative institution, one immediately observes a fundamental ambiguity. It is not clear whether the United Nations should be considered bicameral (with the Security Council comprising the "upper house") or unicameral (with the Security Council considered basically executive in character). But even under the charitable assumption that the Security Council is the second house of its legislature, the United Nations still fails the consociational-federal test. This is because the basis for representation in both the Security Council and General Assembly is the same: the nation-state. There is no "people's house" that corresponds to the lower houses of many parliamentary systems. This has led to occasional calls for the creation of a global assembly based on the principle of one person, one vote (Archibugi 2008).

The status of international courts is a matter of concern for democrats of all stripes. International tribunals seem to hit the limits of their capacity when they confront concrete disputes arising between national actors. International legal structures operate under rules that are sketchy, with no one really in charge of the process, and no central authority to enforce judicial decrees. The ICJ, in particular, seems incapable of rendering definitive decisions and has no power to coerce a country that refuses to accept its jurisdiction (Susskind 1994). It is difficult to imagine that courts facing such limitations could ever accomplish meaningful acts of judicial review. If one reconceptualizes international policymaking as akin to administrative rule making, however, opportunities present themselves for both enhanced democracy and improved reviewability.

It is plausible to envision a system in which transnational networks of environmental policy specialists engage in administrative rule making based on input from citizen juries convened to adjudicate hypothetical disputes—juries crafted to capture the contestations between competing norms of governance or contending models of regulatory policy. The progression from norms of governance to models of regulatory policy (constituting a process of collective will formation) would find a new democratic foundation. Where a transnational consensus on a particular regulatory issue can be discovered or built, the results are available to international tribunals for citation as a general principle of law in support of their resolution of specific environmental disputes (as a substitute for the stare decisis doctrine not formally recognized internationally). The trail of documentation created administratively by this process of will formation renders the regulatory actions of international organizations more easily susceptible to review for their consistency with democratically derived norms and principles of policy.

10

The Calculus of Consensus in Juristic Democracy: Between the Possible and Desirable

A general law, which bears the name of justice, has been made and sanctioned, not only by a majority of this or that people, but by a majority of mankind. The rights of every people are therefore confined within the limits of what is just. A nation may be considered as a jury which is empowered to represent society at large and apply justice, which is its law.
—Alexis de Tocqueville

Both democracy evangelists and democrat theorists of all stripes are eager to hear more whenever the term consensus enters into any conversation. There long have been democrats who harbored serious doubts about the possibility of achieving consensus in politics about anything other than relatively trivial matters. Perhaps the leading contemporary representative of this view is James Bohman (1996, 74), who argues that "if we accept the social facts of pluralism and deep conflict, then we must also wonder whether the scope of what is 'reasonable for all to accept' turns out to be so small as to be irrelevant for most political disagreements." There are two major foundations for these doubts. It could be asserted that modern societies are characterized by a great and growing pluralism that makes general agreement on virtually any substantive matter unattainable. Every important issue of the day can be seen to implicate social, economic, and ideological interests that can only be compromised—never genuinely reconciled. The differences of race, religion, class, and culture create the basis for deep divisions within the modern nation-state. These divides can be bridged with varying degrees of success by preference aggregation—voting of one sort or another. It is even possible, under some circumstances, to encourage citizens to bracket some of their differences enough to find areas of common ground on limited subjects. But these theorists, *pluralist skeptics*, are not encouraged by either the prospects for achieving consensus or usefulness that any achievable consensus may ultimately have.

Another group of skeptics doubts the possibility of consensus for different reasons. These theorists look at the political problems confronting the modern nation-state, and see technical and scientific issues beyond the grasp of most citizens. They point out that specialized units of government have had to be created to deal with fiscal and monetary issues, problems of environmental protection, social development, health, education, law enforcement, dispute resolution, and myriad other challenges to the social order imposed by modernity. In each of these cases, some measure of distance has been imposed between those who decide and those for who the decisions are made. These theorists, *cognitive skeptics*, contend that it could never have been otherwise. The importance of technical expertise and difficulties of social choice make the pursuit of consensus in the modern world a fool's errand, not worth pursuing in today's complex societies (Knight and Johnson 1994). These cognitive skeptics, like their pluralist colleagues, are not necessarily opponents of consensus. They simply harbor profound doubts about our ability to achieve results that would justify the name (or effort).

In much the same way that some democratic theorists question the possibility of achieving consensus, others have cast doubt on whether or not the objective itself is desirable. As with the skeptics, critics of consensus can be distinguished according to the character of their underlying concerns. Some have argued that in complex and diverse societies, any consensus is almost certainly going to come about as a result of the subjugation of one social group at the hands of another. These *pluralist critics* are sometimes the same individuals who express pluralistic skepticism about the possibility of consensus. On those occasions, one could rebuff this criticism by alleging that those leveling it are contradicting their prior skepticism. But that response is not only cheap and trivializing, it is also unpersuasive. There is nothing inconsistent about maintaining that the effort to achieve consensus will both fail in the long run yet produce a harmful and unstable ersatz version of consensus in the short run. Of course, not all pluralist critics are also skeptics. In fact, those who believe that consensus is possible can be some of its most virulent critics. Many point to (and some actually have fled from) the tyranny of political regimes that grounded their claims to power precisely on the degree to which they represented a true consensus among their citizens. The central concern for these critics is that the pursuit of consensus will overprivilege discourses that characterize a single, homogeneous public sphere wherein a dedication to rational unanimity results in the elevation of social hegemony over cultural diversity (Young 1999) along with the imposition of universal identities of rational neutrality in place of the unique and personal (Mouffe 1996).

A different concern animates *cognitivist critics* of consensus. These theorists have no doubt that consensus is possible. Indeed, they often cite compelling real-world examples—all of which lead to disastrously mistaken decisions. The primary mechanism at work is an intragroup dynamic that pushes like-minded persons into more extreme positions when they interact with one another (Sunstein 2009). Whether the context is the corporate boardroom, governmental agency leadership, or political arena, consensus is frequently a prelude to blunder. Organizations and polities of all sorts profit from the error detection service provided by dissenters (Sunstein 2003). It is not enough simply to encourage a decision-making environment marked by candor and openness to diverse perspectives, although that is essential. It is equally vital that decision makers be broken out of their information cocoons, within which they are shielded from inputs that challenge their preexisting notions. Affirmative action must be taken to challenge insular decision process and bring the sum of human knowledge to bear on the challenges confronting modern society (Sunstein 2006). The human predilection for consensus is too strong already, in Sunstein's view, and the temptation to take our ease within the comfortable confines of conventional wisdom must be resisted everywhere it is encountered.

At this point, a graphic representation of the ideas introduced so far may prove useful. The doubts that have been expressed about political consensus can be arrayed as shown in table 10.1.

It should be obvious that these forms of doubt (which often overlap) are far richer and more complex perspectives than portrayed here. Exploring how these doubts relate to the material interests, ideological commitments, ethical concerns, and religious beliefs that divide humankind would clearly require a quite-different (and probably lengthier) volume than this one, but it is possible to suggest how the juristic approach to

Table 10.1
Doubt about Political Consensus

Character of doubt	Pluralism	Cognitivism
Skepticism	Consensus impossible due to social complexity and hyper-pluralism	Consensus impossible due to the limits of rationality
Criticism	Consensus undesirable due to risks of the repression of diversity	Consensus undesirable due to risks of poor decision making

democracy responds to each of these clusters of doubt about consensus, and how those responses can provide the normative framework for an approach to earth system governance.

Responses to Doubt

The doubts about consensus that we have described raise concerns too serious for easy resolution. But the characteristics of juristic democracy offer possible responses to each of these doubts and empirical observations, and when sustained across a sufficient number of replications, constitute realistic grounds for replacing doubt with hope. For example, pluralist skeptics worry that the complexity of modern societies and depth of the conflicts that divide them are too great to allow for consensus on anything other than trivial matters. Citizen juries composed of diverse individuals nonetheless can converge on a limited set of solutions to concrete (but hypothetical) disputes. Existing research on juries in civil and criminal cases indicates that people in those roles are able to perform their deliberative duties in spite of the diverse perspectives they represent—precisely because they are selected for and freely adopt an attitude of impartiality toward their shared tasks. The results of an impartial process of resolving hypothetical disputes could eventually be aggregated into a normative framework offering basic principles for international environmental regimes that would enjoy a more distinctly democratic provenance than those that are either currently in force or under development.

Cognitive skeptics doubt the possibility of achieving political consensus on salient environmental issues because they question the capacity of humans to master the technical intricacies of the subject matter involved.

In response to this concern, juristic democracy employs many of the same techniques that judges, diplomats, and elected officials (few being technical experts) employ in reducing the cognitive demands of their work. Jury research shows that judges and juries in complex cases produce closely similar results. This is possible because the deliberative mechanisms that are brought to bear on concrete disputes simplify and structure the information with which decision makers must work. Using codes of procedure, rules of evidence, and (sometimes) special masters recruited for their technical expertise, courts are able to arrive at credible resolutions of even the most complex and data-dependent disagreements. This is possible, in part, because trial courts are not asked to generalize about the dispute resolutions that they craft. If they were, the reliance on juries would become even more significant because the legitimacy of the resulting generalizations (rules) would come immediately into question. The use of juries closes (to a significant degree) the democratic deficit that would otherwise plague courts. Juries can perform a similar function for the transnational networks of policy specialists charged with the development of global environmental regimes.

The complexity of the social world also provides the foundation for criticizing the results of consensus. Pluralist critics of consensus often do not doubt that consensus is possible. Rather, they think it generally undesirable because it is too likely to result in the repression of diversity—particularly in discrimination against historically neglected and disadvantaged groups and perspectives. But jury research suggests that representatives of minority groups and divergent viewpoints have little trouble participating effectively in real-world jury deliberations. Moreover, the deliberatively constrained environment of juries and jurylike decision environments is more amenable to minority perspectives than other existing political institutions and process that offer only unconstrained aggregation of existing political interests and preferences.

Finally, *cognitive critics* fear that group deliberations such as those used in juristic democracy run an unacceptable risk of producing incorrect decisions. The issues at hand are the problems of groupthink and the tendency of discussion among like-minded individuals to magnify their existing opinions. Yet jury research indicates that verdicts handed down by juries do not differ significantly from those of judges in the same cases. A *recursive* process like juristic democracy can eventually expose disputed issues to a far larger and more varied "cumulative jury" than can simple court proceedings. Juristic democracy is not only recursive, though; it is also *reflexive*. The results can be checked by the use of juries composed for specific analytic purposes. Juries can be composed to maximize inclusivity across any range of demographic or attitudinal variables thought to be of importance. Alternatively, juries of a highly homogeneous character can be used to see whether minority perspectives develop added content and persuasive power if they are allowed to develop in appropriately favorable circumstances. In these ways, investigators can explore the risks posed by small group dynamics to decision-making quality.

It should be remembered that the purpose in this effort is not to sample public opinion. A database of jury results would not pretend to represent environmental viewpoints in proportion to their autonomous incidence in the world population. Nor would it aspire to defuse political conflict by providing an arena in which interests and opinions can exhaust themselves, and eventually, become complacent. In short, it is not the concern of juristic democracy that all and everyone have their say; rather, it is that everything worth saying gets capably said *and heard*. That is the first and most essential requirement for the creation of any form of consensus that might reasonably claim the name.

Consensus Is Where You Find It—but What Then Have You Found?

Certain basic propositions regarding the proper handling of regulatory disputes may recur with a politically significant frequency. The popularity of these propositions may also be cross-cultural as well as largely independent of many demographic and attitudinal differences that social scientists assume are related to political ideologies and policy preferences. This is all to say that when confronted with concrete (but hypothetical) disputes over the regulation of environmental hazards, people may have less trouble finding common ground than one might expect.

What is the fundamental nature of any patterns of normative consensus that we might find? What exactly does it mean when differently situated people in different parts of the world resolve the same dispute in similar ways? If we determine that there are regulatory principles to address environmental problems that can be expected to enjoy broad popular support at the global level, how should we think about those principles? Could it be that they are evidence of a mythology so basic to the human experience that it has left its constituent elements strewn as widely as potsherds in our socioarchaeological record? Or are they even more fundamental than that? Are they evidence of something basic about the way the human mind works when confronted with concrete problems? Or finally, are these continuities actually just emergent qualities of the problems themselves? Are they nothing more than practical responses to real-world challenges that tend to recur across ages and cultures simply because they are, in fact, practical?

Having some working hypotheses regarding these questions is worthwhile for several reasons. First, this kind of inquiry may be helpful in determining how people identify and isolate the specific features of factual situations that pose normatively interesting points of decision. Second, if we better understand where the constituent elements of consensus come from, we will more easily be able to describe and characterize the "rules" that people are using to resolve the disputes presented to them. Third, knowledge of the character and source of the rules that people use to resolve disputes may allow us to better understand the ways they apply those rules to concrete situations. Fourth, a better understanding of how people apply rules to disputes should allow us to more successfully predict how they will resolve problems arising from new factual situations. Fifth, improving our knowledge of these matters should allow us to craft new systems of rules for the anticipatory resolution of disputes (or regulation) that would have a legitimate claim to democratic provenance independent of any plebiscitary or representative mechanism of opinion aggregation—a matter of considerable importance in the realm of international regime development with which we have been concerned. In the next sections, we examine three well-established explanations for the possibility of normative consensus.

Normative Consensus as Cultural Artifact

The *lawgiver* is one of the oldest themes of human mythology. The mythical character who renders decisions, according to Aesop (Gibbs 2002, no. 179), is found even in the animal kingdom:

The wolf had accused the fox of theft but the fox denied that she was guilty of the crime. The presiding judge was a monkey. Each of the plaintiffs pleaded their case and the monkey is then said to have pronounced the following verdict: "As for you, wolf, I do not believe you lost the goods claimed in your suit; as for you, fox, I am convinced you stole the goods, no matter how firmly you deny it."[1]

As is common among the lawgivers of mythology, Aesop's monkey is (wisely) skeptical of both sides. Moreover, mythological verdicts that appear nonsensical or contradictory, like the one handed down by the monkey, are common as well. Recall Solomon's threat to cleave the infant whose parentage was in dispute—a "verdict" calculated to reveal the truth hidden by the dispute rather than actually pronounce judgment on it.

This cultural meme of the wise, skeptical, and inscrutable lawgiver recurs across the length and breadth of the human experience. Sometimes the role of the lawgiver is central to a people's creation mythology. Deganawidah's Great Law united the Five Nations of the Iroquois under a huge, multicompartmented longhouse that extended from the Genesee River in the west to the Mohawk River flowing into the Hudson in the east (Smith 2005). In other traditions, the lawgiver is present both at the beginning and in the next chapter. The Hindu lawgiver, Manu, is both humanity's progenitor and its first earthly king—having stayed around after the creation to set affairs in order and save humankind from the ancient flood foretold to him by Vishnu (Klostermaier 2007). Still other traditions have stories of lawgivers who although not gods themselves, had a heavenly ghostwriter. Both Homer and Thucydides tell of Minos, who ruled Crete and the islands of the Aegean a century before the Trojan War. Some accounts portray Minos as a wise ruler who received the law every nine years in a direct audience with Zeus. Other versions paint a far less flattering portrait of a tyrant feeding young people to the monstrous Minotaur, often on the same curious nine-year schedule (Powell 1998). The mythology surrounding the person and pronouncements of Moses the lawgiver are foundational for all three of the world's major monotheistic faiths. There is no better example than this of a lawgiver myth that influences our contemporary search for normative consensus.[2]

How should we make sense of the process by which mythological themes might find their way into contemporary thinking? If we extend our thinking about Aesop's monkey-judge, we quickly recognize the archetypal character of the wise old man. More than just a stereotype or oversimplification of observed behavior, an *archetype* is a recurrent and universally understood symbol. Carl Jung, while not the first to use the concept, developed the archetype into the basis of an analytic psychology of what he termed the collective unconscious. For Jung, archetypes were universal forms (both part of our culture and transcendent) that lacked any specific content, but still channeled experiences and emotions—resulting in recognizable and typical patterns of behavior with certain probable outcomes. In fact, for Jung (1963, 106) the collective unconscious was personified by the archetype with which we are here concerned—that of the wise old man.

In contrast with the personal unconscious, which is a personal reservoir of experience unique to each individual, the collective unconscious gathers and organizes our personal experiences in similar ways for all members of our species. The archetypes of the collective unconscious must be distinguished from instincts, which Jung took to be biologically determined physical impulses toward particular behaviors. Archetypes, on the other hand, might be thought of as the psychic counterpart of instincts (Friest and Friest 2009). This understanding introduces potential confusions, however. Jung himself offered sometimes-conflicting accounts of what archetypes are. While wishing to distinguish archetypes from genetically transmitted instincts, Jung (1959, 179) argued that the transmission of a *propensity* to generate archetypal representations as unconscious organizers of our ideas was an innate (though not necessarily unique) human characteristic. While this relieved Jung of the necessity of defending archetypes as innate ideas, it was not entirely consistent with his tendency to emphasize the numinous quality of archetypal experiences, or his attraction to the idea that archetypes provide evidence of communion with some divine or world mind (Cook 1987, 405).

In the final analysis, Jung (1978, 76) remained agnostic on the question of the world mind, arguing that neither that hypothesis nor its refutation could be proven. This was probably inevitable given the weight that the archetypes and collective unconscious were to carry in his system of thought. It would not have served his professional interests to alienate either side of that dispute. It is tempting for us to follow his lead, in spite of the fact that there are those who believe that the environmental community has much to be gained from pursuing a Jungian sort of mysticism (Sabini 2002). Given the narrowness of our present interests, though, another course is open to us. Without asserting that there is a mystical communion among all sentient beings (or denying that contention), someone interested only in explaining the fact that humans seem to show a "quasi-instinctual" understanding of the need to resolve disputes under law can look more closely at what sentience itself entails.

Sentience is an unusually important concept in the history of environmentalism. At least since the time of Jeremy Bentham ([1823] 2011), the notion that nonhuman animals share our experiences of pain and pleasure has been used to promote a sentiocentric moral perspective. More recently, sentiocentrism has become a primary challenge to anthropocentrism. In the hands of Tom Regan (2004) and Peter Singer (2009), the logic of this argument leads to a full-blown case for the vegan lifestyle and animal liberation. But we need not take sentiocentrism so far. It is possible to focus more narrowly on the character of sentience as demonstrated by humans. If we take sentience to be the quality that earns other beings a place among our moral concerns, it is worth describing that concern more explicitly. Our sentience, our sense of ourselves as beings with experiences to which we can attach meaning, enables us to see that quality in others. Indeed, an *inability* to see ourselves in others is generally taken to mark one as a sociopath—a personality fundamentally disordered by the inability to form a social identity.

Furthermore, an essential element of the capacity to see ourselves in others is the ability to appreciate that our motives and desires are likely to come into conflict with those of others—necessitating the rule-governed resolution of interpersonal disputes. While it is possible to resolve disputes by force or fiat, a being who can see itself in the others it interacts with will be motivated to avoid those options in favor of rule-governed dispute resolution. This motivation will arise from the recognition that the only genuine solution to interpersonal conflict is a system of rules grounded in reciprocity—a system in which "the foreseeable consequences and side effects of its general observance for the interests and value-orientations of *each individual* could be jointly accepted by *all* concerned without coercion" (Habermas 1998, 42; emphasis in the original). The reciprocity of rule-governed interaction is what marks out the territory of the normative—that realm within which it make sense to describe an action as both free and intentional, on the one hand, and obligatory, on the other. It is this reconciliation of the free and obligatory that sentient beings seek in their interaction with others.

Rule-governed actions as we have described them are not mere behavior, determined either by our genetic makeup or the necessities of our physical environment. Neither are they purely cultural in the sense that they are contingent features of a particular way of life. They are implicit in the human capacity for communicative action (Habermas 1979). In the context of Aesop's fable, both the wolf and fox recognize their need for the monkey to adjudicate their dispute. For his part, the monkey recognizes the futility of adjudicating a dispute in which both parties have dirty hands (or in this case, paws). But from Aesop's perspective, what we can see is the universal and eternal form of the lawgiver as the wise old man as well as the inevitably quizzical nature of his wisdom. We can also see that the archetype of the lawgiver and other instances of normatively governed action, too, are more than mere products of culture. Rather, they are *characteristics of culture as such*. These features of human existence, Aesop, Jung, and Habermas might have agreed, are so fundamental that to ask whether or not they are inherited or learned misses the point. They are simply expressions of who and what sentient beings are (and must be) in the world. The myths that surround these elements of our existence are nothing more (or less) than the stories we must tell ourselves about ourselves.

Consensus as the Intersection of Individual Ideas

At this juncture, the reader might be forgiven for having the sense of having been through the looking glass. The world of the collective unconscious, as Jung describes it to us, is truly a wonderland—stocked with mythical and often-nonsensical characters who seem to evaporate if we question them too closely. These archetypal characters are not the creation of any individual author. They are instead necessary elements of any culture that could be created by sentient creatures like ourselves—creatures who must lead emotional lives characterized by at least a minimal level of organization and order. If this in any way is an accurate portrait of the moral universe in which we live, it would not be surprising if we found some level of concurrence in how people resolved disputes that were hypothetical, that touched their emotional structures only as simple narratives. One might expect to see the Cheshire grin of an archetype of the collective unconscious against precisely this sort of sparse background (if we were ever to see it at all).

Yet an alternative interpretation of moral consensus can be explored on this side of the looking glass. This construal focuses our attention on the consciously developed ideas of individuals along with the possibility that those ideas might cohere in widely supported resolutions to either interpersonal or political disputes. The thesis would be that there is some quality of individual human beings (as opposed to the cultures they create) that lead them to shared moral perspectives. There are at least three venues in which we might look for the source of moral commonality. First, there is the possibility that humans share some sort of *moral sense* that leads them to find similar solutions to a given problem. It also may be that there is some feature of our *moral psychology* that leads us to reason about normative issues in coherent ways. Third, it may be that the very way we articulate moral problems, our *moral language*, promotes consensus among individuals on normative principles.

The chief exponents of the moral sense (in Western philosophy) are David Hume and Adam Smith. They both came to the topic at a time when the scholarly disciplines were freeing themselves from the domain of religion and advancing naturalistic explanations for the questions that concerned them. Once it became possible to put forth a secular answer to a question of physics, it was only a matter of time before other scholars began to claim and exercise the same privilege. But even those who were open to natural explanations for physical and biological processes and events had some trouble imagining how defending the good as well as opposing evil could be possible without God. One response was that human beings are endowed (by their creator perhaps) with a moral sense that allows them to identify the good, and that this sense was subject to investigation like any other. Hume was the most prominent advocate of this view.

Book 3 of Hume's ([1740] 2011, [1759] 2006) *Treatise of Human Nature* and later *An Enquiry concerning the Principles of Morals* advanced the notion that humans possess a moral sense analogous to our senses of sight, sound, and so forth. A careful explication of this perspective would require a far lengthier discussion than can be provided here, but an analogy may prove useful. Each of us (absent illness, accident, or birth defect) has a sense of hearing. We all can, for instance, hear the first four notes of Ludwig von Beethoven's *Fifth Symphony*. Nevertheless, hearing is not identical with the aesthetic sense of music. Even the youngest child can recognize that the first four notes are music and something more is likely to follow. As we grow older, most of us come to understand the first four notes for what they are and form an appreciation of the larger work of which they are a part. Occasionally, someone will find in just such a small fragment of music connections to Greek poetry, the French Revolution, and the very wellsprings of the human imagination (Guerrieri 2012). Where along that progression one might be said to have developed an aesthetic sense of music is, of course, debatable. What is beyond dispute is that the inherent ability to hear discrete sounds and, eventually, identify them as intentionally arranged musical notes is a nearly universal capacity among humans. It is a relatively short step on from there to develop distinct likes and dislikes in music, as our innate capacity combines with experience. Developing that aesthetic sense is almost involuntary.[3] It is an apt analogy for the development of the moral sense that Hume described.

Smith advances a somewhat-different view of the human moral sense, in which moral judgment is a more or less immediate, visceral reaction to an observed or experienced set of circumstances rather than an elemental human capacity that requires prolonged cultivation. Thus, moral judgments are less the product of a single moral sense than they are a collection of moral sentiments extending across a range of moral concerns. The largest part of Smith's ([1759] 2000) *The Theory of Moral Sentiments* is given over to the project of cataloging these sentiments and discussing the effect of external circumstances (fortune, utility, custom, and fashion) on them. The linchpin of Smith's theory, however, is *sympathy*—our capacity to identify with the passions of others and experience a sense of fellow feeling with them. Sympathy gives rise to our sense of the propriety and merit in the actions as well as affections of others. It allows us to condemn wrongdoers while identifying with the outrage and demands for justice of their victims. It even allows us to feel an appropriate passion regarding others who do not feel it themselves, as when we are embarrassed for the boorish guests who are unaware of their own impropriety. It is on the basis of these moral sentiments that we ultimately develop our views of what is praiseworthy and blameworthy, what justice and beneficence require, and how transgressions of the moral order should be dealt with.

Between the empirical version of moral intuitionism espoused by Hume and the moral sentimentalism of Smith, there is much to choose. Hume's single moral capacity grounds judgments of all sorts across the entire range of normative concerns in a unitary intuitive sense that can stand alone as a simple element of human nature. One can then adopt one's own account of its origin, either biblical or Darwinian as the spirit moves. On Smith's account the moral sense is more complicated, and for that reason, harder to attribute to a single source. From where do all of these moral sentiments come? If in our increasingly secular age we discount the possibility that each of these sentiments was planted in the human heart by an all-knowing gardener with a superabundance of time and patience, how did all these sentiments evolve? Smith took great pains to minimize the problem, getting as much moral judgment as possible out of as few basic sentiments as he could manage. But in the hands of those who pursue the study of moral psychology, this kind of self-denial is no virtue. The freedom to roam the vast and varied landscape of human moral judgment is a paramount value.

Moral psychology is both a novel field within psychology and inchoate discipline in its own right, exploring the intersection of ethics, psychology, and philosophy of the mind. It takes as its major topics the formation of moral identity, source and efficacy of moral values, process of moral reasoning, and phenomena of moral behavior. The scholar most widely identified with this field of research is Lawrence Kohlberg (1981, 1984), who used hypothetical moral dilemmas to explore the development of moral reasoning in children and young adults In Kohlberg's view, our capacity for moral reasoning develops along a definable trajectory as we gain both formal education and experience in the world. The mechanism of this moral growth is a process of cognitive–moral conflict that takes place as an individual's beliefs are challenged by their peer group, leading to reflective reorganization that in turn leads the individual from less mature stages of moral development to greater moral sophistication. The organizing value throughout this process is, according to Kohlberg, a core commitment to the idea of justice.

Kohlberg's perspective is not without its critics, of course. Most of these fault Kohlberg for an alleged monological orientation. Chief among these critics is Jonathan Haidt (2001), who complains that Kohlberg's emphasis on moral reasoning does little to explain why people actually engage in what they (and we) might regard as moral behavior. The focus on reasoning distracts us from the complex of emotions and intuitions that are required to form a moral will—a determination to act on our moral precepts. In Haidt's view, sometimes described as social intuitionist, models of moral reasoning are post hoc rationalizations that subjects use to justify their instinctual reactions and that experiments rely on to simplify their analysis. Haidt and his colleague Jesse Graham dissect Kohlberg's master value of justice, producing five substantive dimensions of morality (harm/care, fairness/reciprocity, in-group/loyalty, authority/respect, and purity/sanctity). These dimensions of morality are then used to define competing moral identities, described as "liberal" and "conservative" (Haidt and Graham 2007). This research found that liberals accord justice and its related values a more prominent place in their moral world, and that they value the harm/care and fairness/reciprocity dimensions of justice more highly that do conservatives.

Lest psychology be accused of straying into politics at this point, it is worth considering other research suggesting that moral psychology is driven by something more than an instinct to do justice. Carol Gilligan and Jane Attanucci (1988) conducted experimental work identifying a fundamental alternative to Kohlberg's justice perspective, which they call the care perspective. Using content analysis of narrative responses to moral situations, Gilligan and Attanucci found that a majority of participants in their study employed both the Kohlberg justice perspective and their own care perspective. Furthermore, they discovered that men were prone to rely more on the justice view whereas for women the care perspective loomed larger. One need not engage in gender essentialism to conclude from this that prior research on moral reasoning, to the extent that it focused (as Kohlberg's work did) on males, may have overlooked important variances in patterns of moral reasoning. If we are uncomfortable with the gendered version of this phenomenon, we always have resort to William James's ([1907] 1995, 4) gender-neutral distinction between basic orientations that he characterized as the "tender-minded" and "tough-minded" views of reality.

It is frustrating, from the vantage point of the moral psychology researcher, that James turned his attention to these concerns only late in life. The work for which he is most widely known and appreciated, *The Principles of Psychology* (James [1890] 1990), is nearly silent on the subject. It is possible, however, to tease some of his thinking on the subject out of that massive work. It is revealing that when James does take up the subject of moral principles (if only briefly), he discusses them in connection with aesthetic principles. An aesthetic principle—such as that a note sounds good with its third and fifth—can be explained to some degree as a habitual response. But to explain aesthetic principles entirely in this way would be absurd. James (ibid., 886; emphasis in the original) asks us to consider, "How seldom natural experiences come up to our aesthetic demands.... [The] "*moral* principles which our mental structure engenders are quite as little explicable *in toto* by habitual experiences having bred inner cohesion."

Occurrences common enough to give rise to the linguistic evidence of habitual ways of thought, "popular rhetorical maxims," rarely confront us with serious moral challenges. Moral problems arise from the "unprecedented cases and lonely emergencies" that challenge our "hidden oracle" to speak, "often in favor of conduct quite unusual" and quite unlikely to gain "popular approbation" (886–887). Returning to the language of the musical example of aesthetic principles, James concludes, "No more than the higher musical sensibility can the higher moral sensibility be accounted for by the frequency with which outer relations have cohered" (887). As a result, our moral thinking and actions do not enjoy the same benefit as other realms of human interaction, in which we can rely on a "delicate and incessant" recognition by the mind of the fitness of our use of language. The hazard is not that we will miss errors because we fail to notice discordant or nonsensical assertions. Rather, it is that "sentences with absolutely no meaning may be uttered in good faith and pass unchallenged" merely because their grammar as well as vocabulary are correct—like the "reshuffling of the same collection of cant phrases" at prayer meetings (170).

If, in fact, moral consensus is at least sometimes the product of some quality of sentience (as opposed to a cultural artifact or stimulus–response feature of our interaction with the environment), it presents us with the challenge of avoiding essentialism. Whatever that quality might be, we cannot fall into the trap of assuming that the way it manifests itself is somehow inevitable. Even if the quality of sentience is universal, its products are always going to be contingent—sometimes almost to the point of being unrecognizable.

The notion that we may not be able to rely on moral principles that we have accumulated by long experience and processed through our innate capacity for moral reasoning, and that our discourses on these subjects may betray us at the critical moment, raises a final topic worthy of brief discussion: moral language. R. M. Hare's (1952) analysis of moral language serves as an inescapable reference point.

Hare's *The Language of Morals* is a central text in twentieth-century metaethics.[4] The book is the most general statement of his attempt to develop a form of noncognitivism that accounts for the phenomena of ordinary moral language and argument. But Hare's methods and concerns are different from those of other contemporary metaethicists. His is an argument from the high tide of linguistic philosophy. Hare advances the view that metaethics has one subject: the nature and structure of moral language. His central contention is that moral language should be understood as no more (or less) than one form of prescriptive language. What is characteristic of prescriptive language is its connection to action; there is a conceptual connection between how an agent uses prescriptive language and their motives to act in certain ways.

Hare's analysis starts with the least complicated form of prescriptive language: the language of imperatives. In the first part of his book (chapters 1–4), Hare discusses the proper analysis of imperative language: how we can see it as meaningful, how we can reason about imperatives, how imperatives can stand in logical relations to one another, and so forth. By discussing the logic of imperatives, Hare hopes to suggest that noncognitivism can meet certain traditional objections made against it: that it cannot allow for any sort of moral reasoning, cannot allow for logical relations between moral sentences, and turns ethical language into mere irrational "sounding off." Hare moves on to a substantive account of evaluative language. He offers a purely formal account of moral language according to which there are no content restrictions on what can count as a moral claim. According to Hare, moral claims are universalizable prescriptions. They are universalizable in that an agent must be willing to apply them to all cases that are alike in all the relevant respects. They are prescriptive because sincere moral claims always imply imperatives, and sincerely accepting an imperative involves being motivated to act on it.

Hare does not think that there is a total disconnect between moral (imperative) and nonmoral (descriptive) language. One way that the moral and nonmoral are connected is that moral evaluations are made in response to nonmoral facts. People appeal to nonmoral facts as a reason to hold certain moral evaluations, and must do so since there is a specific requirement that universalizability places on moral judgments; necessarily, if you judge that something is good, you must judge that anything similar in all relevant nonmoral respects is good. Still, Hare denies that we can infer moral facts from nonmoral ones. In addition to one's own views about nonmoral facts, a person has to accept certain principles about the connection between the moral and nonmoral in order to draw a moral conclusion. There is also a link between the descriptive and evaluative meaning expressed in moral claims. Given widely accepted standards, the use of moral language will often convey nonmoral information. There can be a close connection between making certain moral and nonmoral claims, and this is something people know. So at least in particular groups, there are commonly (and often-hidden) descriptive criteria for the application of moral language. Part of the information conveyed in moral discussion, then, is descriptive meaning—but it is secondary to the evaluative meaning. It is always possible for the moral language to retain its evaluative meaning, the primary component, despite a change in or distortion of its descriptive meaning.

This recognition of the special, sometimes-problematic use of moral language among specific groups allows us to make better sense of James's account of the tender-minded and tough-minded approach to moral problems (not to mention the liberal and conservative mind-sets described by moral psychology), and place those conflicting modes of thinking into context. Does it not lead us to ask, "Ought not the existence of the various types of thinking, … each so splendid for certain purposes, yet all conflicting still, and neither of them able to support a claim of absolute veracity, to awaken a presumption favorable to the pragmatistic view that all of our theories are instrumental, are mental models of adaptation to reality, rather than revelations or gnostic answers to some divinely instituted world-enigma?" (James [1907] 1995, 74). Perhaps at long last, we might decide that there are times when it makes sense to demoralize (as we have tried to demythologize) normative consensus?

Normative Consensus as Practical Solutions

A complete departure from the conjectures about normative consensus explored so far is idea that the consensus we tend to find in adjudication is normative in only a limited sense. When a native fisherman tells us that we should stab our spear somewhere other than where the fish appears to be, he is neither communicating a mythical imperative from the darkest reaches of antiquity nor urging on us a moral conviction that fish should be given a fighting chance. He is simply telling us what he has learned from experience: that water distorts the perception of where the fish is, and that if we want fish for dinner, we should take that into account. Stripped of whatever cultural or political adornments they might collect over time, is it possible that many of the normative precepts on which people find themselves in agreement, and on which we rely in adjudicating disputes, are actually of this sort? Might they be no more than pragmatic rules of action that have achieved cultural or political significance precisely because they are so useful?

It is not difficult to find examples of practical rules so overlaid with cultural connotations that the practical reasons for them have become obscured. Two of the most common taboos (so common that Sigmund Freud took them to be universal) are the proscriptions against incest and patricide. The nearly universal revulsion at incest may well be the result of an ancient understanding that intercourse among close relatives is likely to produce ill-favored offspring. The taboo against patricide, strong as its cultural value may be, has obvious practical value for any father who wonders what use his children will see for him in his dotage. There are many other such instances of rules of human conduct so venerable that their original source is no longer known—if it ever was. Our central concern, however, is the circumstance in which normative consensus seems to emerge regarding the allocation of environmental risks and benefits, and whether that sort of consensus can be explained in purely pragmatic terms.

Many such venerable rules play a role in systems that have been referred to as chthonic law—as discussed in chapter 3, ancient systems of law centered on the sacred character of the cosmos (Glenn 2010). The chthonic legal tradition emerged from the most basic of human experiences, primarily with the development of human morality and memory, and was understood as the law of a culture or tribe. From a perspective such as this, it should not be surprising that people from different cultures often resolve environmental disputes in similar ways. They are able, Glenn would argue, to draw on basic precepts of fairness and justice that order their thinking in ways of which they are largely unaware. These ordering precepts continue to structure our thinking not so much because they are grounded in recognized authority but instead because our ancestors found them to be pragmatically useful.

Assuming that Glenn is correct, and that much of the way we respond to concrete disputes relies on traditional and pragmatic principles, how would those precepts express themselves in systems of regulatory rules if such systems were allowed to develop of their own accord? Put differently, can we cite examples of successfully operating systems of environmental governance that rely neither on the wisdom of central governance nor the benevolence of markets? Although it would be foolish to assert that the good people of the earth will reliably husband their resources if they are only left to do it, it is not difficult to offer cases of precisely that kind of successful self-regulation and draw some conclusions about the conditions that promote just such success.

Elinor Ostrom's research is an effort to overcome the assumption that only through either state- or market-centered environmental controls can commonly pooled resources (CPRs) be effectively governed. She writes, "Communities of individuals have relied on institutions resembling neither the state nor the market to govern some resource systems with reasonable degrees of success over long periods of time" (Ostrom 1990, 1). Ostrom's challenge, and ours, is to discover why some groups are able to effectively govern and manage CPRs through consensual arrangements developed over time while other groups are never able to do so.

Both state-based command-and-control systems and privatized property rights regimes are, in Ostrom's (ibid., 1–28) view, likely to prove inadequate over time. Central governmental authorities frequently fail to have the complete and accurate information that their task requires, have only limited monitoring capabilities, and possess a weak sanctioning reliability. For these reasons, a centralized body is likely to govern the commons ineptly and may make bad situations worse. In the case of privatized property rights regimes, Ostrom illustrates two main points. First, they generally assume that property is homogeneous and any division of property will be equitable. This assumption is rarely borne out. Second, privatization will not work with nonstationary "property" (fisheries, say).

Ostrom's diagnosis of the failings of command-and-control regulation and private property regimes, telling as it is, does not commit her (or us) to any particular policy response. Recalling that our objective is to understand instances of naturally occurring consensus on regulatory principles, the tack Ostrom takes is appealing. After discussing the failings of state-controlled and privatization property rights regimes, she examines the circumstances of successful CPR governance. As a representative of the "new institutionalist" school, Ostrom concentrates on the rules, structures, and frameworks within the various CPR governance structures found in real-world cases of self-organized regulation. In the course of this work, she has identified a number of "design principles" within the successful CPR governance cases. They include a clear definition of boundaries; congruence between appropriation and provision rules and local conditions; collective choice mechanisms; a system of monitoring and graduated sanctions; mechanisms controlled by the appropriators used to mediate conflict and, when necessary, change the rules; a recognition of the right to organize; and the use of interdependent, and multilayered "nested" enterprises (88–102).

Ostrom suggests that these design principles form a coherent and cooperative institutional structure. If the correct institutions are in place, the players will see cooperation as the best means to gain optimal outcomes. They will, in other words, arrive at rules for collective self-governance that are mutually agreeable *and* pragmatically useful. Mechanisms of this sort create confidence between players that defections will be minimal and that those who defect will be sanctioned appropriately. Additionally, these institutional structures create an environment in which resources are distributed in such a way that all (or at least most) players benefit. As such, many of these institutional arrangements must be accompanied by a good deal of trust between players. This can only be developed over time and is most likely to succeed when the number of players in the CPR is reasonably small, as is the case among Glenn's people of the earth. For this reason, most of the exemplars that Ostrom offers of such self-generating environmental governance take place in regional and local contexts of traditional societies—where the distinction between a normative rule and a pragmatic one is of less importance than the fact that people grow up knowing how to both spear a fish and preserve a fishery.

Deploying the Models of Consensus

Earlier, we listed five reasons why it would be worthwhile to better understand the source and character of any naturally occurring consensus about environmental governance that researchers might find. For starters, that inquiry might show how people identify and isolate the specific features of factual situations that create points of normative decision (*issues*). Two, understanding where normative consensus comes from may help us to describe and characterize the "rules" that people are using to resolve environmental disputes (*rules*). Three, knowing the character and source of the rules people use to resolve disputes may allow us to better understand the ways that they apply those rules to concrete situations (*application*). Four, an understanding of how people apply rules to disputes should allow us to predict how they will resolve new problems as they are encountered (*conclusions*). And finally, all these improvements in our understanding of normative consensus should allow us to craft new systems of global environmental governance that would have a legitimate claim to democratic provenance, even absent the electoral and legislative elements commonly associated with democracy at the state level (*system*). In turning attention back to those issues, it may be useful to focus on a specific example of normative consensus.

Hypothetical disputes between three fictional countries that share a fictional river border are presented in appendixes B and C. One of these countries is a fully developed, first world nation. The second country has a fast growing economy, but is not yet rich. The third country is relatively impoverished and largely agrarian. One scenario has the first two countries threatening a fishery by raising the river's temperature through the discharge of warm water from geothermal electric-generating plants. The "briefs" filed by each of these countries parallel the arguments both for and against extending the Kyoto Protocol. The developed country acknowledges primary responsibility for the river warming, but insists that each country's remediation obligation (regardless of its state of economic development) should be roughly proportionate to its contribution to the problem. The second country, whose geothermal industry is younger, wants the more developed country to bear a larger share of the remedial burden so that its economic development goals can still be pursued. The poorest of these three neighbors asks that the other two remediate the problem sufficiently that a set-aside for its own future development can be created.

Responses to this problem by deliberators can vary to some degree. But certain, more or less consensual precepts are likely to emerge. Participants can accept or reject the basic concept of common but differentiated responsibility. Citing responsibility (or blame) for the problem as well as the capacity to solve it, they can apportion most of the remedial burden to the fully developed nation. The ideas that any country should stand outside the regulatory system or that environmental remediation should be conflated with economic development probably will generally be rejected. In particular, the suggestion that nations should be allowed to do more damage than they currently do is likely to enjoy little support. Side agreements that provide nonpolluting economic development options may emerge alongside the "common" element of common but differentiated responsibility. What can the cultural, psychological, and pragmatic models of consensus tell us about the issues, rules, applications, conclusions, and systematizations likely to be involved in deliberating the resolution of this along with other such scenarios?

The cultural or mythological account of consensus would suggest that our respondents may access any one of several narratives to help them identify the issues in the dispute. The obvious candidate would be a narrative of fundamental fairness, accounting for both the emphasis on responsibility for the problem as well as the superior problem-solving capacity of the developed nation. Alternately, a narrative of shared fate or collective destiny may be at work. It may also be that a narrative of reciprocity is encouraging participants to imagine themselves in the place of each of the litigants.

Keeping all of these possibilities in mind is important in determining how to frame a rule that would both account for these verdicts and do justice to the cultural values underlying them. For instance, a rule that centered exclusively on retribution against those responsible for an environmental problem might explain these verdicts reached by our jurors and yet likely would offend many of their fundamental normative commitments. To see more vividly how this could be the case, consider the challenge involved in the application of rules of conduct.

The way that we apply any general rule that we might formulate should take account of the multiple narratives about the role that our adjudicators may imagine themselves to be playing. Given the ambiguities of the situation, are they not less likely to imagine themselves as merely looking for a threshold of responsibility than they are to think that they are trying to apply a balancing test to a complex set of competing equities? Are they not more likely to think of themselves as playing the role of mediator in an attempt to restore the conditions of neighborly conduct than to envision themselves administering strict justice in order to punish and deter?

Next, we might ask how powerful are the conclusions that have been reached by our adjudicators? Using a cultural framework, is it not likely that our adjudicators' perspective on the problem at hand is so narrative dependent that even small changes in the facts may make a significant difference in their decisions? If this is true, then the regulatory system we develop is likely to be dense, detailed, and developmental. Many rules of relatively limited application will have to be addressed to a vast array of problems that probably cannot be grouped into a manageably small number of categories. For that reason, our regulatory activity will likely produce an ever-growing web of rules in a constant state of revision.

What, then, does our psychological account of normative consensus indicate about the patterns of normative agreement that we have described? We begin with the premise of Herbert Simon (1996): a human as a behaving system is relatively simple, and the complexity we think we see in human behavior is merely a reflection of the environment. To the extent that is the case, it should be possible to isolate the psychological mechanisms that in the presence of any given pattern of stimuli, produce the consensual response that we seek to explain. Pared of its factual adornments, the issue presented to adjudicators is one of externalities being inflicted by one party on another through the former's exploitation of a common pool resource as a pollution sink. The polluter is being held primarily responsible for remediating the damage, on the basis of a rule that best can be summarized as "polluter pays."

This is the kind of rule that we might expect from any person favored by normal psychological development. It is the product of a fairly simple process of moral reasoning in which a transgression produces a harm that must be remediated by the transgressor. The apparent complications and qualifications noted in the various verdicts are merely decision noise created by the uncertain application of the rule to a complex fact situation. This can be most easily remedied not by the proliferation of first-order rules of obligation but rather by the development of secondary rules that guide legal specialists in dealing with the theoretical niceties of how first-order rules should be concretized (Hart 1994). To the degree that when this process occurs at the international level it suffers from a democratic deficit, the fault lies in the weaknesses of the processes of international legislation and will formation—the problem, in short, is political, not legal.

Once the needed secondary rules are crafted, it will be possible for a relatively small number of primary rules of obligation to guide the process of drawing conclusions about newly arisen factual circumstances. Only the factual features of the original case that were critical to its outcome need be found in a new case for the logic (the rule) of the former case to apply. This approach will obviously allow for an easier route to the systematization of law, which can take on the form of a hierarchy in which the few necessary primary rules will be supplemented as required with inferior rules that draw their legitimacy from the master rules whose administration they support.

Finally, our pragmatic interpretation of normative consensus presents a third possible analysis. The issues at hand have largely to do with the political unsustainability of the resource exploitation involved. A river is a complex CPR. It serves a large variety of needs for those who live along its course, and none of these can reasonably be subordinated to the others when there is a net cost to participants in the community. Unilateral appropriation of the resource as opposed to any specific use is the key problem. The solution, the rule if you will, is for the members of the community to reassert their beneficial interest in the resource and insist that its exploitation be brought into a recognizably equitable alignment.

The rule, equitable use, is nearly as simple as that produced by the psychological model (remediation by transgressors). It is at the level of application that complexities enter. In applying a rule of equitable use, complicating factual circumstances cannot merely be pruned away until the bare form of the transgressor is revealed. Use will always be equitable (or not) and politically sustainable (or not) within a fact-rich context. The conclusions that one draws from an application of that rule will always reflect the variations of the circumstances in which the rule is applied. So the systemization of the regulatory regime will resemble neither the weaving of a web nor raising of a pyramid. Instead, it will involve the construction of a network—with major conceptual nodes at the places where concepts of basic fairness and products of moral reasoning intersect with practical problems like those involved in watershed management.

The Wolf, Fox, and Monkey on the Road from Kyoto

The mythical courtroom where the wolf and fox submit themselves to the sound discretion of the monkey might be taken as another form of the story of the boy who cried wolf. Both of the litigants here have dissembled so often that neither can expect to be believed. Still, this moral is useful only if we care about the complaints that the wolf or fox might advance about the action of the court—an action about which Aesop is less than forthcoming. For the monkey to simply to decline to enter judgment (as the monkey appears to have done) leaves the fox at liberty, which is either just or unjust. It cannot be both, any more than both of the women who argued before Solomon for custody of the child could really have been the mother. This inelegant and ultimately unsatisfying outcome suggests that there may be more to the fable.

The wolf and fox are both committing a wrong against the court by arguing their case to it in the first instance. As the monkey correctly observes, both present themselves for judgment with dirty paws. Both have committed, at one time or another, all the calumnies that they allege against the other. It is an abuse of the judicial process to appear in such a stance, and the fact that refusing judgment appears to favor the fox in this case is mere coincidence. The monkey's "rule" might (and probably will) cut in the other direction when the two appear next.

If this is a more satisfying moral to Aesop's fable, what can it tell us about the normative consensus that our research has begun to reveal? In our hypothetical, as in the world of climate change politics, there are only two sorts of actors. On the one hand, there are those who have contributed much to the problem. On the other hand, there are those who have either contributed something less or would dearly like to contribute something in the future. No party who comes to the court of international public opinion to argue this question comes with clean hands.

Juries have entered verdicts that best can be characterized as efforts to provide some relief to the least guilty parties while addressing the underlying environmental challenge in what is, by their lights, the most reasonable method available. Whatever else might be said of these results, it seems clear that people respond to the challenges of global environmental governance with a good faith effort to find the cultural, personal, and pragmatic grounds that might unite us, rather than focusing on the ethnic, ideological, and political differences that so often divide us. As those who represent the world's citizens in the climate change forum undertake a do-over, it would be well for them to contemplate this before beginning to monkey about again.

Having already argued that moral consensus is at least possible, it remains only to deal with the question of whether moral consensus is desirable. The three views of moral consensus presented above (cultural, psychological, and pragmatic) allow us to do so. If moral consensus, where it exists, is either a cultural artifact or a constituent element of sentience, then the question of its desirability is moot. Humans will, on at least some occasions, find themselves in agreement because the problem at hand touches on an experience so universal that humans have always had a relationship to it or because fundamental features of human consciousness are manifesting themselves as collective choices among behavioral alternatives. If consensus is either cultural or psychological, then it is (at least from time to time) inevitable.

If instead consensus is a result of pragmatic responses to environmental challenges, responses that recur across cultures and populations precisely because they work, then our conclusion is somewhat different. In this case, consensus is desirable because it has practical value—survival potential, to borrow a Darwinian concept. This does not mean that consensus decisions cannot be mistaken. It is only to suggest that instances of consensual error tend to be self-correcting insofar as they are not reinforced. They are, so to speak, unsuccessful adaptations. That being the case, consensual mistakes may recur simply because they are plausible mistakes to make. We would expect to find them infrequently preserved—either in our mythology or genes. This insight is useful for at least two reasons. First, it gives us some basis for optimism about the prospects for our species. Second and perhaps more important, it gives us homework. If the human mind is indeed a mirror in which we can perceive nature in all its complexity, then philosophers and social scientists have a useful purpose to fulfill. It falls to them to continually inspect, maintain, and polish that instrument so that its reliability can be enhanced and its practical value can be maximized (Rorty 1979). Only in that way can mistakes come to be seen as less plausible choices.

A Final Thought

As the social sciences emerged as distinct empirical inquiries, they came to revolve around three questions that seem to lie near the heart of humankind's fundamental concerns. Whether the questions are posed individually, globally, or at some level in between, human beings have long sought to understand who they have been, who they are now, and who they may become in the future. How one answers those questions can have a great deal to do with how one evaluates the human condition and prospect—with the concept of consensus playing a key role. For instance, one's historical perspective may include an account of a shared human identity grounded in a basic consensus about our place in the universe and our relationships with each other. The gradual decline of any such consensus under the attack of modernity may constitute one's view of the present. A pessimistic conception of our future may be based on the assumption that modernity's attack on what remains of our common understandings will likely prove fatal to everything that has ever united us.

In the alternative, a Hobbesian perspective on human history may celebrate the fact that a growing consensus about the necessity of mutual assistance and cooperative effort has allowed us to escape a past in which life was destined to be poor, nasty, brutish, and short. Our present circumstance, through this lens, is not yet characterized by complete social consensus. But extremism, it could be argued, has come to be seen as a negative influence on human welfare to such an extent that consensus building is now regarded as a social good and praiseworthy objective. This essentially progressive view of our present provides the natural foundation for an optimistic perspective about a future in which human disagreements become largely practical (rather than normative) in character, and are subject to resolution by reference to the increasingly sophisticated (and widely accepted) understandings of the social and natural sciences.

The counterpoint of these two vantage points certainly suggests that the concept of consensus could be of critical importance to human beings and their future. Moreover, to the hopeful Hobbesian it also indicates that activity in the international public sphere—marked as it is by an unavoidable search for consensus—may actually lead the way toward more just and democratic resolutions of human disputes, and that it does not have to continue to labor under a democratic deficit. That may be especially true with respect to the discussion of environmental issues, where the fruits of both the natural and social sciences can be brought to bear on processes of solving concrete problems in ways that increasingly square with our basic instincts about right and wrong. An integral component of humanity's refinement of its moral capacities may be our exploration of the normative dimensions of earth system governance.

Appendix A: Using Specific Deliberative Judgments to Identify or Cultivate Global Norms

with Christopher Dennis

Juristic democracy offers a particular form of micropolitical innovation, utilizing "groups small enough to be genuinely deliberative," and suggests a pathway by which these minipublics might be "consequential in democratic practice" in the larger political system, most notably at the transnational level (Goodin and Dryzek 2006, 220–221). Juristic democracy involves the use of jury-size groups of participants presented with hypothetical legal cases. Each "party" to the case advances claims based on an underlying political principle that the researcher has identified as critical to the resolution of an important public policy issue. For instance, imagine a dispute between two countries over the pollution of a river that comprises their shared border. A deliberative exercise can ask participants to choose between one resolution that involves a strictly proportional reduction of pollution and another that requires greater reductions from the wealthier of the two countries (which also is responsible for the longest history of and greatest contribution to the problem according to the fact pattern presented). In this scenario, members of the "citizen jury" are being asked, in effect, whether they support the principle of common but differentiated responsibility that lies at the heart of the Kyoto Protocol (Baber 2010).

As a first step toward moving beyond mere theories and immodest proposals, we have crafted three hypothetical cases to isolate and highlight three real-world normative environmental governance conflicts: the responsibility for shared environmental impacts of development having vastly differential benefits; the adequacy of informed consent as a regulative strategy for trade in hazardous materials; and the appropriateness of alternative regulatory schemes for allocating risks and benefits from the differential transboundary pollution of a common resource. These dispute scenarios are as hypothetical yet concrete as we can make them, but the conflicts are directly analogous to real real-world ones over which no normative consensus appears to have evolved. The purpose is to identify and model normative discourses fundamental to earth system governance, map areas of consensus and disagreement through scenario-based empirical research, and aggregate the findings in a form that will allow for the further progressive development of global environmental norms. These first dispute scenarios along with the procedures for presenting them to citizen juries for possible resolution were test piloted on several juries. For detailed descriptions of the three dispute scenarios and panel deliberation process, see appendixes B and C.

The Hypothetical Scenario: Conflict among the Countries of the Terran Continent

All three of the hypothetical scenarios present jurors with disputes arising on the imaginary continent of Terra. Four nation-states occupy the Terran landmass (although one plays no role in these particular simulations). These nations share an imaginary history of colonial occupation from which they emerged along different trajectories as a consequence of their geographic and demographic diversity as well as different experiences under colonial rule.

The eastern and northern regions of Terra are occupied by Panterra, the largest, most populous, and most economically advanced of the continent's nations. The central region of the continent is shared by two nation-states. Along the southern coast lies the nation of Meerland. This region is not as prosperous as neighboring Panterra, but it is undergoing a period of rapid economic development fueled largely by the use of its forested mountains and unspoiled coast for ecotourism. North of Meerland lies Arroya, a sparsely populated and agrarian nation that is almost entirely desert because it lies behind the rain shield of Meerland's mountains. Arroya's only arable region runs along the banks of the Terra River, which also marks the boundaries of these three countries along their shared borders. For more complete descriptions of these nations and a map of the Terran continent—materials provided to all prior to deliberations—see appendix B.

Ideology and the Deliberative Construction of Norms

Interpreting the results of environmental problem-solving exercises is likely to face insurmountable difficulties if some account is not taken of political ideology. In an exclusively US context, one might be tempted to merely ask participants to self-identify as either liberals or conservatives. But when participants from across the globe are involved, no such culturally specific technique will suffice. An approach to understanding political ideology is available, however, based on the most nearly universal human experience.

George Lakoff (2002) argues that liberalism and conservatism are essentially competing moral systems grounded in the child-rearing experience. This perspective, whatever its other merits, suits our long-range agenda well because what we are advocating is the use of hypothetical test cases to elicit people's moral (as opposed to political or economic) judgments about basic principles of environmental protection. To account for ideological interference in those judgments, our conceptualization and operationalization of ideology must be as nearly universal as possible. According to Lakoff, conservatism is actually a moral perspective that he characterizes as the Strict Father model, whereas he portrays liberalism with the model of a Nurturant Parent. Based on this perspective, we have developed an account of conservatism that contains four conceptual elements, each of which can be measured by asking participants to agree or disagree with statements about the social and natural world. The elements of conservatism we use are:

• Moral absolutism: Good and evil are constants, and people's orientation to them is a social given versus a variable subject to reform. Preserving the moral order is critical to a society's survival, and this requires us to judge each problematic case on its own merits.

• Human depravity: Without the right incentives, people will not behave appropriately nor develop the self-discipline necessary for social stability. So a system of rewards and punishments is necessary.

• Natural adversity: Negative outcomes are to be expected so people need to be self-reliant and self-interested. Competition therefore is both a moral imperative and guarantor of collective survival.

• Social authoritarianism: Disobedience is both morally wrong and socially destructive. Authority figures should be obeyed, and those who refuse must be isolated from society. Human authority extends to control over the nonhuman elements of the world.

This model of conservatism does not implicate specific political or economic issues, nor does it engage interests that may be grounded in class, occupation, or other demographic characteristics. Moreover, this is a model of conservatism that clearly suggests why certain kinds of "conservatives" might adopt environmentally unfriendly positions. People who are morally dedicated to the pursuit of self-interest, certain of the correctness of their own views, hostile to those who question authority, and constantly concerned about adverse social and economic outcomes would not appear to be naturally prone to strong environmentalism. If it turns out that there is a moral matrix so fundamental that it causes some people to be indifferent (or even hostile) to environmental protection, its existence should appear in its clearest form when people are challenged to resolve environmental disputes in which neither they nor anyone they know is involved.

Eureka! But What Is It?

It could be maintained that consensus is "built in" to the experiment by the way that we have structured the problems or framed the arguments of the parties. Two things would have to be true for that to be a telling criticism. First, the structure and framing of the experimental "trial" would have to be invalid in some way. We would have had to characterize the underlying dispute in a way that lacks verisimilitude or frame arguments for contending resolutions of the dispute that misrepresent the reasons that are (or might reasonably be) given by advocates of such solutions. Second, the flaw in the construction of the hypothetical problem has to be determinative of the outcome. Otherwise, we would have only a case of what appellate courts depict as harmless error.

A few observations by way of response are in order. For starters, if either the problem presented by the case or assertions advanced by the parties are thought to be invalid in some way, the clear answer is that repeated experimental deliberations with slight variations in the elements in question should be sufficient to determine that fact. Either varying those inputs will produce different outcomes or variations in those elements will be shown not to be determinative of the experimental outcomes.

Furthermore, tracking the impact of various substantive elements of the case is relatively easy to do. If those elements appear in either the initial responses given by participants in advance of the deliberation or the reasons given by the juries for their ultimate rulings, then their salience is demonstrated and the importance of their validity to the outcome of the experiment can be gauged. So the means of dealing with questions of validity are already part of the experimental design. Third, to the extent that the validity of the case design (or irrelevance of changes in it to the outcome) can be shown, any resulting patterns of consensus that are found would seem to be implicit in the problem being studied rather than the methodology being employed.

Discoveries of that sort are, of course, the objective of this kind of research. They are suggestive of a tacit knowledge of the world finding its way into peoples' practical problem solving (Polanyi [1966] 2009). Increased diversity in a deliberating population brings forth new arguments and additional information that have the potential to improve collective will formation. This is consistent with existing research on small group decision making that emphasizes the risks associated with homogeneity and value of diversity (Sunstein 2006, 2009). It also indicates that regulatory decision making in the international arena, where diversity is at a maximum and the power to coerce is at a minimum, has the potential to produce results of a quality equal (or superior) to that expected at the national level.

With respect to the reasons given by juries in support of their rulings, two things are of singular importance. First, the statements of reason play the same role in this research that written opinions of judges play in the study of law. They provide us with the raw material for generalization. What "rule" is the decision maker employing, what is the decision's reach, and what exceptions to its application might exist? In the law, this sort of analysis underlies the ALI's restatement work. ALI restatements, as noted earlier, are in-depth analyses of decisions in various fields of the common law that summarize and analyze judicial opinions in those areas. The resulting volumes are some of the most widely respected publications in US law, serving as guides for research and teaching, persuasive authority for judges inclined to use them, and points of departure for the construction of model codes and progressive development of the law.

Second, the reasons offered for preferred outcomes of these hypothetical cases, both by individual participants prior to deliberation and juries in their rulings, offer us a catalog of what we might call "discursive threads." These are expressions that call out a feature of the world (as described by the hypothetical) and relate it to some other feature of the world in a way that supports one or another of the claims made by parties to the dispute. Out of these threads, people create discourses through which they organize and attach value to their experiences in ways that supply them with the normative rules they need to resolve particular disputes (theories of the case, as lawyers would portray it). John Dryzek and Simon Niemeyer (2008) have argued that these discourses, as opposed to ideologies, groups, or individual interests, should be the core concern of any form of deliberative representation that we might want to add to (or substitute for) the conventional institutions of liberalism. Cataloging these discourses will allow us to determine when we have compiled a comprehensive list of reasons that might legitimately be given for any specific policy outcome or dispute resolution. By using these discourses to select participants in citizen juries and other deliberative exercises, we can achieve a level of representative legitimacy and discursive accuracy that escapes institutions whose membership is determined by election, self-selection, or random draw.

The hypothetical case for which we have accumulated the largest number of trials so far presents "juries" with a water-warming dispute between three countries that share the Terra River. Arroya has petitioned an international court to roll back warm water emission by 60 percent, which by common agreement would allow the Terra River fisheries to recover. Arroya also asks for sufficient additional reductions in existing emissions to allow it to develop geothermal power (within the 60 percent reduction limit) that would represent a per capita level of production similar to that of Panterra. Panterra has countered this request with one to roll back geothermal production in the region to earlier levels, which would constitute a 60 percent reduction. This would mean the end of Meerland's geothermal industry. Meerland has, for its part, countered with a request to set a 60 percent reduced limit based on per capita production thereby allowing for an increase in Meerland's production.

To date, on twelve occasions citizen panels have deliberated this dispute in the United States and four European countries (Germany, Russia,

Sweden, and the United Kingdom). We cannot generalize from these twelve experimental trials, but they can tell us about the kinds of discourses that ordinary citizens engage in when confronted with this sort of environmental challenge. Perhaps foremost, people take these problems seriously (even when they know them to be hypothetical) and rarely make simple choices among the presented alternatives. They craft their own solutions after considerable personal reflection and discussion among themselves. This fact is evidenced by the large number of imaginative alternatives mentioned in the various judgments, including a regional technology development fund, technology transfer program, regional energy union (reminiscent of the European Coal and Steel Community), regional food assistance program, permanent regional court, and international investment fund for energy diversification. Other discursive elements bear more directly on the issue of common but differentiated responsibility problems of environmental protection.

Every jury that rendered a substantive judgment (eleven of twelve) identified environmental protection as the fundamental policy objective and adopted the emissions target stipulated by the parties as ecologically sustainable in terms of the policy mandate to be satisfied. No jury indicated a willingness to entertain economic growth as an alternate policy narrative, much less a competing policy objective. There was a marked reluctance to impose command-and-control environmental requirements by either judicial decision or the action of a global sovereign. Four of the eleven substantive judgments proposed a system of marketable emissions permits, with initial allotments determined in various ways. Four others proposed a joint negotiation of emission limits, either mediated by the court or organized by a new intergovernmental body. In short, fully two-thirds of the juries predicated a resolution of the problem either on the operation of a market mechanism or attainment of a consensus among the parties in a free and equal deliberative process. Several of the juries called for some form of compensation to the least developed nation involved in the dispute—with suggestions ranging from international education and nutrition funds, to investment banks, technology transfer programs, and direct payments from the polluters. Where implementation of these proposals was discussed, it was generally guided by some concern for the proportionality of the costs based on the benefit derived from the polluting economic activity. In two cases, a temporary court-mandated reduction of 60 percent of emissions (enforced against all current producers) was proposed as an incentive to the parties to engage in negotiations aimed at generating a permanent agreement achieving the necessary limitations.

If we were to "restate" this narrative material in a form that might guide the development of legal obligations for environmental protection, we might frame the matter as follows. With respect to common but differentiated responsibility, where an environmental hazard is created by the behavior of multiple actors, injured parties are entitled to relief consistent with the principles that

- neither the economic benefits of the hazardous behavior nor arguments of economic necessity can be used to offset, counterbalance, or in any way diminish the damage resulting from that behavior
- alleviation of the environmental hazard and its ongoing prevention is to be achieved by a consensus of the parties engaged in the action leading to the hazard along with the parties subject to the hazard, and any interim regulatory standards will be designed so as to redress the environmental hazard in its entirety
- where compensatory policies are involved, these will be structured so as to redound to the benefit of the least favored party (or parties) to the agreement
- parties liable for regulatory expenses or the payment of damages will be entitled to the presumption that their costs will be determined by a standard of proportionality

Needless to say, no such legal regime guides the development of international environmental law today. If such guidance had been in place at the time that the Kyoto Protocol was negotiated, that agreement never would have taken the form in which it was ultimately presented to the world. The protocol would not have excused the climate-damaging behavior of developing nations nor ignored the climate protections already achieved by particular nations in the developed world. In the absence of actually enforceable, draconian interim standards, all parties would have been guided by the realization that a genuine consensus among the parties was necessary.

It is as important to emphasize what these results do not mean as it is to summarize their meaning. We are not producing an account of what is typical (or representative) of public opinion in the countries where we have conducted experimental trials. A far different research design would be necessary for such results. Neither are we producing a description of legal principles that can be found determining (or even influencing) the action of existing nation-states. Our objective is to use the proven techniques of experimental simulation and legal restatement in a new combination to create a discursive map of the policy issues posed. It is essential to master this concept of discursive mapping if the democratic deficit in global politics is to be addressed.

Research of this sort offers at least three crucial advantages over methodologies involving the study of aggregate public opinion. For one, it sometimes can be done where valid measurements of public opinion are difficult for political or methodological reasons. Qualitative methods of this sort also allow us to explore the variable meanings assigned by members of different cultural and national groups to so-called raw facts. Legal scholars already use such methods to study the voluminous legal texts submitted to appellate courts in socially and politically contentious cases (Grover 2010). What this kind of research makes clear is that "facts" are constructed and interpreted in widely differing contexts by various parties involved in cases—either as parties or fact finders.

Finally, empirical research on the normative foundations used by those in various cultures and nations to resolve concrete environmental disputes provides us with the raw materials needed to construct a global constitutional pluralism. It gives us a potential counterweight to the unicivilizational, notably European, bias built into a constitutionalist reading of existing and emergent international law. Reimagining global constitutionalism as a heuristic (or perhaps even hermeneutic) device offers us a response to the new generation of deniers of international law and legitimacy as well as democratic deficit skeptics (Peters 2009). Powerful as these critiques are, we should not allow their significance to deflect us from paths that may lead to more robust and democratic forms of global governance.

Appendix B: The Countries of Eastern Terra: Geography, Politics, and People

Terra

Geography

The continent of Terra comprises 6,356,863 square miles, roughly twice the size of Australia. Like Australia, much of Terra is desert. The southernmost quarter of the island is made up of a heavily forested range of mountains that are volcanic in origin. The south slope of the southern mountains faces into the prevailing winds, creating a rain shield that deprives the northern half of the continent of significant precipitation.

Between the southern mountains and northern desert lies a relatively fertile plain, watered by mountain runoff and the occasional showers that manage to clear the peaks to the south. The other major feature of the continent is the Terra River. The headwaters of the Terra are high in the southern mountains. From there the river runs first north and then west, nearly bisecting the continent. It reaches the ocean near the northern end of the continent's western coast. The areas immediately surrounding the Terra are the only areas of the northern desert (aside from the coastal strip around the mouth of the Terra) that will sustain agricultural activity, and most of that region's sparse population lives within walking distance of the riverbanks.

History

Until nearly the mid-nineteenth century, two competing colonial powers dominated the Terran continent. The eastern half of the continent (roughly speaking) gained its independence in 1832, when the colonial power ceded its sovereignty as a result of its own internal instability and growing pressures for autonomy in its far-flung colonial possessions. The newly independent country took the name Panterra, in recognition of the fact that its territory included the entire eastern bank, approximately one-sixth of the western bank, and the headwaters of the Terra River.

The western half of Terra had to win its independence by a combination of revolution and patience. The westernmost part of this region contained nearly three-quarters of the colonial population, which waged a three-year battle from 1855 to 1858 against colonial rule. At the end of this time, the southwest area of the continent gained its independence as the new nation of Westmare and northwestern area along with the intervening desert region (north of the Terra River) was ceded by the colonial power to Panterra. The central and south-central areas of the continent continued as a relatively unimportant, largely neglected colonial possession for another half century, gaining its independence in 1913 as growing tensions in Europe led its colonial master to divest itself of its overseas possessions.

In surrendering sovereignty over the sparsely populated central and south-central area of the continent, the former owner created two small states, roughly contiguous with the territories of the area's two major ethic groups, but with largely arbitrary boundaries. The southern area now constitutes the nation of Meerland, which consists of a rugged southern oceanfront (with only a small population in a few fishing villages) and fertile highlands area in the north (home to four-fifths of the country's population). The region to the north of Meerland is now the landlocked nation of Arroya, which is entirely desert. Virtually all of Arroya's population lives in the narrow fertile strip along the western bank of the Terra River (which is Arroya's northern and eastern border with Panterra).

Meerland

Meerland is bordered to the east by Panterra, to the north by Arroya, to the west by Westmare, and to the south by the ocean. It is a country dominated by mountains. The southern third of Meerland, which includes its entire coastline, is comprised of a densely forested range of volcanic peaks. Only scattered fishing villages dot the coastline, and the mountains themselves are virtually uninhabited. To the north of the mountains there is a vast expanse of rolling hills and plains, watered by mountain runoff and occasional winter showers. There is a small arid region in the far north, adjacent to Arroya. In this area the border shared by Meerland and Panterra touches the Terra River. There is also considerable geothermal activity in this area, which the Meerland government has recently begun to exploit for electricity generation. Meerland's government is stable and democratic. Its population is relatively homogeneous, comprising a single ethnic group whose members tend to identify with local village life and have, since achieving independence in 1913, taken a growing pride in their national identity. The Meerland constitution establishes a congressional system of government, with a popularly elected president serving one six-year term. Extraordinary majority requirements in both houses of its congress have promoted a consensus-oriented politics, producing a steady consolidation of the federal system without depriving the country's townships of their valued sense of self-determination. A statistical profile of Meerland appears below.

Land   *Area*: 886,700 sq. mi. (2,296,500 sq. km.); *capital*: Kingston (population 426,657).

People   *Population*: 1,680,000; *density*: 1.9/sq. mi. (0.73/sq. km.); *distribution*: 74 percent rural, 26 percent urban; *annual growth*: 2.1 percent.

Education   *Adult literacy*: 90 percent; *universities*: 5.

Health   *Hospital beds*: 55,900; *physicians*: 7,800; *life expectancy*: women 65, men 55; *infant mortality*: 24/1,000 live births.

Economy   *GNP*: $19.3 billion, $1,200 per capita; *labor distribution*: agriculture 40 percent, services 21 percent, government 15 percent, commerce 12 percent, manufacturing 12 percent; *imports*: $74 million; *exports*: $64 million; *principal trade partners*: Panterra and Westmare.

Government   *Type*: republic; *legislature*: congress; *political subdivisions*: 142 townships.

Communications   *Railroads*: none; *roads*: 81,000 mi. (130,350 km.); *major ports*: 0; *major airfields*: 2.

Meerland has recently undertaken two major development projects. The first exploits the geothermal resources of the country's northeastern region for electricity generation. The current electricity usage within the country is small. But electric generation, which had been limited due to the expense of importing oil shipped by pipeline from the eastern coast of Panterra, is growing as geothermal sources come on line. The second project, in its earliest stages, involves the development of a port facility in the southern coast's only shelter anchorage. The objective is not to increase shipping capacity, since there is little population or economic activity in the area but to develop a resort destination and base for the promotion of environmental tourism.

Arroya

Arroya is entirely landlocked. It is bordered on the east and north by Panterra, on the west by Westmare, and on the south by Meerland. This former colonial possession is the poorest nation on the Terran continent. Its territory is almost entirely desert. Only the strip of irrigated land along the Terra River supports agriculture. It also supports the vast majority of Arroya's citizens. The remainder of the country is home only to herders and miners. Arroya is a republic, with eight semiautonomous states. Each state is a homeland to one of the tribes that comprise the ethnic group whose distinctive culture led to the creation of the state by its former colonial master. The central government serves relatively limited functions, largely involving the mediation of disputes between the tribal states that control the country's national assembly. In this, the government enjoys reasonable success. Crime and civil unrest are only limited problems. Political parties are unknown, and the country has neither a military nor a regulatory establishment in the conventional sense. Arroya generally limits its foreign interactions to those required to maintain relations with its immediate neighbors. A statistical profile of Arroya appears below.

Land   *Area*: 674,133 sq. mi. (1,746,000 sq. km.); *capital*: Rivertown (population 876,657).

People   *Population*: 3,300,000; *density*: 4.9/sq. mi. (1.9/sq. km.); *distribution*: 19 percent urban, 81 percent rural; *annual growth*: 3.7 percent.

Education   *Adult literacy*: 38 percent; *universities*: 1.

Health   *Hospital beds*: 6,201; *physicians*: 339; *life expectancy*: women 59, men 51; *infant mortality*: 69/1,000 live births.

Economy   *GNP*: $920 million, $920 per capita; *labor distribution*: agriculture 80 percent, construction/trade/transport 7 percent, government 5 percent, industrial/mining 3 percent; *imports*: $74 million; *exports*: $64 million; *principal trade partners*: Panterra and Westmare.

Government   *Type*: republic; *legislature*: national assembly; *political subdivisions*: 8 states.

Communications   *Railroads*: 1,332 mi. (2102 km.); *roads*: 27,693 mi. (45,000 km.); *major ports*: 0; *major airfields*: 1.

Arroya has an economy based largely on agriculture, made possible by ditch irrigation from the Terra River. The country imports virtually all its manufactured goods. Its principal exports are small quantities of various ores mined in the country's northern half and sold principally to Panterra. There is also a small trade in wool across the Panterra and Westmare borders, but the size of this market can only be estimated because it is a largely informal activity carried on between the indigenous peoples of the two countries. Arroya is, by a small margin, a net importer of foods. These imports are mainly meat products. The Arroyan population's major protein source is Terra River salmon, historically spawned in the middle third of the river's length, just downstream of the rapids that mark its descent from the Meerland plains.

These economic activities have been essentially static since Arroyan independence in 1913. A few development activities have been pursued by international agencies. But the occasional indifference of Arroya's tradition-oriented population, disunity among its tribal states, and limited domestic governmental capacity has hampered these efforts

Panterra

Panterra is the largest and by far most populous country on the Terran continent. The country stretches from the rugged southern coast, across the eastern third of the southern mountains, on to the extreme northern coast of the continent, and west across the northern desert to the western sea. Its official name is the Federated Republic of Panterra, though its twenty-six provincial governments are little more than administrative regions under a central authority. The country enjoys stable and representative government in the form a parliamentary system, including three major parties and several minor ones. It has a respectable record in the area of human rights, but its environmental protection performance is mixed. The country has never participated in a major military operation, is part of no military alliances, and maintains only a small armed force.

In its international relations, Panterra is a firm and longtime advocate of free trade. A statistical profile of Panterra appears below.

Land   *Area*: 3,285,619 sq. mi. (8,511,965 sq. km.); *capital*: Bay City (population 1,576, 657).

People   *Population*: 150,400,000; *density*: 45.8/sq. mi. (17.7/sq. km.); *distribution*: 74 percent urban, 26 percent rural; *annual growth*: 2.1 percent.

Education   *Adult literacy*: 91 percent; *universities*: 88.

Health   *Hospital beds*: 501,660; *physicians*: 198,329; *life expectancy*: women 69, men 65; *infant mortality*: 67/1,000 live births.

Economy   *GNP*: $352 billion, $2,440 per capita; *labor distribution*: agriculture 35 percent; services 40 percent, industrial 25 percent; *imports*: $26.6 billion; *exports*: $ 16.2 billion; *principal trade partners*: United States, European Community, and Westmare.

Government   *Type*: federated republic; *legislature*: parliamentary; *political subdivisions*: 26 provinces.

Communications   *Railroads*: 18,505 mi. (29,871 km.); *roads*: 889,745 mi. (1,448,000 km.); *major ports*: 11; *major airfields*: 24.

Panterra has a large and diverse economy that supports the continent's highest standard of living. Its major exports are natural resources. These exports include timber (28 percent of the total), iron ore (25 percent), machinery and vehicles (13 percent), coffee (12 percent), sugar (5 percent), chemicals (4 percent), other agricultural products (8 percent), and rare minerals and gems (5 percent). Panterra's major import is oil. The country has only small reserves of oil and imports 50 percent of its domestic consumption. This is the major reason for the country's trade deficit along with its status as one of the world's largest debtor nations, in spite of its relatively healthy economy.

In order to reduce its reliance on foreign oil as well as improve the air quality in its capital of Bay City, Panterra has undertaken a major effort to exploit the geothermal resources near its border with Meerland. This area, lying north of the southern mountains and along the Terra River, has great potential for electricity generation. Panterra's Interior Ministry has, with the help of international lending agencies, established several power stations. These stations now generate more than half the electricity used in the capital, which is also Panterra's largest city.

This new source of power also has allowed for the creation of an industrial park to the west of the capital and successful electrification project for the nation's central highland agricultural region. Most significantly, Panterra has been able to reduce its reliance on foreign oil from 80 percent five years ago to 50 percent today while its economy has grown by 9 percent during the same time.

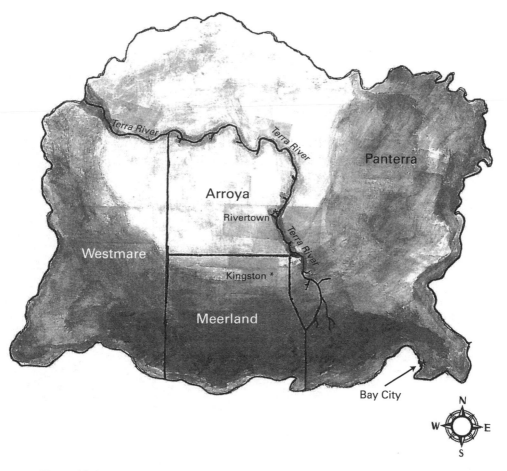

Figure 12.1
Terra

Appendix C: Scenarios 1, 2, and 3

Scenario 1: The Republic of Arroya versus the Federated Republic of Panterra and Republic of Meerland

Facts of the Case

The parties agree that the following facts are accurate:

• The residents of the Republic of Arroya (Arroya) living in the vicinity of the Terra River rely on the Terra River salmon fishery for approximately 80 percent of the protein in their daily diet.

• Throughout the Arroyan people's recorded history, the Terra River salmon have spawned in the area immediately downstream of the Terra rapids near the border between Arroya and the Republic of Meerland (Meerland).

• In 2003, the Federated Republic of Panterra (Panterra) began to develop geothermal electricity-generating facilities on its own territory near the Terra River as well as its borders with Meerland and Arroya. In 2009, Meerland also started to produce geothermal electricity on its territory and discharge water in areas that ultimately drain into the Terra River.

• The geothermal facilities throughout this area discharge large quantities of water into the Terra River. Even when this water is held in catchments and allowed to reach the ambient air temperature, it is still significantly warmer than the Terra River's water.

• Beginning in 2004, measurable increases in the temperature of the Terra River were detected below the Terra falls in the area of the salmon-spawning grounds. These temperature increases have continued since 2004, and by now, the Terra River is without salmon across four-fifths of its length on the Arroyan border.

• If temperature increases continue, wildlife biologists are unanimous in their view that the salmon-spawning grounds will continue to shift downstream and there will be no salmon in the Arroyan segment of the Terra River within five to ten years.

• The parties also share the view that if increases in ambient river water temperature levels could be limited to no more than 0.5°C, salmon would likely return to the Terra River along the entirety of its Arroyan segment. Limiting increases in ambient river water temperature to no more than 0.5°C would require a 60 percent reduction in the geothermal production of electricity, given no changes in currently available technology. Further, the parties agree that no technological innovations that would allow for reductions in the river water temperature without reducing electric production are presently available or foreseeable in the future.

Petition: Arroya

The Republic of Arroya petitions the panel for an order directing the Federated Republic of Panterra and Republic of Meerland to reduce their geothermal electric production by 60 percent from the 2006 levels, and refrain from exceeding that limit in the future. Additionally, the Arroyan petition asks that the court retain jurisdiction for an indefinite period. Arroya argues that it should be allowed to reserve the right to develop geothermal resources equivalent to those of Panterra and Meerland (on a proportionate per capita basis), and the court should use its retained jurisdiction to mandate further reductions in Panterran and Meerlandan production to accommodate Arroyan development as it may occur.

Cross-Petition: Panterra

Panterra opposes the Arroyan petition in its entirety, and in a cross-petition, requests that the panel require all parties to return their geothermal electricity production to 2011 levels (which all parties agree would constitute an overall 60 percent reduction). This remedial measure would, Panterra accurately contends, impose a roughly equal financial loss on both Panterra and Meerland in terms of the total value of the infrastructure investment that would have to be decommissioned.

Cross-Petition: Meerland

In a cross-petition of its own, Meerland requests that the panel mandate a 70 percent reduction in Panterran geothermal production and Meerland be allowed to increase its geothermal production by an amount equivalent to 10 percent of the current Panterran production (thus meeting the 60 percent overall objective). This would permit Meerland to approach a level of geothermal electric production equivalent (as a percentage of its total electric production) to the Panterran electric production profile. This increase in Meerland's electric production would allow it to meet its other economic development objectives.

Meerland vigorously objects to the Panterran remedial proposal on the grounds that 70 percent of its production facilities have been constructed since 2011, whereas only 15 percent of Panterra's much more extensive production capacity has been built during that time. As a factual matter, the Meerland argument is accurate in its description of the history of geothermal development in the Panterra/Meerland region along with the implications of the Panterran proposal.

Charge to the Panel

The task for your panel is to arrive at a resolution of the dispute portrayed above that you can agree is just. You may incorporate any of the reasoning presented above in your judgment, or develop solutions and rationale of your own. After rendering your judgment, you are requested to provide a concise general statement of the reasons for your ruling.

Scenario 2: The Republic of Meerland versus the Federated Republic of Panterra

Facts of the Case

The parties agree that the following facts are accurate:

• The central and northern regions of Meerland, north of the southern mountains, comprise some of the most productive agricultural regions on the Terran continent. Agricultural production in this area constitutes 40 percent of the Meerland economy.

• In addition to satisfying virtually all Meerland's food requirements (with the remainder consisting of fishing along the southern coast), this agricultural production allows Meerland to export food in quantities sufficient to maintain a positive balance of trade, which has contributed to its long-term economic stability.

• Meerland's success in agricultural production is due to two major factors. First, the climate and soil conditions in the region north of its mountains are favorable. Second, the country's farmers have achieved un-usually high levels of productivity through a combination of careful land management along with the aggressive use of chemical fertilizers and pes-ticides. These chemicals are almost entirely imported from neighboring Panterra.

• Imports of agricultural chemicals into Meerland are conducted entirely by private companies (manufactures and retailers) and local farm coopera-tives. Neither government has intervened in this activity beyond the grant-ing of business operating licenses that are typical in other economic sectors.

• Over the years, Meerland's increasingly influential environmental movement has grown concerned about the long-term effects of the coun-try's significant and expanding use of agricultural chemicals. Environ-mentalists point out that the use of these chemicals within their country of origin (Panterra) is far more carefully regulated than it is in Meer-land. Record-keeping standards, limits on application levels, and safety rules for the handling and disposal of chemicals are both demanding and strictly enforced in Panterra. These requirements are part of a rigorous licensing regime that covers the entire life cycle of agricultural chemicals and their use within Panterra's boundaries.

• Between the pressure brought on Meerland's government by the envi-ronmental movement and long-standing hostility toward Panterra among Meerland's political conservatives, the current "hands-off" attitude to-ward the importation of agricultural chemicals has become untenable.

• Nevertheless, this odd coalition of political forces cannot agree on a policy that it wants its government to pursue. Environmentalists want a strict regulatory regime similar to that in existence in Panterra. Conserva-tives want to confront the Panterran government on the issue, but they instinctively rebel at the idea of adopting a strict regulatory regime. They do not want to see so intrusive a level of government intervention in the economy. Moreover, they do not want to pay for the creation of an en-tirely new regulatory agency within the Meerland government. All sides agree that the government currently lacks the expertise and resources re-quired to implement a regulatory system that would approximate that of Panterra. The government, however, believes that it has found an ap-proach that will satisfy both these constituencies and produce the level of environmental protection that citizens of Panterra enjoy.

• Some of the chemicals that Meerland imports are actually banned in Panterra, either totally or for particular uses. In fact, a few of the chemicals in question have been developed entirely for use in the crop and pest conditions in Meerland, and are of no value in any other market. Moreover, Panterra declines to require complete disclosure of all scientific information about chemicals that its manufacturers export, citing patent protection concerns along with the business confidentiality and nondisclosure requirements of this highly competitive industry.

Petition

The Republic of Meerland petitions the panel for an order directing the Federated Republic of Panterra to prohibit any and all trade in agricultural chemicals between individuals, groups, or corporations within its borders as well as those within the borders of Meerland that would not be licensed to engage in the production, distribution, use, or disposal of those chemicals in Panterra. In effect, the government of Meerland is asking the panel to require Panterra to extend its regulatory jurisdiction and enforcement procedures to parties within Meerland. Meerland argues that Panterra is best equipped to license handlers of agricultural chemicals and pledges to conform its business-licensing actions to licensing decisions made by Panterran regulators.

Response

In response to the Meerlandan petition, Panterra makes the following arguments. First, private individuals not in violation of any Panterran law are the ones conducting chemical trades between Meerland and Panterra. Second, the trade in agricultural chemicals between the two countries is free and produces reciprocal benefits. Third, Meerland is better situated to regulate its own citizens. And finally, Panterra argues that it should not be required to bear the financial burden of extending its regulatory jurisdiction to activities by private individuals in Meerland.

As an alternative to Meerland's petition, Panterra proposes a system of prior informed consent. Under this system, Panterra would inform Meerland of proposed exports of chemicals to that country in advance, the quantities and primary characteristics of those chemicals, and the necessary steps for their safe handling. Meerland would also be informed of the identities of the exporting entities and schedules of proposed shipments. It could then grant or withhold its consent for each shipment.

Charge to the Panel

The task for your panel is to arrive at a resolution of the dispute described above that you can agree is just. You may incorporate any of the arguments presented above in your judgment, or develop solutions and rationale of your own. After rendering your judgment, you are requested to provide a concise general statement of the reasons for your ruling.

Scenario 3: The Republic of Arroya versus the Federated Republic of Meerland

Facts of the Case

The parties agree that the following facts are accurate:

• The central and northern regions of Meerland, north of the southern mountains, comprise some of the most productive agricultural regions of the Terran continent. Agricultural production constitutes 40 percent of the Meerland economy.

• In addition to satisfying virtually all Meerland's food requirements (the remainder consisting of fishing along the southern coast), this agricultural production also allows Meerland to export food in quantities sufficient to maintain a positive balance of trade, which has contributed to its economic stability.

• Meerland's success in agricultural production is due to two major factors. The climate and soil conditions in the region north of its mountains are, for one, favorable. Second, the country's farmers have achieved unusually high levels of productivity through a combination of careful land management along with the aggressive use of chemical fertilizers and pesticides.

• The western half of Meerland's agricultural region drains into small creeks and streams, which as they flow north into lower and dryer regions, dissipate as a result of evaporation. No more than 10 percent of these minor waterways reach Meerland's northern border with Arroya.

• Still, the eastern half of Meerland's agricultural region is characterized by wetter conditions and the terrain is steeper, resulting in more rapid runoff. This area drains into the Terra River watershed. Since Meerland began keeping records of chemical concentrations along its small stretch of riverbank in 1989, concentrations of pollutants (residue from the extensive use of fertilizers) have increased dramatically. By 2005, these substances had increased to the point that significant levels of eutrophication (oxygen deprivation) were causing seasonal die-offs of Terra River salmon in the southern regions of Arroya. The problem has grown since that time; the Terra River is now devoid of fish through the southernmost quarter of its Arroyan course.

• The adjacent southeastern area of Arroya is, for climatic reasons, the most productive agricultural region of that country. The government has been trying to encourage greater agricultural productivity in this area to both secure the nation's food supply and generate export food products to help solve the country's persistent balance of trade problems. Part of this effort has been the creation of government subsidies that provide incentives for the development of new ditch irrigation systems and use of fertilizers, both artificial and naturally occurring.

• Arroyan agricultural production has now begun to contribute to the eutrophication problem in the Terra River. Although there is some uncertainty due to a lack of technical expertise in Arroyan government agencies, the country's contribution to the decline in the river's water quality has been estimated by international environmental organizations to be roughly one-tenth that of Meerland's.

• All parties agree that a reduction in pollutant runoff in Meerland to levels observed in 1990 would allow fish to return to the Terra River at least as far south as the border between Arroya and Meerland (assuming no other sources of pollution are added).

Petition

The Republic of Arroya petitions the panel for an order directing the Republic of Meerland to reduce by statute the use within its territory of fertilizers, both artificial and naturally occurring, to 90 percent of the levels reported in 1990. That prohibition would allow for an approximate doubling of runoff from Arroyan sources—an allowance that Arroya contends would permit it to complete its planned expansion of agricultural production in southeastern Arroya. Arroya's contribution of pollutants into the Terra River would still be less than one-quarter the quantity of those contributed by Meerland, despite the fact that Arroya has twice Meerland's population and over a thousand times its river frontage.

Response
In response to the Arroyan petition, Meerland makes the following arguments. First, outright prohibitions of the use of chemical fertilizers are inefficient as a means of controlling pollution because they do not take into account the costs and benefits of the policy. Second, Meerland's farm community should not be required to sacrifice more than farmers are required to do in Arroya to protect Terra River water quality. And finally, Meerland's use of fertilizers in the Terra River watershed has continued unchallenged for so long that it has created an established right to that beneficial use of the resources in that territory.

As an alternative to Arroya's petition, Meerland claims the prior use right to the assimilative capacity of the river up to its 1990 levels of nutrient runoff, but only if Arroya also limits runoff to its own 1990 levels. Meerland proposes to use a permit system to reduce its nutrient runoff over time to 1990 levels by allocating tradable permits at no cost to the current Meerland farmers. It proposes to allow Arroya (or Arroyan citizens) to purchase these permits on the open market that it will establish for their sale at whatever price the market will bear.

Charge to the Panel
The task for your panel is to arrive at a resolution of the dispute described above that you can agree is just. You may incorporate any of the arguments presented above in your judgment, or develop solutions and rationale of your own. After rendering your judgment, you are requested to provide a concise general statement of the reasons for your ruling.

Notes

1 Nature Rules

1. A wide variety of legal orders are associated with the common law tradition. "For most of its history the common law was in the *process* of becoming a common law, and its history is above all one of relations with other laws, themselves also common in considerable measure, both in England and in Europe. This was the case with chthonnic law, its earliest and most significant interlocutor, and then with ecclesiastical law, once the ecclesiastical courts were up and running. In examining the growth of the common law, we have necessarily spoken of unavoidable reciprocal influences and, also, more interestingly, of the underlying harmony of this process.... Rules are not seen as being in conflict if the rules count for less than the facts" (Glenn 2010, 269). Due in part to worldwide colonization by the British Empire (not to mention the English language), there has been "a kind of embedding of common law thinking in a large number of diverse societies around the world" (ibid., 262). Indeed, the very existence of the Westphalian nation-state was (at least conceptually) a Western project—the product of a dynamic interaction between the British common law tradition and continental tradition, much of which was also influenced by its own, often unrecognized, common law (Landauer 2011). In fact, there is a vast source of international norms—what we might call transnational common law—that has long transcended the nation-state altogether. Judicial globalization, domestic treaty enforcement, transnational criminal prosecution, and international and transnational custom count among the principal areas in which the external pressures of foreign affairs developments are profoundly affected by the internal, social commitments of domestic legal systems (Flaherty 2006; Dryzek 2000).

3 Legislation by Consensus

1. Consensus is not a threshold-voting requirement of some sort (plurality, majority, supermajority, or unanimous). It is a shared normative agreement. Benjamin Barber (2003) distinguishes between *generic*, *substantive*, and *creative* consensus. Generic consensus refers to matters of consent such as the underlying agreement

between the sovereign and the governed that establishes the ground of what Barber calls thin democracy. Substantive consensus is composed of those commonly held beliefs and values that underlie unitary democracy (and give consensus its authoritarian overtones for some people). Creative consensus is "an agreement that arises out of common talk, common decision, and common work but that is premised on citizens' active and perennial participation in the transformation of conflict through the creations of common consciousness and political judgment" (ibid., 224). This form of consensus is the foundation of deliberative democracy and what Barber labels *strong* democracy. The juristic democracy we present here is a strategic way to generate creative consensus. It is a politically potent consensus about basic norms that arises from the concrete problem-solving experiences along with shared discourse of average citizens isolated by the decision circumstances from considerations of personal stakes and the influences of special interests. Obstructionist tactics by an individual, group, or country are simply irrelevant. In fact, environmental recalcitrants would have more to fear from juristic democracy than anyone.

2. The institutionalization of legal norms by juries can most easily be seen in the cumulative impact of civil jury verdicts in the United States. Begin with the fundamental proposition that the United States does not have two legal systems—one for litigation and the other for negotiation—but rather a single system that performs both functions simultaneously. To borrow an admittedly inelegant neologism, the United States has a system of "litigotiation." The few jury trials that proceed all the way to a verdict provide systemically critical signals to the entire legal (and business) community that allows actors across the social and political spectrum to estimate what other juries will do, and on that basis, "make decisions and formulate policies about claims, offers, settlements, and trials and even about … investments in safety, disclosure, and so forth." The jury thus "helps retain the salience of the substantive morality embodied in the law—and helps align that morality with the emergent moral sense of the community or communities" (Galanter 1993, 61, 89). In this context, the decline in the number of cases that are tried through to a verdict and increase in negotiated settlements can be seen not as a repudiation of the jury but instead as the surest sign of its success. As surely as executive branch agencies, juries perform a *regulatory* function. Once this is realized, the ascendancy of negotiated settlements in a mature jury system is no more a sign of failure than is voluntary compliance with a system of bureaucratic regulation.

4   Reconciling Diversity and Consensus in Democratic Governance

1. A pendant claim is one that would normally not be actionable, but in fact may be because a cause of action arises from the same set of circumstances that led to a separate claim that is prior and primary. Consequently, a pendant claim is no stronger than the primary claim to which it is joined. If the primary claim fails, so will the pendant claim.

2. The distinction that we draw here between environmental discourses and environmental movements and organizations is critical. A discourse, as we use the

term, is "a shared means of making sense of the world embedded in language." Discourses allow people to "perceive and compile bits of sensory information into coherent stories or accounts that can be communicated in intersubjectively meaningful ways" (Dryzek 2000, 18). Unlike organizations or individuals, discourses do not possess agency. They do, however, possess "the capacity to underwrite or destabilize collective outcomes"—which from the point of view of political legitimacy is the most important feature of agency in the first place (Dryzek 2010, 36). Unlike movements, which are inchoate and often-overlapping aggregations of organizations, networks, and individuals, discourses (political ones at least) normally feature "an ontology of entities recognized as existing or relevant" as well as an ascription of agency to some of these entities and denial of agency to others (ibid., 44). From the perspective of discourses, environmental attitudes and arguments can be seen as the outward manifestations of peoples' attempts to engage each other's moral intuitions. The polarization of attitudes in the United States, for example, about the environment can be explained by the fact that liberals tend to view environmental issues in moral terms, whereas conservatives generally do not. Contemporary environmental discourses are largely based on the moral concern related to "harm and care," which resonates most deeply with liberals. If environmental concerns are reframed (as they can be) in terms of the moral concern for purity, though, they appeal far more to conservatives (Feinberg and Willer 2013). Indeed, the relevance of moral intuitions in this regard is confirmed by the fact that environmental concern on the Right is found largely in religious circles, populated by those who are likely to sense the "purity" theme of environmentalism even when it is not explicitly invoked. Given the relatively small number of these evolutionary-developmental foundations of our moral intuitions (Haidt 2012), anyone interested in using such insights to develop a means of "representing" discourses in a political process must maintain a level of abstraction that often tracks poorly with the complex, convoluted arguments of political actors, organizations, and the movements with which they identify.

3. Accordingly, consider whether or not animal rights activists should have a principle-based preference between two alternate approaches to endangered species protection. The primary mechanism of species protection at the international level is the Convention on International Trade in Endangered Species of Wild Fauna and Flora (CITES). Entering into force in 1975, CITES is an international agreement between governments, the aim of which is to ensure that the international trade in specimens of wild animals and plants does not threaten their survival. CITES subjects the international trade in specimens of selected species to certain controls. A licensing system has to authorize all import, export, reexport, and introduction from the sea of species covered by the convention. Every party to the convention must designate one or more management authority to administer that licensing system, and one or more scientific authority to advise them on the effects of trade on the status of the species. The species covered by CITES are listed in three appendixes, according to the degree of protection they need. A specimen of a CITES-listed species may be imported into or exported (or reexported) from a state that is party to the convention only if the appropriate document (as determined by the state[s] involved) has been obtained and presented for clearance at the port of entry or exit. There is some variation of the

requirements from one country to another, but the basic conditions that apply to this trade is stipulated by the convention, and parties are obligated to respect those fundamental requirements.

The US Endangered Species Act (ESA) of 1973 (16 U.S.C. Sect. 1531 et seq.) represents a different approach to the protection of genetic diversity. The ESA provides a program for the conservation of threatened and endangered plants and animals along with the habitats in which they are found. The lead agencies for implementing the ESA are the US Fish and Wildlife Service and the US Oceanic and Atmospheric Administration Fisheries Service. The Fish and Wildlife Service maintains a worldwide list of endangered species, including birds, insects, fish, reptiles, mammals, crustaceans, flowers, grasses, and trees. The law requires federal agencies, in consultation with this agency or the Oceanic and Atmospheric Administration, to ensure that the actions they authorize, fund, or carry out do not jeopardize the continued existence of any listed species, or result in the destruction or adverse modification of the designated critical habitat of such species. The law also prohibits any action that causes a "taking" of any listed species of endangered fish or wildlife. Likewise, the import or export of, or the interstate and foreign commerce in, listed species are generally prohibited.

Although a number of differences between CITES and the ESA are immediately evident, one stands out as being especially significant for our present purpose. CITES expresses a general interest in the preservation of species, but it only addresses itself to threats to their survival arising from trade, and does so only in a procedural manner. The ESA is far more comprehensive and restrictive. It prohibits the US government from any action that would jeopardize the survival of a listed species or adversely affect its habitat. The act, which has been described elsewhere as an instance of ethical precommitment (Baber and Bartlett 2005), embodies a substantive and enforceable obligation to produce an ecological outcome unaffected by calculations of the relative size of the costs and benefits. While it fails to vest justiciable rights in individual animals, the ESA has fundamentally transformed the relationship between the US government and nonhuman life falling under its jurisdiction. It is, in short, a remarkably biocentric piece of legislation grounded in a quasi-religious emphasis on the sanctity of life (Plater et al. 2004).

So from the perspective of the animal rights movement, what could possibly be wrong with the ESA? It is, in short, that the ESA is grounded in the same utilitarian reasoning that supports all other US policies with regard to animals. No less than animal cruelty laws and agricultural regulations, the ESA is seen by animal rights activists as concerned only with animal welfare within the context of a human-dominated social order (Francione 1996). Were it not for the value that humans attach to biodiversity as an ecological resource, so the argument goes, there would be no rationale for the ESA and no political support for it either. But that of course means only that the ESA is not as selfless as it might be, not that it is less preferable to CITES from a moral perspective. The ESA imposes a strong and uniform obligation on all within the boundaries of its jurisdiction. On the other hand, CITES imposes only a weak obligation on a subset of all possible actors (nation-states). This limitation is based on an acceptance of the debatable proposition that the normative value of sovereignty, when set against that of species protection, should prevail. If environmentalism were armed only with the animal rights discourse, could a judgment that the ESA (as a legal construct) is superior to CITES be made? Regrettably, the answer is far from apparent. It is equally unclear why animal rights advocates should not be asked to bear the deliberative burden of this question.

6   The Citizen Jury as a Deliberative Forum

1. The research and literature on jury behavior has been done mostly in the United States by US researchers, and based mostly on US experiments and experiences with juries. In *comparative* law scholarship generally, US (common law) conceptions of adjudication are associated with a pragmatist approach to judicial lawmaking, a willingness to recognize the policymaking functions of courts, and a "jurisprudential style" that gives much greater weight to substantive values of justice than other legal systems generally do. The European (civil law) legal tradition, by contrast, has long been famous for striving to minimize the scope of judicial discretion and its tendency to rely on codified legal norms for furthering that goal (Aharonson 2013). As a consequence of this limited focus on adjudication per se—one is tempted even to call it an antipathy toward adjudication—interest in the decision processes engaged in by juries along with the impacts of jury verdicts has not featured as prominently in European legal scholarship as it has in the United States. It is, however, entirely possible that this situation is destined to change.

The use of juries outside the common law tradition has been limited (relatively speaking) and tended to use citizen jurors as members of *mixed juries*—bodies composed of both citizens and government officials (judges or bureaucrats). A growing number of countries, though, are committed to significant prodemocracy initiatives, and are developing new ways to incorporate citizens into the legal decision-making apparatus through the use of juries or jurylike arrangements (Hans 2007). Eventually, this process is likely to produce a new interest in the academic study of juries outside the professional communities where that kind of work has been done heretofore. It is critical that this work be done in rigorous and interdisciplinary ways if we are to realize the hope that juries can make legal systems more responsive to community values. A primary challenge to that objective is the fact that while the dispute-resolving function that juries perform is fairly easy to describe and analyze, the role that juries play in institutionalizing legal norms is less obvious but more important from a systemic perspective. Juries do this in at least two ways: by imposing a check on judicial power, and providing normative guidance to the use of that power.

Like other social systems, legal systems sometimes adjust to the circumstances of human life through means other than the procedures for controlled change that are explicitly built into them. A prime example is the jury role in acquittals. The obligation to defer to the court's instructions, while binding on the juror, exists side by side with a protected power and privilege to override that obligation. The result is the legitimated interposition of the juror's judgment between the consequences of the court's instructions and the fate of the defendant. The result is a justified departure from rules by agents acting in role—a possibility that may serve social ends of major significance by institutionalizing powers, rights, privileges, and duties that had previously not existed in the law (Kadish and Kadish 1971). Some, particularly those with political axes to grind, often characterize this informal check on judicial power as "jury nullification" (Conrad 2013). A more measured analysis of the subject suggests that nullification as an act of juror lawlessness is actually quite rare. Far more common is a jury that asserts its independence and authority, ignoring the letter of the law, when "a just and fair law is applied in an unjust manner" (Vidmar and Hans 2007).

10   The Calculus of Consensus in Juristic Democracy

1. Nonhuman primates have been presented as the lawgiver from Aesop's time to the *Planet of the Apes* wherein the lawgiver is portrayed as an orangutan. Of course in that film's dystopian future, all the characters of officialdom were portrayed (with no hint of irony) as simians. But monkeys and orangutans are a storyteller's natural choice as lawgivers because, as we know from song, monkeys are honest and orangutans are skeptical.

2. We will not enter here into the debate over whether Moses was an actual living individual, a conglomeration of historical and/or mythical individuals, or purely a narrative construct. We only observe that the dispute is largely irrelevant to the perspective of the lawgiver as a cultural constant.

3. At least until one encounters opera.

4. The philosophical foundation of Hare's "prescriptivism" (the view that ethical utterances are universalizable imperatives) is the "emotivism" of Alfred Jules Ayer ([1938] 1952) and Charles Stevenson (1944). Contemporary advocates include Singer (2011) and Colin Wilks (2002). For general overviews, see Miller 2013; Schroeder 2010. For critical perspectives, see Holmes 2007; MacIntyre 1984.

References

Abramson, Jeffrey. 1994. *We, the Jury: The Jury System and the Ideal of Democracy*. New York: Basic Books.

Ackerman, Bruce, and James S. Fishkin. 2003. Deliberation Day. In *Debating Deliberative Democracy*, ed. James S. Fishkin and Peter Laslett, 7–30. Malden, MA: Blackwell.

Adams, Kristen D. 2004. The Folly of Uniformity: Lessons from the Restatement Movement. *Hofstra Law Review* 33:423–472.

Adams, Kristen D. 2007. Blaming the Mirror: The Restatements and the Common Law. *Indiana Law Review* 40:205–270.

Agyeman, Julian, and Bob Evans. 2006. Justice, Governance, and Sustainability: Perspectives on Environmental Citizenship from North American and Europe. In *Environmental Citizenship*, ed. Andrew Dobson and Derek Bell, 185–206. Cambridge, MA: MIT Press.

Aharonson, Ely. 2013. Determinate Sentencing and American Exceptionalism: The Underpinnings and Effects of Cross-National Differences in the Regulation of Sentencing Discretion. *Law and Contemporary Problems* 76 (1): 161–186.

Andree, Peter. 2005. The Genetic Engineering Revolution in Agriculture and Foods: Strategies of the Biotech Bloc. In *The Business of Global Environmental Governance*, ed. David L. Levy and Peter J. Newell, 135–166. Cambridge, MA: MIT Press.

Archibugi, Daniele. 2008. *The Global Commonwealth of Citizens: Toward Cosmopolitan Democracy*. Princeton, NJ: Princeton University Press.

Arnold, Jennifer S., and Maria Fernandez-Gimenez. 2007. Building Participatory Capital through Participatory Research: An Analysis of Collaboration on Tohono O'odham Tribal Rangelands in Arizona. *Society & Natural Resources* 20 (6): 481–495.

Ayer, Alfred Jules. (1938) 1952. *Language, Truth, and Logic*. Mineola, NY: Dover Publications.

Baber, H. E. 2008. *The Multicultural Mystique: The Liberal Case against Diversity*. Amherst, NY: Prometheus Books.

Baber, Walter F. 2010. Democratic Deliberation and Environmental Practice: The Case of Natural Resource Management. *Environmental Practice* 12:195–201.

Baber, Walter F., and Robert V. Bartlett. 2005. *Deliberative Environmental Politics: Democracy and Ecological Rationality*. Cambridge, MA: MIT Press.

Baber, Walter F., and Robert V. Bartlett. 2009a. *Global Democracy and Sustainable Jurisprudence: Deliberative Environmental Law*. Cambridge, MA: MIT Press.

Baber, Walter F., and Robert V. Bartlett. 2009b. Race, Poverty, and the Environment: Toward a Global Perspective. *Public Administration Quarterly* 33 (4): 457–480.

Bäckstrand, Karin. 2011. The Democratic Legitimacy of Global Governance after Copenhagen. In *Oxford Handbook on Climate Change and Society*, ed. John S. Dryzek, Richard B. Norgaard, and David Schlosberg, 669–684. New York: Oxford University Press.

Baer, Paul. 2011. International Justice. In *The Oxford Handbook of Climate Change and Society*, ed. John S. Dryzek, Richard B. Norgaard, and David Schlosberg, 323–337. New York: Oxford University Press.

Barak, Aharon. 2006. *The Judge in a Democracy*. Princeton, NJ: Princeton University Press.

Barber, Benjamin R. 2003. *Strong Democracy: Participatory Politics for a New Age*. Berkeley: University of California Press.

Barnaby, Frank. 1988. *Gaia Peace Atlas*. London: Pan Books.

Bartlett, Robert V. 1986. Ecological Rationality: Reason and Environmental Policy. *Environmental Ethics* 8:221–239.

Bell, Daniel A. 1999. Democratic Deliberation: The Problem of Implementation. In *Deliberative Politics: Essays on Democracy and Disagreement*, ed. Stephen Macedo, 70–87. New York: Oxford University Press.

Benhabib, Seyla. 2006a. Democratic Iterations: The Local, the National, the Global. In *Another Cosmopolitanism*, ed. Robert Post, 45–82. New York: Oxford University Press.

Benhabib, Seyla. 2006b. The Philosophical Foundations of Cosmopolitan Norms. In *Another Cosmopolitanism*, ed. Robert Post, 13–44. New York: Oxford University Press.

Bennett, Jane. 2001. *The Enchantment of Modern Life*. Princeton, NJ: Princeton University Press.

Bentham, Jeremy. (1823) 2011. *Introduction to the Principles of Morals and Legislation*. London: British Library.

Berelson, Bernard. 1952. *Content Analysis in Communication Research*. Glencoe, IL: Free Press.

Bessette, Joseph. 1997. *The Mild Voice of Reason: Deliberative Democracy and American National Government*. Chicago: University of Chicago Press.

Bhala, Raj. 1999. The Myth about Stare Decisis and International Trade Law (Part One of a Trilogy). *American University International Law Review* 14:845–956.

Bhala, Raj. 2001. The Power of the Past: Towards De Jure Stare Decisis in WTO Adjudication (Part Three of a Trilogy). *George Washington International Law Review* 33:873–978.

Bickel, Alexander. 1986. *The Least Dangerous Branch: The Supreme Court at the Bar of Politics*. New Haven, CT: Yale University Press.

Biermann, Frank, Michele M. Betsill, Joyeeta Gupta, Norichika Kanie, Louris Lebel, Kiana Liverman, Heike Schroeder, and Bernd Siebenhuner. 2009. *Earth System Governance: People, Places, and the Planet (Earth System Implementation Plan of the Earth System Governance Project*. Bonn: Earth System Governance Project.

Black, Henry Campbell. 1990. *Black's Law Dictionary*. Saint Paul, MN: West Publishing.

Bodansky, Daniel. 1995. Customary (and Not So Customary) International Environmental Law. *Indiana Journal of Global Legal Studies* 3:105–120.

Bodansky, Daniel. 2010a. *The Art and Craft of International Environmental Law*. Cambridge, MA: Harvard University Press.

Bodansky, Daniel. 2010b. The Copenhagen Climate Change Conference: A Postmortem. *American Journal of International Law* 104:230–240.

Bohman, James. 1994. Complexity, Pluralism, and the Constitutional State: on Habermas's *Faktizität und Geltung*. *Law & Society Review* 28:897–930.

Bohman, James. 1996. *Public Deliberation: Pluralism, Complexity, and Democracy*. Cambridge, MA: MIT Press.

Bohman, James. 2007. *Democracy across Borders: From Demos to Demoi*. Cambridge, MA: MIT Press.

Bonnell, Joseph E., and Tomas Koontz. 2007. Stumbling Forward: The Organizational Challenges of Building and Sustaining Collaborative Watershed Management. *Society & Natural Resources* 20 (2): 153–167.

Bookchin, Murray. 1999. The Concept of Social Ecology. In *Ecology*, ed. Carolyn Merchant, 152–162. Atlantic Highlands, NJ: Humanities Press.

Bordens, Kenneth S., and Irwin A. Horowitz. 1989. Mass Tort Civil Litigation: The Impact of Procedural Changes on Jury Decisions. *Judicature* 73:22–27.

Bovbjerg, Randall R., Frank A. Sloan, and James F. Blumstein. 1989. Valuing Life and Limb in Tort: Scheduling "Pain and Suffering." *Northwestern University Law Review* 83:908–976.

Bowers, William J., Benjamin D. Steiner, and Marla Sandys. 2001. Death Sentencing in Black and White: An Empirical Analysis of the Role of Jurors' Race and Jury Racial Composition. *University of Pennsylvania Journal of Constitutional Law* 3:171–275.

Brooks, Rosa Ehrenreich. 2005. Failed States, or the State as Failure? *University of Chicago Law Review* 72 (4): 1159–1196.

Brulle, Robert J. 2000. *Agency, Democracy, and Nature: The U.S. Environmental Movement from a Critical Theory Perspective*. Cambridge, MA: MIT Press.

Brunkhorst, Hauke. 2002. Globalizing Democracy without a State: Weak Public, Strong Public, Global Constitutionalism. *Millennium* 31:675–690.

Bryan, Frank M. 2004. *Real Democracy: The New England Town Meeting and How It Works*. Chicago: University of Chicago Press.

Buchanan, Allen, and Robert O. Keohane. 2006. The Legitimacy of Global Governance Institutions. *Ethics & International Affairs* 20:405–437.

Burch, William R. 1976. The Peregrine Falcon and the Urban Poor: Some Sociological Interrelations. In *Human Ecology: An Environmental Approach*, ed. Peter J. Richerson and James McEvoy, III, 303–321. North Scituate, MA: Duxbury Press.

Button, Mark, and Kevin Mattson. 1999. Deliberative Democracy in Practice: Challenge and Prospect for Civic Deliberation. *Polity* 31 (Summer): 609–637.

Caldwell, Lynton K. 1999. Is World Law an Emerging Reality? Environmental Law in a Transnational World. *Colorado Journal of International Environmental Law and Policy* 10 (2): 227–243.

Camacho, David. 1998. *Environmental Injustices, Political Struggles: Race, Class and the Environment*. Durham, NC: Duke University Press.

Cameron, Chip, Philip Harter, Gail Bingham, and Neil Eisner. 1990. Alternative Dispute Resolution with Emphasis on Rulemaking Negotiations. *Administrative Law Journal* 4:83.

Cantor, Norman. F. 1997. *Imagining the Law: Common Law and the Foundations of the American Legal System*. New York: HarperCollins.

Cawley, R. McGreggor, and William Chaloupka. 1997. American Governmentality: Michel Foucault and Public Administration. *American Behavioral Scientist* 41:28–42.

Champagne, Anthony, Daniel W. Schuman, and Elizabeth Whitaker. 1992. Expert Witnesses in the Courts: An Empirical Examination. *Judicature* 76:5–10.

Cheng, Antony S., and Janet D. Fiero. 2005. *The Deliberative Democracy Handbook: Strategies for Effective Civic Engagement in the 21st Century*. San Francisco: Wiley.

Chesterton, G. K. 1910. *Tremendous Trifles*.

Clark, Jo. 1997. *Strategic Partnerships: A Strategic Guide for Local Conservation Efforts in the West*. Denver, CO: Western Governors' Association.

Conca, Ken. 2005. Old States in New Bottles? The Hybridization of Authority in Global Environmental Governance. In *The State and the Global Environmental Crisis*, ed. John Barry and Robyn Eckersley, 181–205. Cambridge, MA: MIT Press.

Connolly, William. 1991. *Identity/Difference: Democratic Negotiations of Political Paradox*. Ithaca, NY: Cornell University Press.

Conrad, Clay S. 2013. *Jury Nullification: The Evolution of a Doctrine*. Washington, DC: Cato Institute.

Cook, David Angus Graham. 1987. Jung. In *Oxford Companion to the Mind*, ed. Richard L. Gregory, 403–405. New York: Oxford University Press.

Cooper, Philip J. 2007. *Public Law and Public Administration*. Belmont, CA: Thomsom Wadsworth.

Correa, Nestor, Andrew Carver, and Roberto Master. 2008. Strengthening Partnerships for Effective Wildlife Rescue in the Panama Canal Expansion Area. *Human Dimensions of Wildlife* 13:382–384.

Cronin, Amanda E., and David M. Ostergren. 2007. Democracy, Participation, and Native American Tribes in Collaborative Watershed Management. *Society & Natural Resources* 20 (6): 527–542.

Crossen, Teall. 2004. Multilateral Environmental Agreements and the Compliance Continuum. *Georgetown International Environmental Law Review* 16 (3): 473–500.

Dahl, Robert A. 1989. *Democracy and Its Critics*. New Haven, CT: Yale University Press.

Davis, Kenneth Culp. 1969a. *Discretionary Justice: A Preliminary Inquiry*. Baton Rouge: Louisiana State University Press.

Davis, Kenneth Culp. 1969b. A New Approach to Delegation. *University of Chicago Law Review* 36 (4): 713–733.

Davis, Kenneth Culp, Lars Busck, Sabino Cassese, Joachim Herrmann, Karl Matthias Meessen, and Christian Merlin. A.A.M.F. Staatsen, A. B. Ringeling, J.A.J. Scheffers, and R. P. Wolters. 1976. *Discretionary Justice in Europe and America*. Urbana: University of Illinois Press.

Delreux, Tom. 2011. *The EU as International Environmental Negotiator*. Burlington, VT: Ashgate.

Devine, Dennis J., Laura D. Clayton, Benjamin B. Dunford, Rasmy Seying, and Jennifer Pryce. 2001. Jury Decision Making: 45 Years of Empirical Research on Deliberating Groups. *Psychology, Public Policy, and Law* 7:622–727.

Dewey, John. (1929) 1984. *The Quest for Certainty*. Carbondale: Southern Illinois University Press.

Diesing, Paul. 1962. *Reason in Society: Five Types of Decision and Their Social Conditions*. Urbana: University of Illinois Press.

DiMento, Joseph F. C. 2003. *The Global Environment and International Law*. Austin: University of Texas Press.

Dogan, Mattei, and Robert Pahre. 1990. *Creative Marginality: Innovations at the Intersections of Social Sciences*. Boulder, CO: Westview Press.

Dorn, Jonathan G. 2007. NAAEC Citizen Submissions against Mexico: An Analysis of the Effectiveness of a Participatory Approach to Environmental Law Enforcement. *Georgetown International Environmental Law Review* 20 (1): 129–160.

Dryzek, John S. 1987. *Rational Ecology: Environment and Political Ecology.* London: Basil Blackwell.

Dryzek, John S. 2000. *Deliberative Democracy and Beyond: Liberals, Critics, Contestations.* New York: Oxford University Press.

Dryzek, John S. 2001. Legitimacy and Economy in Deliberative Democracy. *Political Theory* 29 (5): 651–669.

Dryzek, John S. 2006. *Deliberative Global Politics: Discourse and Democracy in a Divided World.* Malden, MA: Polity Press.

Dryzek, John S. 2009. Democracy and Earth System Governance. Paper presented at the Amsterdam Conference on the Human Dimensions of Global Environmental Change—Earth System Governance: People, Places, and the Planet, Amsterdam.

Dryzek, John S. 2010. *Foundations and Frontiers of Deliberative Governance.* New York: Oxford University Press.

Dryzek, John S., and Simon Niemeyer. 2008. Discursive Representation. *American Political Science Review* 102 (4): 481–493.

Eckersley, Robyn. 1992. *Environmentalism and Political Theory: Toward an Ecocentric Approach.* Albany: State University of New York Press.

Elliot, Charles. 1994. Towards Moral Communication and Consensus. *Cambridge Journal of Education* 24:393–398.

Ellsworth, Phoebe C. 1989. Are Twelve Heads Better Than One? *Law and Contemporary Problems* 52:205–224.

Elster, Jon. 1997. The Market and the Forum: Three Varieties of Political Theory. In *Contemporary Political Philosophy: An Anthology,* ed. Robert E. Goodin, and Philip Pettit, 128–142. Oxford, UK: Blackwell.

Faber, Daniel, ed. 1998. *The Struggle for Ecological Democracy: Environmental Justice Movements in the United States.* New York: Guilford Press.

Falkner, Robert. 2005. The Business of Ozone Layer Protection: Corporate Power in Regime Evolution. In *The Business of Global Environmental Governance,* ed. David L. Levy and Peter J. Newell, 103–134. Cambridge, MA: MIT Press.

Faure, Michael G., and Jurgen Lefevere. 2011. Compliance with Global Environmental Policy. In *The Global Environment: Institutions, Law, and Policy,* ed. Regina S. Axelrod, Stacy D. VanDeveer, and David Leonard Downie, 172–191. Washington, DC: CQ Press.

Feigenson, Neil. 2000. *Legal Blame: How Jurors Think and Talk about Accidents.* Washington, DC: APA Books.

Feigenson, Neil, Jaihyun Park, and Peter Salovey. 1997. Effects of Blameworthiness and Outcome Severity on Attributions of Responsibility and Damage Awards in Comparative Negligence Cases. *Law and Human Behavior* 21:597–617.

Feinberg, Matthew, and Robb Willer. 2013. The Moral Roots of Environmental Attitudes. *Psychological Science* 24 (1): 56–62.

Feld, Lars P. 2005. The European Constitution Project from the Perspective of Constitutional Political Economy. *Public Choice* 122 (3–4): 417–448.

Fish, Stanley. 1999. Mutual Respect as a Device of Exclusion. In *Deliberative Politics: Essays on Democracy and Disagreement*, ed. Stephen Macedo, 88–102. New York: Oxford University Press.

Fishkin, James S. 1995. *The Voice of the People: Public Opinion and Democracy.* New Haven, CT: Yale University Press.

Fishkin, James S. 1997. *The Voice of the People: Public Opinion and Democracy.* New Haven, CT: Yale University Press.

Fishkin, James S. 2009. *When the People Speak: Deliberative Democracy and Public Consultation.* New York: Oxford University Press.

Fishkin, James S., and Cynthia Farrar. 2005. Deliberative Polling: From Experiment to Community Resource. In *The Deliberative Democracy Handbook: Strategies for Effective Civic Engagement in the Twenty-First Century*, ed. John E. Gastil and Peter Levine, 68–79. San Francisco: Jossey-Bass.

Fishkin, James S., and Robert Luskin. 1999. Bringing Deliberation to Democratic Dialogue. In *A Poll with a Human Face: The National Issues Convention Experiment in Political Communication*, ed. Maxwell McCombs and Amy Reynolds. Mahwah, NJ: Lawrence Erlbaum.

Flaherty, Martin S. 2006. Introduction: "External" versus "Internal" in International Law. *Fordham International Law Journal* 29:447–456.

Forester, John. 1999. *The Deliberative Practitioner: Encouraging Participatory Planning.* Cambridge, MA: MIT Press.

Francione, Gary. 1996. *Rain without Thunder: The Ideology of the Animal Rights Movement.* Philadelphia: Temple University Press.

Freund, Ernst. 1928. *Administrative Powers over Persons and Property: A Comparative Survey.* Chicago: University of Chicago Press.

Friedman, Elisabeth Jay, Kathryn Hochstetler, and Ann Marie Clark. 2005. *Sovereignty, Democracy, and Global Civil Society: State-Society Relations at UN World Conferences.* Albany: State University of New York Press.

Friest, Jess, and Gregory Friest. 2009. *Theories of Personality.* New York: McGraw-Hill.

Frohlich, Norman, and Joe A. Oppenheimer. 1992. *Choosing Justice: An Experimental Approach to Ethical Theory.* Berkeley: University of California Press.

Galanter, Marc. 1993. The Regulatory Function of the Civil Jury. In *Verdict: Assessing the Civil Jury System*, ed. Robert E. Litan, 61–102. Washington, DC: Brookings Institution Press.

Galaz, Victor, Per Olsson, Thomas Hahn, Carl Folke, and Uno Svedin. 2004. The Problem of Fit among Biophysical Systems, Environmental and Resource Regimes, and Broader Governance Systems: Insights and Emerging Trends. In *Institutions and Environmental Change: Principal Findings, Applications, and Research Frontiers*, ed. Oran R. Young, Leslie A. King, and Heike Schroeder, 147–182. Cambridge, MA: MIT Press.

Garrett, Nathaniel. 2005. Life Is the Risk We Cannot Refuse: A Precautionary Approach to the Toxic Risks We Can. *Georgetown International Environmental Law Review* 17 (3): 517–562.

Gastil, John E., E. Pierre Deess, Philip J. Weiser, and Cindy Simmons. 2010. *The Jury and Democracy: How Jury Deliberation Promotes Civic Engagement.* New York: Oxford University Press.

Gastil, John E., and Peter Levine. 2005. *The Deliberative Democracy Handbook: Strategies for Effective Civic Engagement in the Twenty-First Century.* San Francisco: Jossey-Bass.

Gaus, Gerald. 2011. *The Order of Public Reason: A Theory of Freedom and Morality in a Diverse and Bounded World.* New York: Cambridge University Press.

Gearey, Adam. 2005. *Globalization and Law: Trade, Rights, War.* Boulder, CO: Rowan Littlefield.

Gibbs, Laura. 2002. *Aesop's Fables.* New York: Oxford University Press.

Gilligan, Carol, and Jane Attanucci. 1988. Two Moral Orientations: Gender Differences and Similarities. *Merrill-Palmer Quarterly* 34 (3): 223–237.

Giorgi, Liana, and Ronald Pohoryles, J. 2005. Challenges to EU Political Integration and the Role of Democratization. *Innovation* 18 (4): 407–418.

Glaser, Marion, and Rosete da Silva Oliveira. 2004. Prospects for the Co-Management of Mangrove Ecosystems on the Northern Brazilian Coast: Whose Rights, Whose Duties, and Whose Priorities? *Natural Resources Forum* 28:224–233.

Glenn, H. Patrick. 2010. *Legal Traditions of the World: Sustainable Diversity in Law.* 4th ed. New York: Oxford University Press.

Goldsmith, Jack L., and Eric A. Posner. 2005. *The Limits of International Law.* New York: Oxford University Press.

Goodin, Robert E. 2000. Democratic Deliberation Within. *Philosophy & Public Affairs* 29 (1): 81–109.

Goodin, Robert E., and John S. Dryzek. 2006. Deliberative Impacts: The Macro-Political Uptake of Mini-Publics. *Politics & Society* 34 (2): 219–244.

Goodnow, Frank. 1905. *The Principles of Administrative Law in the United States.* New York: Putnam.

Gore, Al. 1993. Report of the National Performance Review. In *From Red Tape to Results: Creating a Government That Works Better and Costs Less.* Washington, DC: Government Printing Office.

Grover, Sonja. 2010. Implicit Informal Qualitative Research Processes Embedded in Legal Proceedings: A Case Example. *Journal of the Canadian Academy of Adolescent Psychiatry* 19 (1): 26–31.

Guerrieri, Matthew. 2012. *The First Four Notes: Beethoven's Fifth and the Human Imagination.* New York: Knopf.

Gupta, Joyeeta. 2008. Global Change: Analyzing and Scaling in Environmental Governance. In *Institutions and Environmental Change: Principal Findings, Ap-*

plications, and Research Frontiers, ed. Oran R. Young, Leslie A. King, and Heike Schroeder, 225–258. Cambridge, MA: MIT Press.

Gutmann, Amy. 1999. *Democratic Education*. Princeton, NJ: Princeton University Press.

Gutmann, Amy, and Dennis Thompson. 1996. *Democracy and Disagreement*. Cambridge, MA: Belknap Press.

Gutmann, Amy, and Dennis Thompson. 2004. *Why Deliberative Democracy?* Princeton, NJ: Princeton University Press.

Habermas, Jürgen. 1979. *Communication and the Evolution of Society*. Boston: Beacon Press.

Habermas, Jürgen. 1984. *The Theory of Communicative Action: Reason and the Rationalization of Society*. Vol. 1. Boston: Beacon Press.

Habermas, Jürgen. 1987a. *The Philosophical Discourse of Modernity*. Cambridge, MA: MIT Press.

Habermas, Jürgen. 1987b. *The Theory of Communicative Action: Lifeworld and System—A Critique of Functionalist Reason*. Vol. 2. Boston: Beacon Press.

Habermas, Jürgen. 1992. *Postmetaphysical Thinking: Philosophical Essays*. Cambridge, MA: MIT Press.

Habermas, Jürgen. 1996. *Between Facts and Norms: Contributions to a Discourse Theory of Law and Democracy*. Cambridge, MA: MIT Press.

Habermas, Jürgen. 1998. *The Inclusion of the Other*. Cambridge, MA: MIT Press.

Habermas, Jürgen. 2001. *On the Pragmatics of Social Interaction: Preliminary Studies in the Theory of Social Interaction*. Cambridge, MA: MIT Press.

Habermas, Jürgen. 2006. *The Divided West*. Cambridge, UK: Polity Press.

Haidt, Jonathan. 2001. The Emotional Dog and Its Rational Tail: A Social Intuitionist Approach to Moral Judgment. *Psychological Review* 108 (4): 814–834.

Haidt, Jonathan. 2012. *The Righteous Mind: Why Good People Are Divided by Politics and Religion*. New York: Pantheon.

Haidt, Jonathan, and Jesse Graham. 2007. When Morality Opposes Justice: Conservatives Have Moral Intuitions That Liberals May Not Recognize. *Social Justice Research* 20 (1): 98–116.

Hans, Valerie P. 2000. *Business on Trial: The Civil Jury and Corporate Responsibility*. New Haven, CT: Yale University Press.

Hans, Valerie P. 2007. Citizens as Legal Decision Makers: An International Perspective. *Cornell International Law Review* 40 (Spring): 300–314.

Hans, Valerie P., and M. David Ermann. 1989. Responses to Corporate versus Individual Wrongdoing. *Law and Human Behavior* 13:151–166.

Hardin, Russell. 2000. Democratic Epistemology and Accountability. *Social Philosophy and Policy* 17 (1):110–126.

Hardy, Scott, and Tomas Koontz. 2009. Rules for Collaboration: Institutional Analysis of Group Membership and Levels of Action in Watershed Partnerships.

Policy Studies Journal: The Journal of the Policy Studies Organization 37 (3): 393–414.

Hare, R. M. 1952. *The Language of Morals*. Oxford, UK: Oxford University Press.

Hart, H.L.A. 1994. *The Concept of Law*. 2nd ed. Oxford, UK: Clarendon Press.

Hawkins, Charles H. 1962. Interaction Rates of Jurors Aligned in Factions. *American Sociological Review* 27:689–691.

Hibbing, John, and Elizabeth Theiss-Morse. 2002. *Stealth Democracy: Americans' Beliefs about How Government Should Work*. New York: Cambridge University Press.

Hofstadter, Richard. 1955. *The Age of Reform*. New York: Random House.

Holmes, Arthur. 2007. *Approaching Moral Decisions*. Downer's Grove, IL: Inter-Varsity Press.

Holmes, Oliver Wendell, Jr. (1881) 1991. *The Common Law*. New York: Dover Publications.

Holsti, Ole R. 1969. *Content Analysis for the Social Sciences and Humanities*. Reading, MA: Addison-Wesley.

Honig, Bonnie. 1993. *Political Theory and the Displacement of Politics*. Ithaca, NY: Cornell University Press.

Huitema, Dave, Marleen van De Kerkhof, and Udo Pesch. 2007. The Nature of the Beast: Are Citizens' Juries Deliberative or Pluralist? *Policy Sciences* 40 (4): 287–311.

Hull, N.E.H. 1990. Restatement and Reform: A New Perspective on the Origins of the American Law Institute. *Law and History Review* 8 (1): 55–96.

Hume, David. (1740) 2011. *A Treatise of Human Nature*. New York: Oxford University Press.

Hume, David. (1759) 2006. *An Enquiry concerning the Principles of Morals*. New York: Oxford University Press.

Humphrey, Matthew. 2007. *Ecological Politics and Democratic Theory: The Challenge to the Deliberative Ideal*. New York: Routledge.

Hunold, Christian. 2005. Green Political Theory and the European Union: The Case for a Non-Integrated Civil Society. *Environmental Politics* 14 (3): 324–343.

Hunter, David, James Salzman, and Durwood Zaelke. 2007. *International Environmental Law and Policy*. 3rd ed. New York: Foundation Press.

Huntington, Samuel. 1996. *The Clash of Civilizations and the Remaking of the World Order*. New York: Simon & Schuster.

Ivkovic, Sanja Kutnjak, and Valerie P. Hans. 2003. Jurors' Evaluations of Expert Testimony. *Judging the Messenger and the Message*. 28:441–482.

Jacobs, Lawrence, Fay Lomax Cook, and Michael Delli Carpini. 2009. *Talking Together: Public Deliberation and Political Participation in America*. Chicago: University of Chicago Press.

Jaffe, Louis L. 1969. Book Review: *Discretionary Justice* by Kenneth Culp Davis. *Villanova Law Review* 14:773-778.

James, William. (1890) 1990. *The Principles of Psychology.* Chicago: Encyclopaedia Britannica.

James, William. (1907) 1995. *Pragmatism: A New Name for Some Old Ways of Thinking.* New York: Dover Publications.

Jayasuriya, Kanishka. 2005. *Reconstructing the Global Liberal Order.* New York: Routledge.

Jung, Carl Gustav. 1959. *Aion.* London: Pantheon.

Jung, Carl Gustav. 1963. *Mysterium Coniunctionis.* London: Pantheon.

Jung, Carl Gustav. 1978. *Man and His Symbols.* London: Pantheon.

Kadish, Mortimer, and Sanford Kadish. 1971. The Institutionalization of Conflict: Jury Acquitals. *Journal of Social Issues* 27 (2): 199–217.

Kalven, Harry, Jr., and Hans Zeisel. 1966. *The American Jury.* Boston: Little, Brown.

Kant, Immanuel. (1794) 1994. *Perpetual Peace: A Philosophical Sketch.* New York: Cambridge University Press.

Kay, David H., and George F. Sensabaugh, Jr. 2000. Reference Guide on DNA Evidence. In *Reference Manual on Scientific Evidence*, 2nd ed. 485–576. Washington, DC: Federal Judicial Center.

Kelsen, Hans. (1949) 2006. *General Theory of Law and State.* New Brunswick, NJ: Transaction Publishers.

Kennedy, David. 1997. New Approaches to Comparative Law: Comparativism and International Governance. *Utah Law Review* 1997:545–637.

Kenyon, Wendy. 2005. A Critical Review of Citizens' Juries: How Useful Are They in Facilitating Public Participation in the EU Water Framework Directive? *Environmental Planning and Management* 48 (3): 431–443.

Kenyon, Wendy, Nick Hanley, and Ceara Nevin. 2001. Citizen Juries: An Aid to Environmental Valuation? *Environment and Planning C: Government and Policy* 19:557–566.

Keohane, Robert O., and Joseph S. Nye, Jr. 2003. Redefining Accountability for Global Governance. In *Governance in a Global Economy: Political Authority in Transition*, ed. Miles Kahler and David A. Lake, 386–411. Princeton, NJ: Princeton University Press.

Kerwin, Cornelius M. 1994. *Rulemaking: How Government Agencies Write Law and Make Policy.* Washington, DC: Congressional Quarterly Press.

Klinghoffer, Arthur, and Judith Klinghoffer. 2002. *International Citizens' Tribunals: Mobilizing Public Opinion to Advance Human Rights.* New York: Palgrave.

Klostermaier, Klaus. 2007. *A Survey of Hinduism.* Albany: State University of New York Press.

Knight, Jack, and James Johnson. 1994. Aggregation and Deliberation: On the Possibility of Democratic Legitimacy. *Political Theory* 22 (2): 277–296.

Knox, John H. 2001. A New Approach to Compliance with International Environmental Law: The Submissions Procedure of the NAFTA Environmental Commission. *Ecology Law Quarterly* 28 (1): 1–122.

Kohlberg, Lawrence. 1981. *The Philosophy of Moral Development: Moral Stages and the Idea of Justice*. New York: Harper and Row.

Kohlberg, Lawrence. 1984. *The Psychology of Moral Development: The Nature and Validity of Moral Stages*. New York: Harper and Row.

Koskenniemi, Martti. 2001. *The Gentle Civilizer of Nations: The Rise and Fall of International Law, 1879–1960*. Cambridge: Cambridge University Press.

Krippendorf, Klaus. 2004. *Content Analysis: An Introduction to Its Methodology*. 2nd ed. Thousand Oaks, CA: Sage.

Kuhn, Thomas S. 1970. *The Structure of Scientific Revolutions*. 2nd ed. Chicago: University of Chicago Press.

Kuhn, Thomas S. 2000. *The Road since Structure: Philosophical Essays, 1970–1993, with an Autobiographical Interview*. Chicago: University of Chicago Press.

Lakoff, George. 2002. *Moral Politics*. Chicago: University of Chicago Press.

Landauer, Carl. 2011. Regionalism, Geography, and the International Legal Imagination. *Chicago Journal of International Law* 11 (2): 557–595.

Landis, James M. 1938. *The Administrative Process*. New Haven, CT: Yale University Press.

Larmore, Charles. 2008. *The Autonomy of Morality*. New York: Cambridge University Press.

Larson, Eric Thomas. 2005. Why Environmental Liability Regimes in the United States, the European Community, and Japan Have Grown Synonymous with the Polluter Pays Principle. *Vanderbilt Journal of Transnational Law* 38:541–575.

Laslett, Peter. 2003. Environmental Ethics and the Obsolescence of Existing Political Institutions. In *Debating Deliberative Democracy*, ed. James S. Fishkin and Peter Laslett. Malden, MA: Blackwell.

Leach, William D., and Neil W. Pelky. 2001. Making Watershed Partnerships Work: A Review of the Empirical Literature. *Journal of Water Resources Planning and Management* 127:378–385.

Lempert, Richard. 1993. Civil Juries and Complex Cases: Taking Stock after Twelve Years. In *Verdict: Assessing the Civil Jury System*, ed. Robert E. Litan, 181–212. Washington, DC: Brookings Institution Press.

Leonard, People v. 1962. *People v. Leonard*, 207 Cal. App. 2d 409; 24 Cal. Rptr. 597; 1962 Cal. App. LEXIS 1924.

Lijphart, Arend. 1977. *Democracy in Plural Societies: A Comparative Exploration*. New Haven, CT: Yale University Press.

Lijphart, Arend. 1984. *Democracies: Patterns of Majoritarian and Consensus Government in Twenty-One Countries*. New Haven, CT: Yale University Press.

Lijphart, Arend. 1999. *Patterns of Democracy: Government Forms and Performance in Thirty-Six Countries*. New Haven, CT: Yale University Press.

Lijphart, Arend. 2008. *Thinking about Democracy: Power Sharing and Majority Rule in Theory and Practice*. New York: Routledge.

Lindblom, Anna-Karin. 2005. *Non-Governmental Organizations in International Law*. New York: Cambridge University Press.

Lipset, Seymour Martin, and Stein Rokkan. 1967. *Party Systems and Voter Alignments: Cross-National Perspectives*. New York: Free Press.

Lo, Ying-Jen. 2005. *Human Rights Litigation: Promoting International Law in U.S. Courts*. El Paso: LFB Scholarly Publishers.

Lowi, Theodore J. 1979. *The End of Liberalism: The Second Republic of the United States*. New York: W. W. Norton.

Lubell, Mark, Mark Schneider, John T. Scholz, and Mihriye Mete. 2002. Watershed Partnerships and the Emergence of Collective Action Institutions. *American Journal of Political Science* 46 (1): 148–163.

Lupoi, Maurizio. 2007. *The Origins of the European Legal Order*. New York: Cambridge University Press.

Lutz, Robert E., II. 1976. The Laws of Environmental Management: A Comparative Study. *American Journal of Comparative Law* 24 (3): 447–520.

MacIntyre, Alasdair. 1984. *After Virtue: A Study in Moral Theory*. 2nd ed. Notre Dame, IN: Notre Dame University Press.

Mansbridge, Jane. 1983. *Beyond Adversary Democracy*. Chicago: University of Chicago Press.

Mansbridge, Jane. 1990. Feminism and Democracy. *American Prospect* 1:126–139.

Matthews, Freya. 1991. Democracy and the Ecological Crisis. *Legal Services Bulletin* 16 (4): 157–159.

Mburu, John, and Regina Birner. 2007. Emergence, Adoption, and Implementation of Collaborative Wildlife Management or Wildlife Partnerships in Kenya: A Look at Conditions of Success. *Society & Natural Resources* 20:379–395.

McCarthy, Thomas. 1978. *The Critical Theory of Jürgen Habermas*. Cambridge, MA: Polity Press.

McCarthy, Thomas. 1994. Kantian Constructivism and Reconstructivism: Rawls and Habermas in Dialogue. *Ethics* 105:44–63.

McCormick, John. 2011. The Role of Environmental NGOs in International Regimes. In *The Global Environment: Institutions, Law, and Policy*, ed. Regina Axelrod, Stacy D. VanDeveer, and David Leonard Downie, 92–110. Washington, DC: CQ Press.

McKeone, Dermot. 1995. *Measuring Your Media Profile: A General Introduction to Media Analysis and PR Evaluation for the Communications Industry*. London: Gower Press.

Meidinger, Errol. 2008. Competitive Supragovernmental Regulation: How Could It Be Democratic? *Chicago Journal of International Law* 8 (2): 513–534.

Miller, Alexander. 2013. *Contemporary Metaethics*. New York: Polity Press.

Miller, David. 2003. Deliberative Democracy and Social Choice. In *Debating Deliberative Democracy*, ed. James S. Fishkin and Peter Laslett, 182–199. Malden, MA: Blackwell Publishing.

Minteer, Ben A. 2006. *The Landscape of Reform: Civic Pragmatism and Environmental Thought in America*. Cambridge, MA: MIT Press.

Mize, Gregory E. 1999. On Better Jury Selection: Spotting UFO Jurors before They Enter the Jury Room. *Court Review* 36:10–15.

Moore, Elizabeth A., and Tomas M. Koontz. 2003. A Typology of Collaborative Watershed Groups: Citizen-Based, Agency-Based, and Mixed Partnerships. *Society & Natural Resources* 16 (5): 451–460.

Moravcsik, Andrew. 2005. Is There a "Democratic Deficit" in World Politics? A Framework for Analysis. In *Global Governance and Public Accountability*, ed. David Held and Mathias Koenig-Archibugi, 212–239. Malden, MA: Blackwell Publishing.

Mouffe, Chantal. 1996. Democracy, Power, and the "Political." In *Democracy and Difference: Contesting the Boundaries of the Political*, ed. Seyla Benhabib, 245–256. Princeton, NJ: Princeton University Press.

Mouffe, Chantal. 1999. Deliberative Democracy or Agonistic Pluralism? *Social Research* 66 (3): 745–758.

Mouffe, Chantal. 2000. *The Democratic Paradox*. London: Verso.

Munger, Michael. 2000. *Analyzing Policy: Choices, Conflicts, and Practices*. New York: W. W. Norton.

Mutz, Diana C. 2006. *Hearing the Other Side: Deliberative versus Participatory Democracy*. New York: Cambridge University Press.

Najam, Adil. 2011. The View from the South: Developing Countries in Global Enviromental Politics. In *The Global Environment: Institutions, Law, and Policy*, ed. Regina Axelrod, Stacy D. VanDeveer, and David Leonard Downie, 239–258. Washington, DC: CQ Press.

Nelson, William Edward. 1975. *Americanization of the Common Law: The Impact of Legal Change on Massachusetts Society, 1760–1830*. Cambridge, MA: Harvard University Press.

Neuendorf, Kimberly A. 2002. *The Content Analysis Guidebook*. Thousand Oaks, CA: Sage.

Nisbet, Matthew, and Teresa Myers. 2007. Twenty Years of Public Opinion about Global Warming. *Public Opinion Quarterly* 71 (3): 444–470.

O'Leary, Rosemary. 1993. *Environmental Change: Federal Courts and the EPA*. Philadelphia: Temple University Press.

Ophuls, William. 1997. *Requiem for Modern Politics: The Tragedy of the Enlightenment and the Challenge of the New Millennium*. Boulder, CO: Westview Press.

Ostrom, Elinor. 1990. *Governing the Commons: The Evolution of Institutions for Collective Action*. New York: Cambridge University Press.

Park, Jacob, Ken Conca, and Matthias Finger. 2008. *The Crisis of Global Environmental Governance: Towards a New Political Economy of Sustainability.* New York: Routledge.

Parkinson, John. 2006. *Deliberating the Real World: Problems of Legitimacy in Deliberative Democracy.* New York: Oxford University Press.

Patterson, Charles. 2002. *Eternal Treblinka: Our Treatment of Animals and the Holocaust.* Herndon, VA: Lantern Books.

Pederson, William F., Jr. 1975. Formal Records and Informal Rulemaking. *Yale Law Journal* 85:38–88.

Peel, Jacqueline. 2011. Environmental Protection in the Twenty-First Century: The Role of International Lsw. In *The Global Environment: Institutions, Law, and Policy,* ed. Regina S. Axelrod, Stacy D. VanDeveer, and David Leornard Downie, 48–69. Washington, DC: CQ Press.

Pennington, Nancy, and Reid Hastie. 1991. A Cognitive Theory of Juror Decision Making: The Story Model. *Cardozo Law Review* 13:519–551.

Perdue, Wendy C. 1990. Commentary: Finley v. United States: Unstringing Pendent Jurisdiction. *Virginia Law Review* 76:539–573.

Perlman, Cary. 2009. *Environmental Litigation: Law and Strategy.* New York: American Bar Association.

Peters, Anne. 2009. The Merits of Global Constitutionalism. *Indiana Journal of Global Legal Studies* 16 (2): 397–411.

Plater, Zygmunt J. B., Robert H. Abrams, William Goldfarb, Lisa Heinzerling, David Wirth, and Robert L. Graham. 2004. *Environmental Law and Policy: Nature, Law, and Society.* 3rd ed. New York: Aspen Publishers.

Polanyi, Michael. (1966) 2009. *The Tacit Dimension.* Chicago: University of Chicago Press.

Posa, Mary, Arvin Diesmos, Navjot Sodhi, and Thomas Brooks. 2008. Hope for Threatened Tropical Biodiversity: Lessons from the Philippines. *Bioscience* 58 (3): 231–240.

Posner, Richard A. 1981. *The Economics of Justice.* Cambridge, MA: Harvard University Press.

Posner, Richard A. 1990. *The Problems of Jurisprudence.* Cambridge, MA: Harvard University Press.

Posner, Richard A. 1995. *Overcoming Law.* Cambridge, MA: Harvard University Press.

Posner, Richard A. 1999. *The Problematics of Moral and Legal Theory.* Cambridge, MA: Belknap Press.

Posner, Richard A. 2008. *How Judges Think.* Cambridge, MA: Harvard University Press.

Powell, Barry. 1998. *Classical Myth.* Upper Saddle River, NJ: Prentice Hall.

Putnam, Hilary. 1995. *Pragmatism: An Open Question.* Cambridge, MA: Blackwell.

Rabkin, Jeremy A. 2005. *Law without Nations? Why Constitutional Government Requires Sovereign States*. Princeton, NJ: Princeton University Press.

Rawls, John. 1971. *A Theory of Justice*. Cambridge, MA: Harvard University Press.

Rawls, John. 1993. *Political Liberalism*. New York: Columbia University Press.

Rawls, John. 1999. *The Law of Peoples*. Cambridge, MA: Harvard University Press.

Regan, Tom. 2004. *The Case for Animal Rights*. Berkeley: University of California Press.

Rhodes, Edwardo Lao. 2003. *Environmental Justice in America: A New Paradigm*. Bloomington: Indiana University Press.

Ringquist, Evan J. 2003. Environmental Justice: Normative Concerns, Empirical Evidence, and Government Action. In *Environmental Policy: New Directions for the Twenty-First Century*, ed. Norman J. Vig and Michael E. Kraft, 249–273. Washington, DC: CQ Press.

Rorty, Richard. 1979. *Philosophy and the Mirror of Nature*. Princeton, NJ: Princeton University Press.

Sabatier, Paul A., Will Focht, Mark Lubell, Zev Trachtenberg, Arnold Vedlitz, and Marty Matlock. 2005. *Swimming Upstream: Collaborative Approaches to Watershed Management*. Cambridge, MA: MIT Press.

Sabini, Meredith, ed. 2002. *The Earth Has a Soul: C. G. Jung on Nature, Technology, and Modern Life*. Berkeley, CA: North Atlantic Books.

Sanders, Lynn. 1997. Against Deliberation. *Political Theory* 25 (June): 347–376.

Scanlon, Thomas M. 1998. *What We Owe to Each Other*. Cambridge, MA: Harvard University Press.

Scanlon, Thomas M. 2008. *Moral Dimensions: Permissability, Meaning, Blame*. Cambridge, MA: Harvard University Press.

Schapp, Andrew. 2006. Agonism in Divided Societies. *Philosophy and Social Criticism* 32:255–277.

Scharpf, Fritz. 1999. *Governing in Europe: Effective and Democratic?* New York: Oxford University Press.

Schlosberg, David. 1998. Resurrecting the Pluralist Universe. *Political Research Quarterly* 51:583–615.

Schlosberg, David. 1999. *Environmental Justice and the New Pluralism: The Challenge of Difference for Environmentalism*. New York: Oxford University Press.

Schoenbaum, Thomas J. 2006. *International Relations: The Path Not Taken*. New York: Cambridge University Press.

Schroeder, Mark. 2010. *Noncognitivism in Ethics*. New York: Routledge.

Schuck, Peter H. 2000. *The Limits of Law: Essays on Democratic Governance*. Boulder, CO: Westview Press.

Sen, Amartya. 2009. *The Idea of Justice*. Cambridge, MA: Belknap Press.

Shaffer, Gregory C., and Mark A. Pollack. 2010. Hard vs. Soft Law: Alternatives, Complements, and Antagonists in International Governance. *Minnesota Law Review* 94:706–799.

Shandas, Vivek, and W. Barry Messer. 2008. Fostering Green Communities through Civic Engagement: Community-Based Environmental Stewardship in the Portland Area. *Journal of the American Planning Association* 74 (4): 408–418.

Simon, Herbert A. 1996. *The Sciences of the Artificial*. 3rd ed. Cambridge, MA: MIT Press.

Singer, Peter. 2002. *One World: The Ethics of Globalization*. New Haven, CT: Yale University Press.

Singer, Peter. 2009. *Animal Liberation*. New York: Harper Perennial.

Singer, Peter. 2011. *Practical Ethics*. 3rd ed. New York: Cambridge University Press.

Slaughter, Anne-Marie. 2004. *A New World Order*. Princeton, NJ: Princeton University Press.

Smith, Adam. (1759) 2000. *The Theory of Moral Sentiments*. Amherst, NY: Prometheus Books.

Smith, Brian. 2005. He Who Has Lost Something but Knows Where to Find It: Iroquois "Law" and the Withdrawal of the Origin. *Dialogue and Universalism* 5 (3–4): 147–159.

Smith, Graham. 2009. *Democratic Innovations: Designing Institutions for Citizen Participation*. New York: Cambridge University Press.

Smith, Vicki L. 1991. Prototypes in the Courtroom: Lay Representations of Legal Concepts. *Journal of Personality and Social Psychology* 61:857–872.

Snidal, Duncan, and Alexander Thompson. 2003. International Commitments and Domestic Politics: Institutions and Actors at Two Levels. In *Locating the Proper Authorities: The Interaction of Domestic and International Institutions*, ed. Daniel Drezner, 197–230. Ann Arbor: University of Michigan Press.

Sofaer, Abraham D. 1972. Judicial Control of Informed Discretionary Adjudication and Enforcement. *Columbia Law Review* 72 (1293): 1296–1297.

Sommers, Samuel R. 2006. On Racial Diversity and Group Decision Making: Identifying Multiple Effects of Racial Composition on Jury Deliberation. *Journal of Personality and Social Psychology* 90:597–612.

Sørensen, Eva, and Jacob Torfing. 2008. Governance Network Research: Towards a Second Generation. In *Theories of Democratic Network Governance*, ed. Eva Sørensen and Jacob Torfing, 1–21. New York: Palgrave Macmillan.

Soroos, Marvin S. 2011. Global Institutions and the Environment: An Evolutionary Perspective. In *The Global Environment: Institutions, Law, and Policy*, ed. Regina Axelrod, Stacy D. VanDeveer, and David Leonard Downie, 24–47. Washington, DC: CQ Press.

Stavins, Robert N., and Robert C. Stowe. 2010. What Hath Copenhagen Wrought? A Preliminary Assessment. *Environment* 52 (3): 8–14.

Stevenson, Charles L. 1944. *Ethics and Language*. New Haven, CT: Yale University Press.

Stewart-Harawira, Makere. 2005. *The New Imperial Order: Indigenous Responses to Globalization*. New York: Zed Books.

Stone, Deborah. 2002. *Policy Paradox: The Art of Political Decision Making*, rev. ed. New York: W. W. Norton.

Sunstein, Cass R. 1993. *The Partial Constitution*. Cambridge, MA: Harvard University Press.

Sunstein, Cass R. 1996. *Legal Reasoning and Political Conflict*. New York: Oxford University Press.

Sunstein, Cass R. 1999. Agreement without Theory. In *Deliberative Politics: Essays on Democracy and Disagreement*, ed. Stephen Macedo, 123–150. New York: Oxford University Press.

Sunstein, Cass R. 2002. The Law of Group Polarization. *Journal of Political Philosophy* 10:175–195.

Sunstein, Cass R. 2003. *Why Societies Need Dissent*. Cambridge, MA: Harvard University Press.

Sunstein, Cass R. 2005. Group Judgments: Statistical Means, Deliberation, and Information Markets. *New York University Law Review* 80:962–1049.

Sunstein, Cass R. 2006. *Infotopia: How Many Minds Produce Knowledge*. New York: Oxford University Press.

Sunstein, Cass R. 2009. *Going to Extremes: How Like Minds Unite and Divide*. New York: Oxford University Press.

Susskind, Lawrence S. 1994. *Environmental Diplomacy: Negotiating More Effective Global Agreements*. New York: Oxford University Press.

Taylor, Dorceta. 1999. Environmentalism and the Politics of Inclusion. In *Confronting Environmental Racism: Voices from the Grassroots*, ed. Robert Bullard and Benjamin Chavis, 53–62. Cambridge, MA: South End Press.

Thompson, Dennis F. 1999. Democratic Theory and Global Society. *Journal of Political Philosophy* 7 (2): 111–125.

Thompson, William C., and Edward L. Schumann. 1987. Interpretation of Statistical Evidence in Criminal Trials: The Prosecutor's Fallacy and the Defense Attorney's Fallacy. *Law and Human Behavior* 11:167–187.

Tocqueville, Alexis de. (1835) 1994. *Democracy in America*. Vol. 1. New York: Everyman's Library.

Tomuschat, Christian. 2006. An International Law Commission: An Outdated Institution. *German Yearbook of International Law* 49:77–105.

Torgerson, Douglas. 1997. Policy Professionalism and the Voices of Dissent: The Case of Environmentalism. *Politiy* 29:345–374.

Tully, James. 1995. *Strange Multiplicity: Constitutionalism in an Age of Diversity*. New York: Cambridge University Press.

Turner, John C. 1987. *Rediscovering the Social Group: A Self-Categorization Theory*. New York: Blackwell.

Valadez, Jorge M. 2001. *Deliberative Democracy: Political Legitimacy and Self-Determination in Multicultural Societies*. Boulder, CO: Westview Press.

VanDeveer, Stacy D. 2003. Green Fatigue. *Wilson Quarterly* 27 (4): 55–59.

Vidmar, Neil, and Shari Seidman Diamond. 2001. Juries and Expert Evidence. *Brooklyn Law Review* 66:1121–1180.

Vidmar, Neil, and Valerie P. Hans. 2007. *American Juries: The Verdict*. Amherst, NY: Prometheus Books.

Waltzer, Michael. 1999. Deliberation, and What Else? In *Deliberative Politics: Essays on Democracy and Disagreement*, ed. Stephen Macedo, 58–69. New York: Oxford University Press.

Weber, Max. 1978. *Economy and Society: An Outline of Interpretive Sociology*. Berkeley: University of California Press.

Wechsler, Herbert. 1969. The Course of the Restatements. *American Bar Association Journal* 55:147–201.

Weiler, Joseph. 1999. *The Constitution of Europe*. New York: Cambridge University Press.

Weiss, Edith Brown, Stephen C. McCaffrey, Daniel Barstow Margraw, and A. Dan Tarlock. 2007. *International Environmental Law and Policy*. 2nd ed. New York: Aspen Publishers.

Wenz, Peter. 1988. *Environmental Justice*. Albany: State University of New York Press.

Wilks, Colin. 2002. *Emotion, Truth, and Meaning: In Defense of Ayer and Stevenson*. Boston: Kluwer.

Williams, Melissa. 2000. The Uneasy Alliance of Group Representation and Deliberative Democracy. In *Citizenship in Diverse Societies*, ed. William Kymlicka and Wayne Norman, 125–152. New York: Oxford University Press.

Williams, Stephen F. 1975. "Hybrid Rulemaking" under the Administrative Procedure Act: A Legal and Empirical Analysis. *University of Chicago Law Review* 42:401–456.

Wilson, Matthew A., and Richard B. Howarth. 2002. Discourse-Based Valuation of Ecosystem Services: Establishing Fair Outcomes through Group Deliberation. *Ecological Economics* 41:431–443.

Wirth, David A. 1996. Public Participation in International Processes: Environmental Case Studies at the National and International Levels. *Colorado Journal of International Environmental Law and Policy* 7 (1): 1–38.

Woll, Peter. 1963. *Administrative Law: The Informal Process*. Berkeley: University of California Press.

Wright, J. Skelly. 1972. Beyond Discretionary Justice. *Yale Law Journal* 81:575–597.

Yokota, Yozo. 1999. International Justice and the Global Environment. *Journal of International Affairs* 52 (2): 583–598.

Young, Iris Marion. 1996. Communication and the Other: Beyond Deliberative Democracy. In *Democracy and Difference: Contesting the Boundaries of the Political*, ed. Seyla Benhabib, 120–135. Princeton, NJ: Princeton University Press.

Young, Iris Marion. 1999. Justice, Inclusion, and Deliberative Democracy. In *Deliberative Politics: Essays on Democracy and Disagreement*, ed. Stephen Macedo, 151–158. New York: Oxford University Press.

Young, Iris Marion. 2000. *Inclusion and Democracy*. New York: Oxford University Press.

Young, Iris Marion. 2007. *Global Challenges: War, Self-Determination, and Responsibility for Justice*. Cambridge, UK: Polity Press.

Young, Oran R. 1994. *International Governance: Protecting the Environment in a Stateless Society*. Ithaca, NY: Cornell University Press.

Young, Oran R. 2008. Institutions and Environmental Change: The Scientific Legacy of a Decade of IDGEC Research. In *Institutions and Environmental Change: Principal Findings, Applications, and Research Frontiers*, ed. Oran R. Young, Leslie A. King, and Heike Schroeder, 3–45. Cambridge, MA: MIT Press.

Young, Oran R. 2011. Improving the Performance of the Climate Regime: Lessons from Regime Analysis. In *Oxford Handbook on Climate Change and Society*, ed. John S. Dryzek, Richard B. Norgaard, and David Schlosberg, 625–638. New York: Oxford University Press.

Zürn, Michael. 2004. Global Governance and Legitimacy Problems. *Government and Opposition* 39 (2): 260–287.

Index